herbivoracious

herbivoracious

a flavor revolution, with 150 vibrant and original vegetarian recipes

MICHAEL NATKIN

The Harvard Common Press
Boston, Massachusetts

The Harvard Common Press
535 Albany Street
Boston, Massachusetts 02118
www.harvardcommonpress.com

Printed in the U.S.A.
Printed on acid-free paper

Library of Congress Cataloging-in-Publication Data
Natkin, Michael.
  Herbivoracious : a flavor revolution, with 150 vibrant and original vegetarian recipes /
Michael Natkin.
     p. cm.
  Includes index.
  ISBN 978-1-55832-745-0 (hardback)
  1. Vegetarian cooking. 2. Cookbooks. I. Title.
  TX837.N276 2012
  641.5'636--dc23
                              2011030819

Special bulk-order discounts are available on this and other Harvard Common Press
books. Companies and organizations may purchase books for premiums or resale, or may
arrange a custom edition, by contacting the Marketing Director at the address above.

Book design by Elizabeth Van Itallie
Front cover photograph and prop styling by Sabra Krock; food styling by Roscoe Betsill
Cover recipe: Basil Gnudi with Summer Squash, page 162
Author photographs by Brian Smale

10 9 8 7 6 5 4 3

For my mother, Lois Natkin, whom I lost far too soon

contents

acknowledgments

This book would never have happened without the love and support of my wife, Sarina. She's done so much to make *Herbivoracious* (both book and blog) successful, helped me make the tough decisions, and worked extra-hard so that I would have the time to follow my dreams. Our two beautiful girls, Zoey and Olivia, both love to cook with their dad and know more about food than lots of grownups.

My mom, Lois, taught me the basics of cooking and always encouraged me to experiment in the kitchen. I became a vegetarian when she was fighting breast cancer and trying a macrobiotic diet. Luckily, my dear friend Nicole Moore was already a vegetarian and a good cook who showed me the ropes. Sadly, Mom passed away when I was only 18, so we didn't get the opportunity to share an adult life together. It would be wonderful to be cooking with her today.

My father, Jerry, has always been my biggest fan. He taught me to see the world with a scientific bent and always believed that any chance I took, no matter how outlandish, would turn out well. I couldn't ask for a better stepmom than Yudit, who looks after a big brood of grandchildren with so much love. My in-laws, Suzanne Morhaime and Howard and Lynn Behar, have been incredibly generous with their advice, support, and belief in what I'm doing.

My brother, Joel, and his wife, Sara, have been along for this journey as well, tasting and critiquing many of the recipes at our regular Sunday suppers. In the time it took to write this book, their baby, Asa, graduated from a dairy diet to gleefully smashing pesto and watermelon all over himself.

My grandparents, Ann and Ben Rosenbaum and David and Yetta Natkin, all loved food in their own ways, and we frequently shared their table. Grandpa Ben, especially, was a terrific cook and an early role model for me of a man comfortable in the kitchen. I've also been lucky enough to marry into a family where Sarina's grandmother Sophie still presides over a traditional Sephardic kitchen at age 93, feeding anyone who walks through the door the most delicious *bulemas* and *borekas* imaginable.

Spending months in restaurants has expanded my skills and perspective on cooking. I owe a big debt of gratitude to chef Janine Doran and owner Nat Stratton-

Clarke of Café Flora in Seattle, chef Jason Franey and owners Brian and Mark Canlis of Seattle fine-dining landmark Canlis, and chef/owner Amanda Cohen of New York's Dirt Candy for allowing me to intern in their kitchens.

Seattle, not to mention the Internet, is blessed with an incredible food community. I can't even begin to thank all of the farmers, foragers, purveyors, home cooks, chefs, scientists, and fellow bloggers who are my teachers. Whether I want to know how to work with an obscure wild mushroom, how to hand-form a Chinese dumpling, or how to infuse ginger into bourbon using a cream-whipper, these people are incredibly generous with their time and expertise.

Bruce Shaw, Adam Salomone, and my editor, Dan Rosenberg, from The Harvard Common Press have been phenomenal to work with. They helped shape the vision for this book and showed me the ropes of the publishing business. Keren Brown, Seattle's Frantic Foodie, connected me with Bruce and Adam and for that, and the hundred other ways she's helped Herbivoracious grow, I can't thank her enough. Roy Finamore and Jane Dornbusch provided additional editorial assistance. Their depth of experience in writing recipes has improved the text tremendously.

One of my oldest friends, David Harpe, taught me a lot about photography. Without his advice, I would never have been able to take my own pictures for the book. James Eddleman, whom I've known since fourth grade, has always been there for me through thick and thin. My buddies Dave Simons and Dan Wilk have put up with me babbling endlessly about food.

Finally, none of this could have happened without the readers of the Herbivoracious blog. From all over the world, they have created a community with me that loves great food. We learn together as they share their thoughts, opinions, and family foodways. Many readers stepped forward to test the recipes for this book, and their comments and suggestions were invaluable in making sure that each dish tastes just right and has easy-to-follow directions.

introduction

I grew up in Louisville, Kentucky, in the 1970s and early 1980s. It was not exactly a hotbed of haute cuisine. Everyone ate fast-food hamburgers, and vegetables were boiled until they begged for mercy. I remember the house of one friend in particular, whose mother would invariably be chain smoking and cooking a giant skillet of canned ham.

I visited this same friend a few years ago. His mom, quite old now, had just returned from Whole Foods with several bags full of fresh produce. This moment crystallized for me just how radically our food habits have changed. Vegetarian food and cooking have played a big part in these changes. The confluence of our interests in personal health, the environment, and animal welfare has caused even diehard carnivores, like my friend's mom, to include meatless meals in their diets.

Vegetarian cooking has come a long way. If you are old enough to remember the 1970s, you might recall the horror of mushy loaves of lentils and wheat berries or meals so loaded with carbs that you needed a long nap afterward. The 1980s and 1990s brought an increased awareness and availability of global ingredients and recipes, although a lack of context, and of in-depth knowledge of the cuisines from which they came, led to frightening "fusion" foods. Care for a curried endive pizza with Thai-spiced hummus, Oaxacan pesto, and a drizzle of Moroccan olive tapenade?

Over the past few years, as we've all become more sophisticated about food, vegetarian cooking in the West has reached a new level of quality and taste. Locally made tofu, preserved lemons, and whole black cardamom seeds are available in most cities—and are easily found online. Farmers' markets offer us tomatoes worth eating, a dozen varieties of radishes, and strawberries still warm from the field. Most communities are much more diverse, too, giving many of us the opportunity to experience authentic Singapore noodles or Ethiopian *injera* without a transcontinental flight. We learn cutting-edge methods from world-class chefs, whether they are vegetarian or not. We've come to understand that traditional flavor combinations and recipes are delicious because they have been honed over the course of centuries; we can (and should) always experiment, but they provide a foundation of reliable inspiration to which we can always return.

The upshot of all of these changes is that good vegetarian food is now just good food, period. This is a golden age for creative, intelligent vegetarian cuisine. Never again need anyone say, "That wasn't bad, for a vegetarian meal."

My own obsession with cooking is inextricably linked with vegetarian food. When I was 18, my mom was dying after a decade-long battle with breast cancer. She had decided to try a macrobiotic diet, but she was too weak to do much cooking. My girlfriend at the time (and still great friend), Nicole, was a vegetarian and a good cook. She taught me how to make flavorful, homey meals. I took over our kitchen and started to do all the cooking for my family. I continued to do so after my mom passed, until I took off for college, and thereafter during vacations. In those early years, I subjected my dad and brother to some ghastly combinations. I'll never forget a pot of wheat berries, peas, and plums (!) that was so bad we all took one bite, laughed, and dumped it in the garbage.

In spite of that rocky beginning, I persevered and became a good cook. I read hundreds of cookbooks and books about food. At college in Providence, Rhode Island, I had the opportunity to eat a range of foods, including Italian, Indian, Thai, Armenian, and Portuguese, that I never could have found in Louisville. One year I lived in a co-op house with 13 other students and we rotated cooking, which taught me how to feed a crowd and produced lots of instant feedback. These days, I get even more feedback from the readers of my blog, Herbivoracious.

Inspired by Ed Brown's *The Tassajara Bread Book* and *Tassajara Cooking*, I took a break from college and ended up at Green Gulch Farm, which, like Tassajara, is part of the San Francisco Zen Center. I spent several months working the fields of the stunning farm, which is nestled into a valley on the Marin County coast. I planted and later plucked potatoes, greens, and vegetables, which we would often eat that same day. Then I transferred to the kitchen, which was my first professional experience as a cook. I'll never forget the awesome power of the wok burner, the sunlight streaming in through the translucent roof, and the piles of still-warm vegetables with dirt clinging to their roots. I was hooked and transformed.

Life has its twists and turns, and I was drawn back into the world of software that I had been profoundly engaged with since the age of 14. I helped make dinosaurs and Terminators come to life at George Lucas's Industrial Light & Magic and worked on an early interactive television system at Silicon Graphics; for the past 12 years, I've been at Adobe Systems.

Through all of that, the food bug never left. On vacations I ate my way through Japan, India, Italy, France, Spain, Portugal, Holland, the Czech Republic, Mexico, and 48 of the United States as well. I dreamed of opening a restaurant. I continued to intern at restaurants, including Café Flora and Canlis in Seattle and Dirt Candy in New York City. I started my blog, Herbivoracious, as an outlet for all of this passion, never imagining that it would be the beginning of a community of tens of thousands of readers who use and comment on the recipes and share their own ideas. The blog has become an incredible catalyst for me to refine and improve my cooking; I never want to post a dish that doesn't taste terrific and look beautiful on the plate.

Through all of these journeys, I've learned that I'm nowhere near alone in my devotion to food. I've met hundreds of fellow travelers who plan their vacations around green markets and restaurants, who can easily tell you where the best Indian groceries are in their city or exactly which months local chanterelles will be available. These folks aren't driven by a desire to one-up their less-informed brethren. They simply find every aspect of food fascinating and are insatiable in their quest to cook and eat better. This isn't just a modern Western conceit. Great-grandmothers in Bangalore will talk endlessly about how to make the best *dosa*, and in Tel Aviv you could start a fistfight arguing about which stall has the tastiest falafel.

I've learned, too, that much of our current deepening interest in food comes from a growing understanding of the tremendously important social and environmental issues surrounding it. How much petroleum did it take to grow this pound of corn, grind it into meal, and ship it to me? How many pesticides leached into groundwater in the process? Were family farmers put out of work by an agribusiness conglomerate that sold them patented, genetically modified corn seeds? And is it self-indulgent of me to worry about these issues when there are people starving? *This book won't answer any of those questions.* That's not because they aren't crucially important. They are, and I encourage you to learn about them and figure out for yourself where you stand.

My mission is a good deal simpler. I propose to bring you a collection of vegetarian recipes that are so full of flavor, so pleasurable to make and to eat, and so satisfying that, if you are an omnivore, you won't give a second thought to the fact that they contain no meat. If you are a vegetarian, you'll be able to greatly expand your repertoire of everyday and special-occasion dishes.

I like to think that being mindful of the implications of what one cooks and eats is not an *ascetic* practice but an *aesthetic* pleasure. When you get used to great peaches from the local farmers' market, you may find you can't bear to eat the grainy, flavorless forgeries that were trucked in across continents. You'll look forward to those few weeks a year when they are sweet, perfumed, and tender. When you start to learn about ingredients from cultures beyond your own, food becomes a bridge that builds mutual respect. When your meals are well crafted and convey big, bold flavors, you may find that you are satiated without overeating or reaching later for highly processed snacks. Food is wonderful because maximizing your own pleasure and doing good can be very much aligned.

Some of the dishes in this book are culinary "deep tracks," by which I mean authentic versions of lesser-known traditional foods from around the world that were always vegetarian or can be made vegetarian without losing their essence. You'll find Mexican dishes way beyond the burrito and Middle Eastern meals without a hint of hummus. Many others recipes are my own ideas and improvisations using traditional or modern flavor profiles. I've thoroughly tasted and tested them all, and then readers of Herbivoracious double-checked and critiqued them, so you can be sure they work well and produce delicious results.

At the core of this book, you will find more than 40 hearty entrées, divided into baked dishes, pastas, stews, and sandwiches. Most of them, like Pappardelle with Eggplant Ragu and Fresh Ricotta (page 172), are substantial enough to serve as a one-dish meal, and many can either be made ahead or are quick enough to do for a weekday dinner. Soups and salads include both filling recipes like Red *Pozole* with Beans (page 100) as well as lighter fare like Roasted Maitake Mushrooms in Smoky Tea Broth (page 80). The appetizer chapter includes many dishes that work well with a glass of wine or as the first course of a dinner party, such as the Chèvre with Sautéed Grapes (page 46). On the far side of the entrées you'll find a repertoire of side dishes that you'll want to have in your quiver as you plan a meal. The breakfast chapter includes updated classics like Buckwheat Buttermilk Pancakes (page 304), along with what I think are some real showstoppers, like the Manouri Cheese Blintzes (page 313) with Rosemary-Blueberry Sauce (page 333). Of course I wouldn't leave you without a few unusual desserts, such as Seckel Pears with Cinnamon Pastry Crumbs (page 290). The final chapter includes recipes for basic sauces, condiments, and doughs that are used throughout the book. See pages 153, 183, and 227 for sample menus and tips on how to plan your own.

Why vegetarian? Because vegetarian meals are good for you, tread more lightly on our planet's resources, and are kinder to animals. And, personally, I figure that because I am a vegetarian I have a little leeway to indulge in extra chocolate, cheese, or French fries without overdosing on saturated fats. Whether you are a full-time lacto-ovo vegetarian, a flexitarian, or just someone who is looking to incorporate more meatless meals into your family's routine (and who isn't?), I think that you will find a lot of exciting dishes in these chapters.

Vegans and cooks who avoid gluten will find plenty of recipes in these pages as well. I've indicated throughout which recipes fit into one of these categories or can be made to do so through simple changes (like replacing milk with soy milk). Of course, you will need to be the final judge of whether any particular recipe meets the dietary requirements or preferences of you and your fellow diners.

I'm excited to put this collection of recipes into your hands, and I'd love to hear from you. At herbivoracious.com you will find contact information and extended features, including videos for some of the recipes and photos that didn't fit in the book. See you there, and happy cooking and eating!

A NOTE ABOUT THE PHOTOGRAPHY. As a blogger, I started taking my own photographs out of necessity. Over the course of a few years I graduated from a point-and-shoot to a DSLR with professional lenses and studio strobe lights, and I learned on the job about composition, lighting, and post-processing. I did all of my own photography for this book.

You will probably notice that the look of these shots is a bit different from that of most cookbook photos. I do very little with props and food styling, preferring to focus on the dishes as they really look. There are no scoops of "ice cream" made out of Crisco or perfectly arranged piles of napkins in soft focus. I hope you will find these honest, unadorned photos appealing and that they'll serve as a helpful guide to how the dishes should look when you make them in your own kitchen.

some notes about ingredients

This is not an exhaustive list of ingredients used in the recipes in this book. Instead, I have focused on two things: introducing ingredients that may be unfamiliar and providing tips for finding, buying, and working with more-common items. Additional notes about ingredients can be found in boxes throughout the book and in the head-notes of individual recipes.

AVOCADOS. You may find several types of avocado in your grocery, but generally the Hass variety has the best flavor. If you want to use avocados the day you buy them, they must already be soft enough to yield a bit to a gentle press with your thumb but not so soft that they have shrunken pockets of skin. For use a day or two later, you can choose firmer ones and let them ripen on the counter—although this is never a certainty. You can't make good guacamole from bad avocados, so take your time and select nice ones.

BEANS (AND LENTILS). Without exception, legumes that are cooked at home will have a better flavor and, especially, texture than canned beans. That said, canned beans are awfully convenient. When you do use them, be sure to rinse off all of the mucilaginous goo. If you have a pressure cooker, you can use it to make perfect beans rapidly and without the need to presoak.

BROTH. It is handy to have a multipurpose, clear, somewhat neutral vegetable broth to use as a background in soups and sauces. Some things that are sold as broth are really more like pureed soups and are therefore much less useful, and others have unpleasant chemical flavors or too much salt. My personal preferences among vegetarian broths are Seitenbacher broth mix, which has a clean, round, but unassertive flavor and is good enough to drink by itself, and Better than Bouillon Vegetable Base, which has a richer, more oniony taste.

BUTTER. Whenever butter is called for in a recipe, we want unsalted sweet-cream butter, though cultured butter generally works as well, as long as its very slightly sour flavor is appropriate. Pay close attention to the temperature of butter. It must be extremely cold for pie crust and near room temperature but definitely not melted for a cake.

BUTTERMILK. Buttermilk has a wonderful way of adding richness, body, and mild acidity. In a pinch you can substitute 1 cup of whole milk mixed with 1 tablespoon of white vinegar, or a mixture of milk and yogurt or sour cream—but it is never quite the same.

CANNED TOMATOES. My favorite canned tomato products are whole tomatoes, diced tomatoes in juice, and tomato puree. I find less use for tomato sauce. For Italian food, nothing beats the flavor of canned tomatoes that have been grown in San Marzano, but you will pay a premium price for the pleasure. You can also find fire-roasted canned tomatoes that add a delicious smoky flavor; I especially like them in Mexican dishes. Tomato paste is wonderful when added to onions and browned.

CHEESES. Most aged cheese is coagulated using rennet. Traditional rennet comes from a calf's stomach. These days, a great deal of rennet is from vegetable, micro-bial, or synthetic sources. Unfortunately, it can be hard to find out what is used in a particular cheese, especially with artisanal products. My personal choice is to allow this one gap in my otherwise firm vigilance about eating vegetarian, but you will have to decide for yourself how you want to handle this issue. If you want to avoid animal rennet, look for "vegetable rennet" on package labels, ask your cheesemonger, or do some research on the Web.

CHILE PEPPERS, FRESH AND DRIED. Fresh and dried chiles are two completely different things; dried peppers aren't meant to serve as a substitute when you can't find the fresh. You should use dried peppers when you want ripe, round, fruity, and raisiny flavors along with heat and fresh peppers to add sharp, green, vegetal flavors. If you like heat, it is easy and fun to get hooked on buying new varieties, and there are an endless number to choose from. Check out ethnic markets to see what types of whole fresh and dried chiles, as well as chile flakes, powders, and traditional spice blends, they sell.

Chile peppers vary wildly in their heat level, even within the same variety. I've had some jalapeños, poblanos, and serranos that were mild as bell peppers and others that were smoking hot. Taste a tiny bit, and add them gradually to your food if you have any doubts about what your diners will enjoy. You can reduce the heat of peppers somewhat by removing the seeds and ribs, which contain much of the concentrated capsaicin.

When you work with peppers, it is always wise to wear food-safe rubber gloves. It is far too easy to rub the hot oils in your eyes accidentally. Always wash your cutting board and utensils thoroughly before moving on to the next task.

CHOCOLATE. If you haven't yet added high-quality cooking chocolates to your pantry, you'll be amazed at the difference they make. There are much better cocoa powders, unsweetened chocolates, high-cacao-percentage bittersweet chocolates, and even milk chocolates available today than the ubiquitous supermarket brands you probably knew as a kid. Of course you will pay a premium, but I'm pretty sure that after your first batch of brownies made with higher-quality chocolate, you won't want to go back.

COCONUT MILK. Choose pure coconut milk with no added thickeners or sweeteners; a small amount of preservative is okay, however.

CUCUMBERS. To remove the seeds from a cucumber, slice it in half lengthwise and use a spoon to scrape the seeds out.

EGGS. Like many vegetarians, I feel a little dubious about eating eggs. My personal choice, both ethically and for flavor, is to buy the most responsibly produced eggs I can find. When possible, I buy them directly from a farmer at a farmers' market. Failing that, I look for organic eggs from cage-free hens that are fed a vegetarian diet with no hormones or antibiotics.

FRESH GINGER. Some folks like to peel fresh ginger by scraping it with a spoon, though I personally don't find that to be super efficient and will usually use a knife or peeler. If you have a Microplane grater (and you should), it is often possible to grate ginger with the skin on. It gets cut so finely that it will cause no problem in a recipe.

HERBS. In most cases, fresh and dried herbs are not substitutes for each other. For example, dried mint doesn't bear even a passing resemblance to the fresh leaf. Dried parsley is, in my view, completely worthless. On the other hand, dried oregano is needed for a typical Italian-American tomato sauce. You could use fresh oregano, but you'd be making a different dish. A small herb garden with basic items like parsley, cilantro, and basil will save you lots of money while giving you the freshest possible flavors. If you don't have garden space, many herbs will grow well in pots or containers on a windowsill or porch.

LEMONS. I'm never without fresh lemons, because almost every dish needs acidity for balance and citrus is often the ideal option. When I can get them, I prefer Meyer lemons for their floral scent and slightly sweeter taste. Nothing beats a pitcher of lemonade made with Meyer lemons. Don't even think about buying prepackaged lemon juice. It is a sad shadow of the real thing and will ruin your food.

Do not forget about the zest of your lemons. Small amounts of lemon zest add fragrance and puckery freshness to garnishes, sauces, and desserts.

LETTUCES. It is worth choosing the right variety of lettuce for a given salad, sandwich, or wrap. Tender, subtle butter lettuce goes well with mild flavors like pear, while romaine has the body to stand up to an intensely flavored , creamy dressing. The slightly bitter greens you will find in a typical lettuce mix play well against sweet beets or candied nuts. And don't write off iceberg lettuce! It got a bad rap when it was the only lettuce a lot of Americans ate for a miserable 30 years in the last century, but it is actually uniquely crisp, cool, and refreshing on a hot day.

MANGOES. Mangoes can be as frustrating as they are delicious. They are usually quite expensive, they don't always ripen when bought firm but may be rotten when bought soft, and they are sometimes excruciatingly stringy. You may want to consider buying mangoes at ethnic grocers, where customers will demand good quality and a low price. If you do end up with an underripe mango, try the Green Mango Salad on page 106.

In India, there are hundreds of mango varieties, each delicious in its own way. Sadly, we get only a few types here, but try as many as you can find.

MAPLE SYRUP. Always use real maple syrup. The U.S. Grade B is generally preferable in cooking to Grade A, because it has a good deal more flavor.

MEXICAN OREGANO. Mexican oregano is not closely related to European oreganos and tastes completely different. If you want your Mexican food to taste authentic, it is well worth picking up a 99-cent packet at your local *tienda*.

MICROGREENS. Microgreens are no longer just for fine-dining restaurants and chefs. Those tiny little leaves of anything from cilantro to shiso have started to show up in regular groceries. Seek them out for beautiful, interesting, and highly flavorful garnishes.

MIRIN. Mirin is a sweet rice wine that is used in many Japanese recipes for everything from glazes to salad dressings and broths. It is readily available at Asian groceries as well as natural foods stores. Look for brands that aren't made with corn syrup.

MISO. Miso is a traditional Japanese fermented paste made from soybeans and various grains. There are many varieties, ranging from mild white shiro miso to dark brown, smoky hatcho miso. Each has a distinct taste that is worth exploring. Beyond forming the base for miso soup, miso paste can be used in salad dressings, marinades, sauces, dips, and pickles.

MUSHROOMS, DRIED. Dried mushrooms are a wonderful source of complex, umami-rich flavors, especially in brothy soups and sauces. I'll typically rehydrate them in just enough boiling water to cover, then strain and use both the mushrooms and the soaking liquid. Some mushrooms, like porcini, are completely different (but delicious) when dried, while others, like morels, retain more of their original character. Dried shiitakes are by far the least expensive item in this group, and they add tremendous flavor to Asian dishes.

MUSHROOMS, WILD(ISH). The term "wild mushroom" is used loosely to refer to anything other than your basic button, crimini, and portobello, although many "wild" varieties (such as oyster mushrooms and shiitakes) are actually cultivated. Whatever the source, they offer distinctive flavors and textures and are well worth getting to know. When you buy more expensive varieties, use them in dishes that will really highlight the mushrooms.

MUSTARD SEEDS. Common yellow mustard seeds and Indian black mustard seeds are not interchangeable. The Indian ones are much more versatile. They are typically added to the hot oil at the beginning of a dish and cooked for just a few seconds, until they start to change color and pop. Add the next set of ingredients immediately so that the mustard seeds don't burn.

NUTMEG. Nothing elevates a creamy sauce like a healthy pinch of nutmeg. It is really worth finding the whole seeds and grating them as needed, as the flavor is much better. You don't need one of those special nutmeg graters; a regular Microplane does a terrific job.

OLIVE OIL. I always keep at least two varieties of extra-virgin olive oil on hand: an inexpensive one for cooking and a very delicious and rather expensive one for drizzling and other raw uses where the flavor will come through clearly. Try to taste a few brands and settle on one that you like in each category. I wouldn't recommend non-extra-virgin olive oils, as they tend to have unpleasant flavors from poor processing methods.

VEGETABLE OIL. Throughout the recipes in this book, I use the term "vegetable oil" to mean any refined, neutrally flavored oil. My personal choice is safflower oil, because it is reasonably priced and high in healthy monounsaturated fats. It is important to choose a refined oil with a high smoke point so that it doesn't burn when cooking at high temperatures.

ONIONS. I often specify white onions instead of yellow onions, because I find them to have a slightly better flavor and a little less bite. They are also traditional in Mexican cuisine. That said, white onions are usually a bit more expensive and harder to find, so feel free to use yellow if that is what you have on hand.

Red onions and the various varieties of sweet onions (such as Vidalias and Walla Wallas) are usually reserved for raw use. If you are eating a white onion raw, you may want to soak the cut pieces in cold water for a short while before serving to reduce their sharp edge.

PANKO. Panko is a Japanese-style bread crumb that is all white and very airy. It has become fairly commonplace even at basic grocery stores; look in the Asian foods aisle. Panko is most useful for breading foods to be fried, where it creates a phenomenally crisp, uniform crust. I prefer traditional homemade bread crumbs for adding bulk and body to the interior of a food. There are instructions for how to make them on page 345.

PARSLEY. Parsley got a bad reputation when sprigs of the curly variety were used as irrelevant plate decorations for several sad decades. Flatleaf parsley is tasty and versatile. It can be used in fresh sauces like Chimichurri (page 328), and a shower of the minced leaves adds a fresh, aromatic top note to a wide range of Mediterranean dishes. If you have a garden, parsley is easy to grow, and that makes it easy to pick just a few stalks as you need it.

PASTA. Many folks are under the mistaken impression that fresh pasta is automatically superior to dried pasta. In fact, they are just different, and each works best with particular sauces. Fresh pastas are often served with butter-based sauces and light condiments, while dried pastas can work with either olive oil or butter and can stand up to heartier treatments. But there are exceptions: See the Pappardelle with Eggplant Ragu and Fresh Ricotta on page 172 for a delicious case of a robust condiment with fresh noodles.

PEPPER, BLACK. Freshly ground black pepper is incomparably more interesting than the preground powder. It has a bright, floral aroma that disappears within just a few moments of grinding. You should always have a pepper mill at hand to put the finishing touch on your dishes just before serving.

POMEGRANATE MOLASSES. Pomegranate molasses isn't molasses at all; it is simply pomegranate juice that has been boiled down to a thick syrup. It is used throughout the Middle East when a tart, fruity flavor is wanted. You can find pomegranate molasses at Middle Eastern grocers and use it for sauces, salad dressings, glazes, and even as a final drizzle, much as you would an aged balsamic vinegar. Try a tablespoon or so in a glass of seltzer for a refreshing beverage, too, and if you want to add something stronger to that glass, don't let me stop you!

PRESERVED LEMONS. Preserved lemons are whole lemons that have been packed in salt and water and allowed to pickle for a month or two. You can find them at Middle Eastern stores and increasingly at any place that carries gourmet groceries. The peel, or sometimes the whole lemon, is minced and used as a condiment or in sauces and stews.

RICE. There are so many varieties of rice available these days, each with its own uses. I like to stock larger quantities of the types I use most and buy others as I need them for particular meals. I always have basmati, Thai jasmine, sushi rice, and a short-grained brown rice on hand. I'll pick up a smaller bag of one of the many excellent risotto or paella rices as needed, or experiment occasionally with more unusual types such as Wehani, Chinese forbidden rice, or pecan rice.

RICOTTA. The best fresh ricotta tastes pure, sweet, and milky, not at all sour. You may find a local artisanal product. If not, keep your eye out for the Calabro brand, which is delicious.

SAFFRON. Saffron is the world's most expensive spice by weight. It consists of the stigmas and styles of a particular variety of crocus, and it takes 150 flowers to produce a single gram of the spice. Fortunately, it takes only a pinch to add a beautiful orange hue and unique, slightly bitter flavor with a hint of iodine. Always buy whole threads of saffron, not powdered saffron, as there is a good chance the powdered version will have been adulterated to increase profits.

SCALLIONS. I love to use scallions (green onions) as a garnish on a wide range of Asian dishes to add that final note of crunch and freshness. Always use only the white and light green parts, and peel off any tough or slimy outer layers.

SESAME OIL. Untoasted, light-colored sesame oil has a mild, sweet flavor that you might enjoy in delicate salad dressings. Dark, toasted sesame oil, on the other hand, is used in many Asian cuisines to add a heady, nutty aroma. In most dishes it is used as an accent, with just a few drops or perhaps as much as a teaspoon drizzled in at the end. Occasionally, especially in Korean cuisine, it can be the main cooking oil used in a dish.

SESAME SEEDS. Pale brown sesame seeds, often sold as "white" sesame seeds, are available both hulled and unhulled. The hulled seeds are smaller and have a more distinctive flavor, while the unhulled seeds have a better crunch and more nutritional value. Black sesame seeds are also popular, especially for Asian dishes. They taste similar to the lighter seeds but add a nice contrasting color to many dishes. In all cases, it is best to buy raw seeds and toast only the amount you need. They can be toasted in just a couple of minutes in a dry skillet or toaster oven on medium heat, and are done when they darken a bit and smell fragrant.

SMOKED PAPRIKA. Smoky flavors can be hard to come by in vegetarian foods. Smoked paprika (such as *pimentón de la vera* or *pimentón dulce*) is one of the most versatile ways to add them. I use it both in cooking (for vegetarian paella or rich stews) and as a table condiment for pizza and quesadillas.

SOY SAUCE, TAMARI, SHOYU. Look for soy sauces that are naturally brewed, not made from hydrolyzed vegetable protein, which is a shortcut that produces inferior flavor. It is helpful to have both a Chinese soy sauce and a Japanese shoyu on hand for their somewhat different tastes. Some Japanese tamari is wheat-free, which makes it a good substitute for those who can't tolerate gluten. If you're avoiding gluten, this is one ingredient that requires you to do your research carefully. Indonesian *kecap manis* is a very sweet soy sauce that works well as a glaze on tofu because it caramelizes rapidly.

SUMAC. Ground sumac is a spice made from the fruits of a flowering plant. It is available at Middle Eastern markets and adds a tart flavor. It is often used to garnish hummus and other dishes because it adds a beautiful maroon color.

TOFU. Tofu is a misunderstood ingredient. Many people think of it as a modern meat substitute, when in fact it has thousands of years of history in Asia as an artisanal, delicious, and high-protein food in its own right. It is well worth seeking out a local producer of tofu, for the freshest product is much more delicious than one that's been sitting in a plastic, water-filled box for weeks (or, heaven forbid, in a shelf-stable package for months). Firm or extra-firm tofu is the most useful for stir-fries, curries, and so forth. Soft tofu is most often used in soups.

TORTILLAS. A really fresh corn tortilla should be supple enough for you to roll without it cracking. If you live in a major city, you can probably find a local *tortilleria* that makes them fresh daily. Flour tortillas are wonderful, too, and the grocery-store brands are generally fine for these.

VINEGAR. There are as many kinds of vinegar as there are foods that can be fermented. Everything from pears to barley can be turned into the sour stuff. A minimal set to have on hand should include white distilled, apple cider, red wine, and rice vinegars. Real balsamic vinegar, which has been aged for years in the traditional process, is a complex, syrupy, sweet-sour revelation if you are only familiar with the thin grocery-store stuff; you'll pay dearly for it, but it is also dosed out in drops, so you can make the pleasure last. If you want to splurge, look for artisanal vinegars that are made from single, high-quality base ingredients rather than those that have been flavored with herbs and spices. (You can add those yourself, according to your own tastes.) Some of my favorites are sherry vinegar, champagne vinegar, and specific varietal apple vinegars.

YOGURT. Thick, Greek-style yogurts are widely available now. They are much creamier than typical yogurt. Beyond enjoying these yogurts straight with some berries or brown sugar, you can use them in everything from baking to sauces. Beating thick yogurt with a whisk will thin it out considerably, so always do that first before adding water to a sauce that seems too thick.

ABOUT MEAT SUBSTITUTES. Commercial meat substitutes are billed as a convenience and an easy way to introduce vegetarian meals to folks who are used to having a piece of meat in the middle of their plates. These substitutes have come a long way, evolving from ghastly burgers-in-a-box ("Just add water!") to quite tasty applewood-smoked "sausages" made from wheat.

I have nothing against these foods, and we do eat them occasionally in my family. They are certainly handy when visiting friends for a summer barbecue. You won't find any recipes using meat substitutes in this book, however. I would rather focus on making delicious food from vegetarian ingredients than attempt to emulate meat. (After all, if I were a meat-cooking chef, I wouldn't try to make ground beef look and taste like carrots!)

Note that I don't consider foods such as tofu and tempeh to be meat substitutes. These are traditional ingredients with thousands of years of history that are craveable in their own right. In general, I like to eat them in their traditional contexts—tofu with nori, or with chiles and peanuts, or in a red curry, for example, but not as a replacement for ricotta in a cheesecake or as fake mozzarella in a lasagna.

some notes on cooking equipment

Kitchen stores are filled with semi-useless gadgets that can perform only a single task, won't stand up to heavy-duty use, or are just plain poorly designed. It is perfectly possible to make great food with a *batterie de cuisine* consisting of nothing more than a knife, a cutting board, a skillet, and a pot.

Still, there are a number of tools that will make it easier and faster to prepare delicious meals. Here is my very personal, idiosyncratic list of items that have stood the test of time in my kitchen. Though useful for any cook, many are particularly valuable for vegetarian meals, where there is more produce to break down efficiently. You don't need to own everything on this list, but you might consider acquiring a few items each year.

KNIVES AND THEIR FRIENDS

CHEF'S KNIFE. No other kitchen tool is more important or personal than your chef's knife. Whole books have been written about what makes a great knife, but the most important things are that it is razor-sharp and feels good in your hand. See page 135 for more information. Treat your knife with respect; it should never go in the dishwasher or the sink, or in a drawer where it can bang against up against other stuff that will dull the edge. When you are done using a knife, wash it by hand and put it in a block or on a magnetic rack.

OTHER KNIVES. You'll want to have a small paring knife and a good serrated bread knife. If you were to add just one more knife, especially for vegetarian cooking, I would make it a "tomato knife," which is a little larger than a paring knife but serrated to slice easily through the tough skins of tomatoes, grapes, and the like.

SHARPENING STEEL. You should have a metal or ceramic "steel" that can be used in between sharpenings to keep an edge on your knife. Dragging the edge of your knife against the steel removes any burrs and realigns the cutting edge. Using a steel is a lot easier to do than to describe, so ask a knowledgeable friend or a cutlery-store staffer to show you the proper technique.

KNIFE SHARPENING. If you check the knives of 10 home cooks, nine will be so dull that they are bludgeoning food, not cutting it. The easiest option for sharpening is to find a professional service in your town and have all of your blades done, say, two to four times per year, depending on how much you cook. You can also sharpen knives at home. Very few people are willing to take the time to learn to sharpen correctly on oilstones or waterstones, so there are dozens of gadgets that have been invented to make the job fast and foolproof. The device I rely on is made by Chef's Choice; it has three wheels of different grit levels, each with built-in angle guides. The finest grit is pretty much equivalent to a steel, so it can be used frequently and produces a razor edge. The same manufacturer also makes a handheld, non-motorized sharpener that is quite effective. I bring that one on trips so I can sharpen whatever knives I find in a rental apartment.

HEAVY-DUTY CUTTING BOARD. You and your knives deserve a flat, stable, comfortable platform on which to chop, with a surface gentle enough not to dull a blade. I personally prefer thick cutting boards made of maple, but plastic is used in almost all restaurant kitchens and is a viable option as well. If your board won't stay still, place a moist kitchen towel under it, laid out flat.

HAND TOOLS

MICROPLANE. Microplane graters are one of the greatest kitchen inventions of the late twentieth century. Originally developed as woodworking tools, they are covered with tiny, ultrasharp teeth that make quick work of grating hard cheese, ginger, citrus zest, nutmeg, and just about anything else you can think of. They come in a variety of shapes and hole sizes, but the most useful is about 8 inches long and 1 inch wide and has very small teeth.

MANDOLINE. A mandoline is simply a blade mounted on a flat platform, with adjustable screws to set the depth of cut, allowing you to make thin, consistent slices very quickly. Extra attachments allow for a variety of julienne cuts. The inexpensive Japanese models are just as good as, if not better than, the $100-plus European varieties. You might also like to buy a Kevlar kitchen glove (available from the Microplane company as well as others) to keep your fingers safe from the blade.

THIN METAL SPATULA. It is frustrating to try to flip ingredients in a skillet using a blunt-edged spatula that won't actually get under the food. You should own at least one metal spatula with a very thin leading edge that is easy to insert. There is another useful variety, known in the trade as a fish spatula, which has a thin edge and slots that allow oil to drain back into the pan, essentially combining the virtues of a spatula and a slotted spoon.

HEATPROOF SILICONE SPATULAS. Silicone spatulas are versatile. It is worth owning a few in different sizes and shapes, because they can scrape out containers with various contours, mix ingredients for baking, and stir hot ingredients. They are also safe for use in nonstick skillets, because they won't damage the coating.

MINI OFFSET SPATULA. These little spatulas are workhorses for pastry chefs. The offset-handle design keeps your hands out of the way of the work and lets you reach down into baking pans and get right up to the edge.

SILICONE PASTRY BRUSH. Silicone pastry brushes are better than the old paintbrush style for brushing on butter, oil, or glazes. They don't soak up the food and can go right in the dishwasher for thorough cleaning.

INSTANT-READ THERMOMETER. Many kitchen tasks are made simpler if you can take an accurate temperature reading. For example, a casserole is hot enough to serve if it is 160°F inside. Baked custards must be stopped well below 185°F or the egg proteins will become tough and weep liquid. Food that is going to be unrefrigerated for an extended period of time must be kept above 140°F or below 40°F, and an instant-read thermometer will let you know right away whether you are in the safe range.

SQUEEZE JUICER. I've tried any number of citrus juicers over the years. By far my favorite, for ease of use, ease of cleanup, good extraction, and seed removal, is the type that consists of two handles with a pivot pin at the end. Half of a citrus fruit goes in a perforated bowl at the end of the handle and a mating part provides the pressure to squeeze out the juice. You can get the most juice by squeezing each half twice, inverting the fruit in between.

BOARD SCRAPER. A board scraper is simply a rectangular piece of metal or plastic with an integral handle. I use it constantly to remove all the little scraps of food from my cutting board and to transfer vegetables to the stove.

VERTICAL VEGETABLE PEELER. Vegetable peelers whose blade is perpendicular, rather than parallel, to the handle, make for faster, more efficient work. They shouldn't cost more than, say, $8, and they should be replaced once or twice a year when they become dull.

SERRATED PEELER. Serrated peelers are useful for removing skin from soft fruits such as pears, peaches, or mangoes. The tiny, sharp teeth catch the skin and take it right off.

WHISKS. You should have at least one full-size and one quite small whisk, each with thick, ergonomic handles that let you get right in there and take a sauce to task. If you have any wimpy ones with thin wire handles lying around, get rid of them.

TONGS. Please lose those goofy 1950s-style tongs with their metal loops at both ends. They are way too flimsy and awkward to use. A good pair of 12-inch solid-metal tongs with a spring-loaded, lockable handle will set you back about $10. You'll wonder how you ever tossed pasta with a sauce before.

PORTION SCOOPS. You don't really need several portion scoops with their little thumb levers for releasing the contents, but they can be pretty handy for making consistently sized cookies, balls of ice cream, and patties. I have several different sizes and love them all.

MORTAR AND PESTLE. Spices always taste better when freshly ground. A small mortar and pestle is ideal for this job, because it lets you control texture precisely and cleans up in just seconds. You can also use an electric coffee grinder reserved for spices. That tends to be more efficient for very hard spices, but it is more of a pain to clean up.

POTATO RICER. I don't know how I went so many years without a potato ricer. I always figured that a handheld potato masher was just as good. Wrong. The ricer produces a light, fluffy texture with minimal risk of gumminess. It is also useful for squeezing the water out of raw, grated potatoes for latkes and out of spinach for lasagna and other fillings. You'll want to buy a heavy-duty ricer that won't fail under pressure.

SMALL APPLIANCES

MINI FOOD PROCESSOR. Full-size food processors are wonderful, but they take up a lot of counter space and are a pain to clean up. They don't work well when you need to make a small amount of sauce, because the ingredients won't reach the blade. Mini food processors typically hold only a cup or two, which makes them ideal for small quantities of sauces like *Chermoula* (page 331), Lemon-Mustard Vinaigrette (page 327), or the pureed chiles for Red *Pozole* with Beans (page 100).

IMMERSION BLENDER. Immersion blenders, also known as stick blenders, let you bring the power tool right to the ingredient, rather than having to set up and clean a full-size blender. They can even work right in a pot to puree a soup (but turn off the heat first, and be careful if the soup is still hot). For a bit more money, you can find an immersion blender with multiple attachments, including a mini food-processor base, allowing you to combine these two very useful tools.

PRESSURE COOKER. Pressure cookers no longer deserve the reputation they once had for exploding. The modern pressure cooker is as safe as any other cooking utensil as long as you follow the instructions. Whether you choose an electric or a stovetop model, it will use a great deal less energy than conventional cooking. My favorite use for the pressure cooker is cooking dried beans. Even chickpeas take just 40 minutes once they are up to pressure and don't require an overnight soak to reach the perfect texture.

RICE COOKER. Cooking rice on the stove isn't difficult, but it does require a bit of attention. In countries where rice is a staple, almost everyone who can afford it uses an electric cooker, because it produces perfect rice every time. The thing to understand about rice cookers is that they measure temperature, not time. When the temperature goes above 212°F, that means all the water is gone, and the machine shuts off. So to adjust the texture of your rice, just add a little more or less water. I'm particularly fond of rice cookers that have a timer setting, so you can put rice and water in the pot in the morning and come home to a steaming hot batch ready for dinner. The soaking time only improves the texture.

DIGITAL SCALE. Cooks in the U.S. tend to rely much more on volume measurements than weight. Measuring by weight has many advantages, though, including precision, and, if you use the metric system, the ability to quickly scale recipes up or down. Choose a model that can measure weights up to at least 1 kilogram (2.2 pounds) with an accuracy of 1 gram (0.05 ounces) and has easy controls for zeroing (taring) and switching between grams and ounces. This needn't cost more than $25.

OTHER EQUIPMENT

CAST-IRON SKILLET. One of the most popular posts I ever wrote on Herbivoracious was about the deep bond I feel with my 12-inch cast-iron skillet. It has pride of place in my kitchen, living on the stove at all times. I love how it heats up fast, holds that heat, puts on a beautiful sear or crust, never sticks, and cleans up easily. I use it as part of cooking virtually every meal, because I know exactly how it will respond. Dozens of readers wrote in to share their own, similar feelings. There are some things cast iron isn't good for, especially acidic foods like tomato sauce. If cast iron isn't for you, I understand, but I hope you will find a skillet or wok with which you can have a similar connection!

DUTCH OVEN. My love for my 5½-quart, enameled-steel Dutch oven is second only to my feelings for the aforementioned cast-iron skillet. It is heavy enough to hold heat, so the temperature doesn't drop drastically when you add cold ingredients, it can go from the stove to the oven, and it has a tight-fitting lid. I use it for soups, stews, and curries, and for deep-frying, boiling small amounts of pasta, and even baking no-knead bread.

CHINOIS. Professional kitchens almost exclusively use conical strainers, known as chinois, rather than the sieves and colanders we find at home. Chinois come in a range of mesh sizes. The conical shape makes for efficient drainage, and the handle and hook allow them to be rested in most sinks for hands-free use.

SHEET PANS. I am not sure why, but there are a lot of thin, odd-size, poorly designed sheet pans on the market. A proper half-size sheet pan, also known as a jelly-roll pan, should be 13 x 18 inches in size and made of heavy-duty, uncoated aluminum, with a rim all the way around. You can use them for baking cookies, roasting vegetables, catching messes under a lasagna, holding ingredients before cooking, and a hundred other everyday tasks. I highly recommend owning silicone pan liners for when you want a nonstick surface and easy cleanup without the waste of parchment paper.

A NOTE ABOUT INGREDIENTS AND SPECIAL DIETS.
To the best of my knowledge, all of the recipes in this book are lacto-ovo vegetarian. I indicate dishes that I believe to be vegan and/or gluten-free, or easily modifiable to be so. Of course, you are responsible for following your own diet and reading product labels since manufacturers can change ingredients and information can become outdated. Remember that ingredients can be added to a product intentionally, or through cross-contamination, or as a result of the manufacturing process.

appetizers
and small dishes

tea-smoked lychees

VEGAN

GLUTEN-FREE

SERVES 4

20 MINUTES,
PLUS CHILLING
TIME

NOTE:
Genmaicha tea is
available at good
groceries, health
food stores, tea
shops, and Japa-
nese markets.

If you haven't had fresh lychee fruit, seek them out at a good Asian grocery or high-end produce shop in early summer. I've even seen them at Trader Joe's. They are miles beyond the fairly sad canned fruit that sometimes appears in perfunctory desserts at Chinese restaurants.

Without a doubt the best use of these gems is to eat them out of hand, lazily peeling one at a time on a hot day. The flavor is quite sweet, but with a perfumed and slightly smoky note, which inspired this surprising little bite. This dish is meant to be an *amuse bouche*—a tiny taste to whet the appetite for an exciting meal.

I smoke the lychees with *genmaicha* tea (a green tea with toasted brown rice), then serve them chilled with an infusion of the same tea, a bit of grated ginger, and micro shiso leaves. If you can't find micro shiso, you could use any other micro-green, a chiffonade of full-size shiso, or the tiniest leaves of cilantro you can cull from a regular bunch.

4 fresh lychee fruits
4 tablespoons *genmaicha* tea (see Note)
1 cup boiling water
½ teaspoon peeled and grated fresh ginger
Micro shiso (see headnote for substitutions)
Flaky sea salt (such as Maldon)

1 Peel the lychees. Use a paring knife to split the fruit in half; working as carefully as possible, remove the pit. This will give you 8 halves, so that you can serve the 4 best-looking ones. It is the cook's prerogative to eat the halves that look less lovely.

2 Place 3 tablespoons of the tea in a small heavy pot with a lid. Put the lychee halves on a folding steamer or inverted metal cup inside the pot. Cover and set over the lowest heat on your stove. After about 5 minutes, lift the lid and be sure there is some smoke being generated. If not, raise the heat a bit. Smoke the lychees for about 10 more minutes.

3 Carefully remove the lychee halves from the smoker and chill them thoroughly.

4 Meanwhile, steep the remaining 1 tablespoon of tea in the boiling water for a few minutes, then strain and chill.

5 To serve, place one lychee half in each of four Chinese soup spoons or tiny bowls. Sauce with a spoonful of the tea, then top each piece of fruit with a tiny pinch of the grated ginger, a leaf or two of the greens, and a couple flakes of salt.

spicy nori seasoning for popcorn

VEGAN OPTION

GLUTEN-FREE

MAKES ENOUGH
TO SEASON
AT LEAST 10
QUARTS

10 MINUTES

I think you'll enjoy this unusual but simple seasoning on popcorn. The Japanese inflection from the nori makes the spiced popcorn a nice snack with ice-cold sake and the perfect accompaniment to an anime marathon.

Technically, what we are making here is a very simple *furikake*, a dry seasoning usually used on rice but delicious in many contexts (the *gomashio* on page 346 is another example of a *furikake*). A good Japanese grocer will sell many pre-made *furikake*, some vegetarian and others not (non-vegetarian versions may contain ground dried seafood). Making your own opens up a world of possibilities.

Grinding the seasoning very finely helps it adhere to the popcorn. This will work best if the popcorn has at least a little oil or butter on it.

2 sheets nori seaweed
1 dried chile pepper of your choice, seeds and ribs removed
½ teaspoon sea salt (*fleur de sel* is a good choice)
Freshly popped popcorn (with a little butter or oil added if air-popped)

1 Hold a sheet of nori in a pair of tongs and toast lightly over a burner on medium heat, being careful not to set it on fire or burn your hands. Toast until it darkens slightly (about 20 seconds), moving it around to toast the whole sheet. Repeat with the second sheet.
2 Repeat the toasting process with the chile pepper.
3 Break up the nori and the chile pepper coarsely, so they will fit into a spice grinder. Add the salt, and grind thoroughly, until the mixture forms a very fine powder. Pass through a sieve if it isn't evenly ground. Taste and adjust salt as needed.
4 Sprinkle to taste on freshly popped corn, tossing to coat. You probably won't need all of the seasoning for one batch of popcorn; it will keep for a few days in a sealed container at room temperature.

GRINDING SPICES. Even if you don't grind your own coffee beans, a small coffee grinder is an invaluable kitchen tool. It makes short work of grinding whole spices to a fine powder. I love my mortar and pestle, but there are times when I just want to get the job of grinding spices done quickly and efficiently.

You'll either want to dedicate a separate coffee grinder for spices or clean your grinder thoroughly after using it for non-coffee purposes. To clean the grinder, spin a tablespoon of kosher salt or a little piece of white bread in it, then wipe it out with a paper towel.

grapefruit and avocado crudo

VEGAN

GLUTEN-FREE

SERVES 4

15 MINUTES

The idea for this dish came while I was experimenting with different ways to cut a red grapefruit. Cutting straight through the fruit vertically produced beautiful shimmering slabs that were visually reminiscent of raw fish. Playing off that idea, I treated them like *crudo* (the Italian equivalent of sashimi).

Crudo is typically dressed with olive oil, sea salt, and a citrus juice, which in this case is built in. I added avocado, capers, and chervil.

Don't put this dish together in advance! The grapefruit will start to break down into a juicy mess on your plate. You can cut the grapefruit ahead of time (and refrigerate it in a covered bowl), but wait until the last minute to assemble the platter.

2 Ruby Red grapefruit
1 ripe avocado, thinly sliced
About 12 sprigs fresh chervil
1 tablespoon capers, briefly soaked to remove some salt and drained
2 tablespoons fruity extra-virgin olive oil
Flaky sea salt (such as Maldon)
Freshly ground white or black pepper

1 To cut the grapefruit, use an extremely sharp chef's knife. Cut a ½-inch slice from the top and bottom, to expose the flesh. Resting the grapefruit on one of the cut ends, remove all the skin and pith by making four vertical cuts, producing a rough cube. Now slice vertically into ⅓-inch-thick slices, avoiding the core. (If you get just a little bit of core, you can put that side down on the plate.) Slicing grapefruit in this way produces a lot of waste material, so be sure and juice the rest for a cook's treat. If you don't care so much about creating the thin slices, you can cut the grapefruit into supremes (see the box on page 125).

2 Arrange the grapefruit slices pleasingly on a large platter.

3 Top each slice with 1 piece of avocado, 1 chervil sprig, and a few capers.

4 Drizzle with the olive oil.

5 Add a few grains of sea salt and a grinding of pepper to each slice.

seared tofu poke

VEGAN

GLUTEN-FREE
OPTION

SERVES 4

20 MINUTES

Poke (pronounced POH-keh) is the Hawaiian equivalent of sashimi or *crudo. Poke* is typically raw fish, seasoned with soy and onion, often on a bed of seaweed. This vegetarian version is made with seared tofu, which pairs perfectly with those Asian flavors.

For the seaweed, the best option is any fresh variety that is thin enough to eat raw. Keep your eye out for Sea Tangle brand in the refrigerated foods section of health food stores or Asian groceries; they make a delicious fresh mixed seaweed that is packed in salt. You simply rinse it and enjoy. The other option is dried *hijiki*, which must be rehydrated.

You can serve this *poke* at room temperature or chilled.

1 cup *ogo, limu kohu, hijiki*, or mixed seaweed (see headnote)
2 tablespoons vegetable oil
8 ounces firm tofu cut into 2 x 1 x ½-inch rectangles, thoroughly patted dry
1 tablespoon toasted sesame oil
1 tablespoon sweet soy sauce or *kecap manis* (use a wheat-free version for gluten-free)
1 tablespoon shoyu (use a wheat-free version for gluten-free)
1 teaspoon grated fresh ginger
1 teaspoon sriracha or similar thick Asian chile sauce, or wasabi paste (optional)
¼ cup thinly sliced scallions or sweet onions, such as Maui or Vidalia
Half a jalapeño pepper, thinly sliced (optional)
1 cup mung bean sprouts (or try *kaiware* radish sprouts for a spicy variation)
Sea salt (preferably Hawaiian)

1 Rinse or hydrate the seaweed according to the package directions. If it isn't thinly sliced, make it so.

2 Place a large, preferably cast-iron, skillet over high heat. Add the vegetable oil. When the oil shimmers, add the tofu pieces in a single layer and fry until well browned on both sides, about 5 minutes. Transfer to paper towels.

3 Whisk together the sesame oil, sweet soy sauce, shoyu, fresh ginger, and sriracha, if using, in a medium bowl. Toss the tofu in the sauce and let rest for 3 minutes. Use a slotted spoon to transfer the tofu to another bowl (reserve the sauce) and toss the tofu with most of the scallions and jalapeño, if using, reserving a little for garnish.

4 To serve, divide the bean sprouts among four bowls. Drain the seaweed as needed, pat it dry, and place a small mound of it atop the bean sprouts. Cover that with the tofu and drizzle on some of the reserved sauce. Garnish with the reserved scallions and jalapeño and a few grains of sea salt.

broiled tofu with miso jam (tofu dengaku)

VEGAN

MAKES 12
PIECES,
SERVING 4 TO 6

15 MINUTES

These tofu skewers, grilled over wickedly hot charcoal, are a popular street food in Japan. You can create a similar effect using your broiler.

Of course, if you have a grill going, go ahead and use it for the smoky flavor. Just oil the tofu well so it doesn't stick, and thread the tofu on pre-soaked skewers before grilling.

Be sure to use the firmest tofu you can find, and dry the surface thoroughly. Otherwise, it will keep leaching out water and refuse to brown properly.

If you are mainly familiar with miso in soup form, it might be a little bit of a surprise to experience the almost chocolaty intensity it packs when eaten practically straight.

2 tablespoons red miso
1 tablespoon mirin
1 tablespoon sake or dry sherry
1 teaspoon sugar
1 (14- to 16-ounce) block extra-firm tofu
Vegetable oil, for brushing
1 tablespoon toasted sesame seeds

SPECIAL EQUIPMENT: 24 short bamboo skewers (optional)

1 Preheat the broiler and position one of the oven racks 3 to 4 inches from the broiler element.
2 Whisk together the miso, mirin, sake, and sugar in a small bowl.
3 Wrap the tofu in a clean kitchen towel or paper towels for a minute or two to remove excess water from the outside. Cut into 6 slabs (about ¾ inch thick), then cut each slab in half to produce approximately 1½-inch squares. Lay all the pieces out in a single layer and pat firmly with a towel to dry the surfaces, then flip and pat again.
4 Place the tofu on a baking sheet and brush the tops with oil. Broil until well browned, about 5 minutes. Flip and broil until the other side is browned, about 3 minutes. Remove the pan from the oven and brush each piece of tofu with 1 teaspoon of the sauce. Return the tofu to the broiler until the sauce is bubbling, about 1 minute.
5 If using the skewers, insert two into each piece, parallel to each other and about ½ inch apart.
6 Sprinkle on the sesame seeds and serve immediately.

grilled treviso radicchio

GLUTEN-FREE

SERVES 4

5 MINUTES, IF
YOU HAVE A HOT
GRILL

Treviso is a type of radicchio that is hugely popular in Italy and is becoming easier to find at farmers' markets in America. Treviso, like all radicchio, is quite bitter. I find a few bites of it invigorating, but it might be too much for some folks. A milder alternative is to use a small head of romaine lettuce for this dish, removing the coarse outer leaves first.

Grilled treviso makes a great first course when you already have a grill fired up for your entrées. You can serve it as is or with grilled bread for an unusual bruschetta. A few toasted walnuts make a spectacular addition.

If you don't have a grill going, a grill pan on the stovetop can work as well.

1 head Treviso radicchio, round radicchio, or romaine lettuce (see headnote)
1 tablespoon extra-virgin olive oil
Aged balsamic vinegar or thick balsamic reduction (see page 72)
About 12 thin slices of Parmigiano-Reggiano, cut with a vegetable peeler
1 handful toasted walnut halves
Flaky sea salt (such as Maldon)
Freshly ground black pepper

1 Prepare an outdoor grill or a heat a cast-iron grill pan on your stovetop to a medium-hot temperature.

2 Cut the head of radicchio in half lengthwise, straight through the stem. Do not cut off the stem; you need it to hold the head together.

3 Brush the cut sides of the radicchio with the olive oil. Place on the grill, cut side down, and press down firmly with a spatula to maximize contact area. Grill until nicely seared and starting to wilt, about 2 to 3 minutes.

4 Remove from the grill and place on a serving platter. Cut into bite-size pieces and top with a generous drizzle of vinegar, the cheese, walnuts, a sprinkle of sea salt, and freshly ground pepper. Serve immediately.

chèvre with sautéed grapes

GLUTEN-FREE

SERVES 4

10 MINUTES

I love this appetizer because it comes together in minutes and tastes amazing, and the sautéed grapes provide an element of surprise and pleasure. It is a riff on a popular dish from Seattle's Osteria La Spiga, where they do it with Toma cheese wrapped in grape leaves.

This version is even simpler. You should feel free to try it with other cheeses and other herbs. Mint or basil would be delicious. How about grilled Halloumi cheese instead of the chèvre?

Serve with a crusty baguette or grilled flatbread.

8 ounces fresh, soft chèvre (goat cheese; I'm partial to the Laura Chenel brand)
2 tablespoons extra-virgin olive oil
1½ cups seedless red grapes, halved
1 tablespoon fresh chives, minced
1 tablespoon chive blossoms, pulled apart into individual florets (optional)
1 tablespoon fresh oregano leaves
Flaky sea salt (such as Maldon)

1   Cut the chèvre into 8 pieces and roll into balls. Arrange on a serving platter.

2   Just before you are ready to serve, heat 1 tablespoon of the olive oil in a medium sauté pan over medium-high heat. When it is hot, add the grapes and sauté them for 30 seconds, then pour them over and around the chèvre. (You only want to warm the grapes through, not cook them until they start to break down.)

3   Drizzle with the remaining 1 tablespoon olive oil. Top with the chives, chive blossoms (if using), oregano, and sea salt, and serve immediately.

KIMCHI is a Korean pickled and fermented side dish; the most common type is made with napa cabbage, but there's an enormous variety prepared with other vegetables—and even fruits. It is reputed to be very healthful because of the live beneficial bacterial cultures that thrive in it.

If you are vegetarian, you'll want to look closely at the ingredients of kimchi; many kimchis include shrimp or other seafood, but you can find vegetarian options. Explore different brands to find one you like. They are not all the same, by any means!

Asian grocers are likely to carry a selection of kimchis, but another place to look is your local farmers' market. There's been a recent surge in interest in fermented foods, and you may find local varieties with a lot more character than prepackaged brands.

king oyster mushroom lettuce wraps with ssamjang

VEGAN

MAKES 8
WRAPS,
SERVING 4 TO 8

10 MINUTES,
PLUS RICE
COOKING TIME

Ssamjang is a crazy delicious Korean condiment made from fermented bean paste, chile paste, and aromatics. The name literally means "wrapping sauce," which gives you a good clue as to how it is normally used. For this recipe, I double it up, as a grilling sauce and for passing at the table. You'll find it at Korean markets and online.

Korean markets are also good places to find king oyster mushrooms (*Pleurotus eryngii*, otherwise known as a king trumpet or French horn). They tend to be much less expensive there than at fancy grocers. They are big, meaty mushrooms with a mild flavor. Even folks who are skeptical about wild mushrooms will enjoy them.

¼ cup plus 1 tablespoon *ssamjang*
2 teaspoons mirin *or* 2 teaspoons dry sherry plus 1 teaspoon sugar
1 tablespoon vegetable oil
½ teaspoon toasted sesame oil
2 teaspoons sugar
½ teaspoon kosher salt
4 large king oyster mushrooms, halved lengthwise
2 cups cooked Calrose or jasmine rice, warm but not hot
8 leaves red-leaf or similar lettuce, washed and thoroughly dried
***Kaiware* radish sprouts**
6 tablespoons minced kimchi

1 Whisk 1 tablespoon of the *ssamjang* with the mirin until it starts to thin out, then whisk in the vegetable oil, sesame oil, sugar, and salt. Taste and adjust the seasoning. Toss the mushrooms with the sauce.

2 Heat a grill pan or large cast-iron skillet over medium-high heat. Add the mushrooms in one layer and cook until caramelized, about 2 minutes, then turn and cook until the other side is caramelized. Remove from the heat.

3 Whisk the remaining ¼ cup *ssamjang* with a little water if needed to reach a dipping-sauce consistency.

4 To serve, place ¼ cup of the rice in the middle of a lettuce leaf. Top with one oyster mushroom half, a small handful of *kaiware*, and a couple teaspoons of minced kimchi. Let diners roll up the leaves and dip in the *ssamjang*.

smoked asparagus with a panko-crusted egg

This dish is a little showy but not at all difficult. Make it as a first course for your next dinner party and you'll surprise and delight your guests. Eggs and asparagus have a natural affinity, and I've reinforced the smokiness of the asparagus with the addition of smoked paprika. The crunchy panko is an interesting counterpoint to the soft, smooth hard-cooked egg. And the sherry *gastrique*—a sauce made by reducing a flavorful vinegar with sugar—adds complex sweet, sour, and caramelized notes.

In this recipe, I show you how to smoke the asparagus with an improvised setup on your stovetop. If you have a commercial stovetop smoker or like to smoke foods on a barbecue, feel free to do that instead. Cherry is my favorite wood for smoking asparagus, but mesquite or alder is delicious, too.

3 large eggs
24 fat spears asparagus
Extra-virgin olive oil
½ cup sugar
1 cup sherry vinegar
Kosher salt
½ cup cornstarch
½ cup panko bread crumbs
Vegetable oil, for shallow frying
Smoked Spanish paprika
Flaky sea salt (such as Maldon)

SPECIAL EQUIPMENT: ½ cup wood chips, preferably cherry wood

1 Hard-cook 2 of the eggs (see page 51).

2 Choose a pot that you don't mind staining on the inside, has a tight-fitting lid, and is large enough to hold a steaming rack containing all of the asparagus in no more than a double layer. Wrap the wood chips loosely in aluminum foil, leaving the ends open. Poke several large holes in the top. Put the foil packet in the bottom of the pot. Place a steamer basket on top of that. Toss the asparagus lightly with olive oil and arrange in the steamer basket. Cover the pot and turn the heat to medium-high.

3 Smoke the asparagus for 5 minutes. Carefully lift the lid (it will be very hot), and poke a spear of asparagus with the tip of a knife to see if it is tender, with just a bit of resistance remaining. If not, keep cooking until they are done, checking every couple of minutes. When you lift the lid, if you don't get a whiff of smoke aroma, raise the heat a bit (and conversely, if you are getting a lot of smoke, lower the heat). When the asparagus is done, remove it from the smoker and set aside on a plate.

4   Simmer the sugar, sherry vinegar, and a pinch of salt in a small pot over medium heat until it is reduced enough to coat a spoon lightly when allowed to cool for 20 seconds. This should take about 5 minutes. Set the *gastrique* aside.

5   Set up 3 shallow bowls for breading. Put cornstarch in the first, a beaten egg in the second, and the panko, seasoned with salt, in the third. Fill a small skillet with ½ inch vegetable oil for frying, and heat over medium heat. Peel the hard-cooked eggs and cut them in half lengthwise. Dip the outside, rounded part of each egg first in cornstarch, then beaten egg, and finally panko. Try not to get any breading on the flat side of the egg. Pan-fry, rounded side down, until the breading is browned and crispy, about 2 minutes. Use a spatula to tilt the eggs gently to brown all of the panko up to the edge.

6   Reheat the asparagus with a very quick sauté in a bit of olive oil in a skillet over high heat.

7   To serve, put a light circular dusting of smoked paprika on a salad plate and top with the egg. Next to that, put down a teaspoon or so of the *gastrique*. Place 6 spears of the smoked asparagus on top of the *gastrique* in a pyramid.

8   Drizzle the asparagus with a bit of extra-virgin olive oil, season with a few grains of flaky sea salt, and serve immediately.

HARD-COOKED EGGS. To make perfect hard-cooked eggs, put raw eggs in a large pot with enough cold water to cover them by ½ inch. Cover the pot, bring to a boil, and immediately remove from the heat. Sprinkle in a little salt and leave covered for exactly 20 minutes. Drain the eggs and put them in an ice bath to stop the cooking. Peel. The result will be fully cooked but tender whites and yolks that are just set, with absolutely no green ring.

tomato confit and roasted garlic bruschetta

VEGAN

SERVES 4

1 HOUR
(10 MINUTES
ACTIVE)

Have you ever wondered what the difference is between crostini and bruschetta? A crostini is generally a small, crispy toast that is often served at room temperature. A bruschetta is a larger piece of grilled bread that is served warm or hot.

The mint adds an unexpected twist to this topping, but feel free to switch to oregano, basil, or parsley if you prefer. A few chopped black olives can be added as well.

1 head garlic
Extra-virgin olive oil
8 Tomato Confit halves (page 343), finely chopped
1 tablespoon finely sliced fresh mint leaves
¼ teaspoon kosher salt
4 thick slices rustic bread
Flaky sea salt (such as Maldon)

1 Preheat the oven to 300°F. Cut the top ¼ inch off the head of garlic, making sure to expose the top of each clove. Rub with a little olive oil and wrap in aluminum foil. Roast until the garlic is completely soft, about 45 minutes.

2 Squeeze all of the garlic cloves out of their skins and finely chop them. Mix with the tomato confit, mint, and kosher salt. Set aside.

3 Heat a grill pan over medium-high heat (use an outdoor grill if you have it going or a toaster oven as a last resort). Brush the bread generously on both sides with olive oil. Grill until well browned, with nice grill marks, about 2 minutes. Flip and grill the other side in the same manner.

4 Divide the topping among the four pieces of bread, season with a few flakes of sea salt, and serve immediately.

braised belgian endive with sauce gribiche

I first tasted the classic French *sauce gribiche* when I was interning at Seattle's landmark Canlis restaurant. *Gribiche* is powerfully flavored with mustard, vinegar, *cornichons*, capers, and a lot of fresh herbs. Chef Franey serves it with asparagus, which is superb. I like it equally well with quickly braised Belgian endive or steamed artichoke hearts. You'll want to have good bread on hand to mop up the extras.

The method for making the sauce is similar to that for homemade mayonnaise, but it isn't necessary to achieve a perfect emulsion; it is just fine for the olive oil to be partially separated.

FOR THE ENDIVES
2 tablespoons olive oil
Kosher salt
8 Belgian endives, halved lengthwise (don't trim stem end or they will fall apart)
¼ cup water

FOR THE SAUCE
1 large egg, hard-cooked (see page 51)
1 teaspoon Dijon mustard
¼ cup extra-virgin olive oil
2 teaspoons red wine vinegar or champagne vinegar
2 *cornichons*, very finely diced
1 teaspoon capers, very finely diced
¼ cup minced fresh chervil or fresh flatleaf parsley leaves, or a combination
1 teaspoon minced fresh tarragon
Freshly ground black pepper
Kosher salt

1 *For the endives:* Put the olive oil in a very large skillet over medium-high heat. Sprinkle in a big pinch of kosher salt. When the oil is hot, add the endives in a single layer, cut side down. Cook for 3 minutes, until beginning to brown, then add the water, cover, and reduce the heat to low. Cook until tender, about 10 minutes. Set aside to cool to room temperature, or refrigerate.

2 *For the sauce gribiche:* Separate the yolk and white of the hard-cooked egg. Finely dice the egg white. Force the yolk through your finest-mesh sieve into a bowl. Whisk the yolk with the Dijon mustard until it forms a paste. While whisking, slowly drizzle in the olive oil, as if you were making a mayonnaise. Don't worry if it is somewhat separated.

3 Whisk in the vinegar, *cornichons*, capers, chervil, tarragon, diced egg white, and a generous grind of black pepper. Taste and add salt if needed.

4 To serve, place the endives on a platter. Give the sauce a final stir, and spoon it over the endives.

cheddar-battered onion rings

SERVES 4
30 MINUTES

The idea for these rings came from a daydream on the way home from work. What if I could make perfect tempura-battered onion rings and somehow get them to taste like aged cheddar? I didn't want to create a melty mess and ruin the crunch, though.

I ended up broiling the cheese like I would for a *frico* (cheese crisp), and then grinding it into a powder to add to an otherwise standard tempura batter. The broiling cheese is pretty cool to watch; it looks like the surface of a boiling alien planet as all the moisture cooks off and the fat separates.

The basic batter is based on Chef Morimoto's (of *Iron Chef* fame) small-batch tempura, with a pinch of xanthan gum (which is available in many large markets and health food stores) added. That is optional but really helps with cling.

Try serving these with Stout Chocolate Malt (page 298) for an *Alice in Wonderland* spin on traditional diner food.

2 cups grated extra-sharp cheddar
1 large egg yolk
2 tablespoons vegetable oil
1 teaspoon kosher salt
1 big pinch xanthan gum (optional, see headnote)
1 cup all-purpose flour
¾ cup seltzer, plus additional as needed
Vegetable oil, for deep-frying
2 large white onions, peeled and cut into thick rings
All-purpose or rice flour, for dredging
Flaky sea salt (such as Maldon)

1 Preheat the broiler and position one of the oven racks 3 to 4 inches from the broiler element. Line a baking sheet with a silicone baking mat or parchment paper. Spread the cheddar cheese in a thin layer on the sheet. Watching rather closely, broil until the cheese is starting to brown, about 4 minutes. Allow to cool completely. Pat off excess oil. Using a spice grinder or mortar and pestle, crush the cheese into a fine powder.

2 Whisk together 3 ounces (a scant ½ cup) of the cheese powder, the egg yolk, 2 tablespoons vegetable oil, kosher salt, xanthan gum (if using), 1 cup flour, and seltzer. The batter should be rather thin, the consistency of crêpe batter, not thick pancake batter. Add more seltzer as needed.

3 In a large saucepan, heat 3 inches of oil to 360°F. Working in small batches, dredge each onion ring in flour, shake off the excess, dip in the batter, allow the excess to drip off, and add to the oil. (I find this easiest to do with chopsticks.) Deep-fry until golden brown; remove to paper towels to drain. Pat lightly to remove excess oil. Season with sea salt. Serve immediately.

caramelized apple and blue cheese crostini

These crostini are a cinch to make, and they will surprise your guests with the unexpected combination of caramelized apple, blue cheese, and tarragon. Serve them with a crisp, dry white wine for an elegant pre-dinner snack.

I prefer a creamy blue cheese that will get a little melty on the warm apples, such as Bleu de Causses, but any blue cheese will work. Instead of tarragon, you could use basil or even arugula.

If you have any fancy finishing salts (which you can find at high-end food retailers), this is the perfect dish to use them on. A few grains will sit beautifully on top of the apples and add a bit of extra crunch and interest.

½ cup loosely packed fresh tarragon leaves
2 tablespoons extra-virgin olive oil
16 thin slices crusty baguette
1 tablespoon unsalted butter
2 small apples (such as Pink Lady), each cored and cut into 16 wedges
Tiny pinch of cayenne pepper
Freshly ground black pepper
¼ cup blue cheese (such as Bleu de Causses or Gorgonzola Dolce),
    at room temperature
Flaky sea salt (such as Maldon) or large-crystal sea salt
    (such as red Hawaiian salt)

1 Preheat the oven or toaster oven to 400°F.

2 Set aside 32 nice-looking tarragon leaves. In a mortar and pestle or mini food processor, coarsely puree the remaining tarragon with the olive oil.

3 Brush the baguette slices with the tarragon oil, reserving the crushed tarragon. Arrange on a baking sheet and toast in the oven or toaster oven until golden brown and crispy, about 5 minutes.

4 Melt the butter in a large skillet over medium heat. Cook the apples in a single layer, turning once (work in batches if needed), until both sides are golden brown and somewhat tender, about 5 minutes. Season with a pinch of cayenne pepper and several grinds of black pepper.

5 To serve, arrange 2 slices of cooked apple on each piece of toast. Top with ½ teaspoon of the blue cheese, a speck of the crushed tarragon, 2 whole tarragon leaves, and a few grains of sea salt.

chana chaat with pappadams

VEGAN OPTION

GLUTEN-FREE

SERVES 4

20 MINUTES

Chaat is a whole family of delicious Indian snacks, generally served cold or at room temperature, either as street food or in shops that specialize in these treats. They aren't very well known in America, but you can sometimes find a few such items on a menu, especially at South Indian restaurants.

Pappadams are lovely, crispy thin crackers made from lentil flour; you've probably had them as a free appetizer at Indian restaurants. Here I top them with spicy chickpeas, yogurt, tamarind, and candied ginger.

Chaat masala is a spice mixture that can be found in packets at any Indian grocery. If you don't have it, you can make a fine approximation by grinding together equal parts toasted fennel and cumin seeds, *amchoor* (dried mango) powder if available, cayenne pepper, and a pinch of ground ginger.

2 tablespoons boiling water
2 tablespoons tamarind concentrate
2 teaspoons sugar
4 black pepper (or other flavor) *pappadams*
2 cup cooked and cooled (or rinsed and drained canned) chickpeas
2 tablespoons *chaat masala*
1 teaspoon kosher salt
½ cup yogurt (omit for vegan)
1 teaspoon mild chili powder
A few sprigs of fresh cilantro
4 pieces of crystallized (candied) ginger, thinly sliced

1   Stir together the boiling water, tamarind paste, and sugar in a small bowl until the tamarind is dissolved. Taste and add more sugar if needed. Reserve in the refrigerator.

2   Heat a heavy skillet over high heat. Toast a *pappadam* by pressing it onto the skillet with a spatula or another pan until golden brown, flipping once and blistering on both sides, about 2 minutes. Remove and repeat with the remaining *pappadams*.

3   Mix the chickpeas with the *chaat masala* and salt. You could also add diced cucumbers, potatoes, or onions. Taste and adjust the seasoning.

4   Place a *pappadam* on each of four serving plates and top each with one-quarter of the chickpeas, 2 tablespoons yogurt, a bit of chili powder, and cilantro. Drizzle a little tamarind sauce on the plate, scatter with a few pieces of the crystallized ginger, and serve immediately.

TALKING WITH MY BLOG READERS. Feedback from my blog readers really helped out with this recipe! In my original version, the *pappadam* was formed into an edible bowl, and the tamarind was lightly gelled with agar-agar. While this made for a beautiful presentation, it was fussy and more trouble than most folks wanted to go to. I love the updated version of this *chaat*, which is much more accessible and tastes just as good.

chanterelle banh mi bites

VEGAN OPTION

MAKES 12
SMALL PIECES

30 MINUTES
(15 MINUTES
ACTIVE)

Banh mi are Vietnamese sandwiches that have taken the West Coast by storm. They are served on crusty baguettes, spread with a little mayo, and stuffed with pickled vegetables and a filling of your choice. Tofu is usually on the menu, though vegetarians still have to watch out for fish sauce.

I've adapted the traditional *banh mi* into a little two-bite crostini that makes a great appetizer. It will really wake up your palate with bright flavors and crunchy textures. If you can't find chanterelle or other wild mushrooms, a thin slab of well-fried tofu would also be delicious, or you could use portobello mushrooms, cut into pieces that will sit nicely atop your baguette slices.

FOR THE PICKLED VEGETABLES
½ cup rice vinegar
¼ cup sugar
½ teaspoon kosher salt
1 whole star anise
Freshly ground black pepper
12 thin round slices daikon
½ cup julienned carrot (about one 6-inch carrot, cut into pieces about 1½ inches
    long then thinly sliced)

FOR THE SEASONED MAYONNAISE
⅓ cup mayonnaise or vegan mayonnaise
1 teaspoon sriracha or similar thick Asian chile sauce

TO COMPLETE THE DISH
2 teaspoons vegetable oil
1 teaspoon minced lemongrass, tender white parts only (see page 253)
12 small chanterelle mushrooms (or cut larger ones to appropriate size)
Kosher salt
12 slices baguette, each about ⅜ inch thick
12 slices cucumber, peeled if the skin is tough
12 sprigs fresh cilantro (smaller than your baguette slices)
12 paper-thin slices jalapeño pepper, seeds removed
Flaky sea salt (such as Maldon)

▼ ▼ ▼

1. *For the pickled vegetables:* Combine the rice vinegar, sugar, kosher salt, star anise, and a few grinds of black pepper in a small saucepan. Cook over medium heat until the mixture is nearly boiling and the sugar is dissolved. Turn off the heat and stir in the daikon and carrot. Cool to room temperature, then refrigerate for at least 20 minutes or up to 1 day.
2. *For the seasoned mayonnaise:* Mix together the mayonnaise and hot sauce.
3. *To complete the dish:* Place a small skillet over medium-high heat. Add the vegetable oil and when it is hot, add the lemongrass, chanterelle mushrooms, and a pinch of kosher salt. Cook, stirring a couple of times, until the mushrooms are tender and lightly browned, about 3 minutes.
4. Toast the baguette slices until very lightly browned. They should still be more soft than crunchy.
5. Spread each piece of baguette with 1 teaspoon of the seasoned mayonnaise. Top with 1 slice of the pickled daikon and 1 slice of cucumber, followed by a few pickled carrots. Top that with 1 mushroom, a sprig of cilantro, a slice of jalapeño, and a few flakes of sea salt. Serve immediately.

GET ORGANIZED. There are a lot of ingredients to put on each crostini, so have them all lined up and ready to go. It will be more efficient if you first spread all the crostini with the mayo, then add the daikon to all of them, and so forth.

paella cakes with manchego and marmalade

MAKES 12,
SERVING 6 TO 12
AS AN APPETIZER
OR 4 TO 6 AS A
MAIN COURSE

45 MINUTES

Everyone agrees that the best part of paella is the *soccarat*, the crispy crust formed where the rice sticks to the bottom of the pan. Frying the rice as a patty creates even more surface area for that deliciously toasted flavor.

I learned about the combination of smoked paprika (*pimentón*) and cinnamon from an Amsterdam-based blogger named Mem, who writes Vegetarian Duck. The pairing sounded surprising to me, but when I tried it, I was blown away. Rather than tasting like two spices, it comes across as a unified, individual flavor.

The marmalade provides an interesting sweet-tart counterpoint to the rice and Manchego cheese. My favorite brand, June Taylor, has large pieces of orange peel, but if you can't find that, just use a small amount of any brand of Seville orange marmalade that you prefer. Another option would be a little bit of minced preserved lemon.

¼ cup extra-virgin olive oil
Half a white onion, finely diced
Half a red bell pepper, finely diced
2 cups short-grain Spanish rice (a type sold for paella; in a pinch you
    could use an Italian variety like Arborio)
3½ cups vegetable broth or water
2 teaspoons smoked paprika
1 big pinch of saffron
Kosher salt
2 large eggs
2 cups Homemade Bread Crumbs (page 345) or panko bread crumbs
Vegetable oil, for pan-frying
12 slices Manchego cheese

TO SERVE
1 teaspoon smoked paprika mixed with ¼ teaspoon ground cinnamon
About ¼ cup Seville orange marmalade
Flaky sea salt (such as Maldon)
Freshly ground black pepper

1 In a large saucepan with a tight-fitting lid, heat the olive oil over high heat. Cook the onion and bell pepper for 3 minutes. Add the rice and cook, stirring, until slightly translucent, about 2 more minutes.

2 Add the vegetable broth, smoked paprika (taste it first; if yours is hot, adjust down unless you like that sort of thing), and saffron. If the broth isn't salted, add 2 teaspoons kosher salt. Bring to a boil, cover, and reduce to a bare simmer.

▼ ▼ ▼

3 Cook until all of the water is absorbed. Taste a few grains. If they aren't fully cooked, add a bit more water. They should be just slightly al dente, not mushy.

4 Allow the rice to cool. If you are in a hurry, spread it on a sheet pan and refrigerate.

5 Taste the rice and adjust the seasoning, if necessary. Place the rice in a large bowl. Beat the eggs and mix them in. You should have a mixture that you can just barely squeeze into a patty in your hands. Spread the bread crumbs in a flat dish.

6 Heat a large, heavy skillet over medium heat. Add about ⅛ inch of oil to the pan. Working quickly, grab a handful of rice, form it into a rough patty, press it into the bread crumbs on each side, and add to the skillet. Use a spatula to gently shape into a nice cake, not too thick— you want the eggs to set inside.

7 Fry until quite crispy and brown on one side, 2 to 3 minutes, then flip and top immediately with a piece of Manchego. Fry until the other side is also crispy and browned; transfer to paper towels. Continue making and frying patties, adding more oil to the skillet as needed.

8 *To serve:* Lightly dust serving plates with the paprika-cinnamon mixture, add the patties, and top each with about 1 teaspoon of the marmalade, some sea salt, and a few grinds of black pepper.

tempeh-filled potstickers (gyoza)

VEGAN

MAKES
ABOUT 48

1½ HOURS
(FASTER AND
MORE FUN IF
YOU GET
SOME HELP
FORMING THE
DUMPLINGS)

The first rule of potstickers is that you can never make enough of them—at least in my family. We fight over the last few like seagulls over a spilled bag of kettle corn.

If you haven't had them, potstickers are Chinese or Japanese pan-fried dumplings with a savory filling, dipped in a soy, vinegar, and sesame oil sauce. What's not to like? Plan on making a minimum of 4 per person as an appetizer; but really, you could make a whole meal of a big plate of potstickers along with a salad or two and a beer, and I bet you wouldn't get any complaints.

Potstickers get their name because of the unusual cooking technique. The dumplings are first fried in a lightly oiled pan until they brown and stick a bit. Then water is added and the pan covered to steam the tops and release the bottoms. Finally, the lid is removed and the remaining water cooked off.

Where most vegetarian potstickers go wrong is by trying to use too many vegetables in the filling. I've had terrible versions stuffed with spinach, or lots of water chestnuts and so forth. This is not the place for a distracting crunch, and you certainly don't want your dumplings leaching water. My filling of choice is tempeh. I sauté it first to develop the flavor, and then crumble it and mash it with the other ingredients. It gives just the right bite.

If for some reason you don't need the whole batch at once, place them on a baking sheet in a single layer without touching each other, freeze, then transfer them to a zipper-top plastic bag when fully frozen. They can be cooked later without defrosting; just allow a little more time.

FOR THE SAUCE
¼ cup good-quality soy sauce, shoyu, or tamari
2 tablespoons rice vinegar
1 teaspoon hot-chile sesame oil *or* 1 teaspoon toasted sesame oil
   and ½ teaspoon chile paste
1 scallion, whites part only, cut into tiny, thin rings

▼ ▼ ▼

FOR THE POTSTICKERS
3 tablespoons vegetable oil, plus additional as needed
1 pound tempeh, cut into thin slabs
1 cup very thinly sliced napa or green cabbage
6 scallions, white and light green parts only, minced
4 teaspoons Chinese rice wine (dry sherry is a good substitute)
2 tablespoons soy sauce
Kosher salt
1 tablespoon cornstarch
48 (about 1 typical package) potsticker wrappers (also called gyoza wrappers;
   if possible, choose a thick variety)
1/3 cup water, plus additional as needed

1 *For the sauce:* Combine the soy sauce, vinegar, hot-chile sesame oil, and scallion in a small
   bowl. Taste and adjust for salt/vinegar/heat balance and set aside. I like mine pretty vinegary.
2 *For the potstickers:* Heat a large skillet, preferably cast iron, with a tight-fitting lid, over medium-
   high heat. Add 2 tablespoons of the oil. Fry the tempeh in a single layer, working in batches if
   needed, until golden brown on both sides. Set aside to cool.
3 In the same skillet, adding a bit more oil if needed, fry the cabbage until it's browned and most
   of its water has cooked out, 4 to 5 minutes. Turn off the heat.
4 Thoroughly crumble the tempeh into a bowl. Mix it with the cabbage, scallions, rice wine, and
   soy sauce. Taste and add salt as needed. You can also add more rice wine or soy, but don't
   make it too wet. When you are satisfied with the taste, sprinkle in the cornstarch and toss thoroughly to combine. (This will absorb any water released when the dumplings are cooking).
5 To form the potstickers, take one potsticker wrapper and moisten the entire edge with a finger-
   tip or pastry brush dipped in water. Place a heaping teaspoon of filling in the center. Pick it up,
   fold in half, and seal the edge. Decoratively crimp the edge if you like. Set on a plate or sheet
   pan, seal side up; press down gently to flatten the bottom.
6 To cook the potstickers, heat that big skillet back up again over medium-high heat and add the
   remaining 1 tablespoon of oil. Add the potstickers in a single layer, flat side down, not touching
   (but they can be close). You will probably need to do two or more batches. Fry until they are
   dark golden brown on the bottom, 1 to 2 minutes. Add 1/3 cup of water and cover the pan. Cook
   for about 3 minutes. Remove the lid and keep cooking until the water is totally gone—otherwise
   they won't be crispy. Repeat the process for the remaining potstickers, adding 1 tablespoon oil
   to the skillet for browning and 1/3 cup water for cooking.
7 Serve hot, with the dipping sauce.

chickpea fritters

These little chickpea cakes are versatile; you can serve them as an appetizer, a side dish, or as the protein-packed star of the show. They are somewhat like a pan-fried falafel, but without a deep-fried crust, so we amp up the internal flavoring. Try them with Tomato Jam with Rosemary and Saffron (page 344) for a big flavor combination.

3 cups cooked chickpeas (or two 15-ounce cans, rinsed and drained)
½ cup scallions, white and light green parts only, very thinly sliced
5 garlic cloves, minced
¼ teaspoon minced fresh rosemary leaves
¾ teaspoon kosher salt
Grated zest of 1 lemon
Juice of half a lemon
1 egg, lightly beaten
½ cup all-purpose flour
¼ cup Homemade Bread Crumbs (page 345)
¼ cup toasted sesame seeds
Vegetable oil, for shallow frying
Flaky sea salt (such as Maldon)

1 Combine the chickpeas, scallions, garlic, rosemary, kosher salt, lemon zest and juice, egg, flour, bread crumbs, and sesame seeds in a food processor and buzz until you have a fairly uniform mixture, but stop before you make a smooth puree; you want to leave some texture. You should be able to form it into a ball that holds its shape. It should be neither crumbly nor a batter. Add liquid or bread crumbs as necessary to reach the right moisture level.

2 Heat a few tablespoons of oil in a large skillet, preferably cast iron, over medium-high heat. Take a golf ball–size piece of dough, press it in your hands into a flattened 3-inch patty, and place in the skillet. Repeat with as many as will fit comfortably. Fry on one side until golden brown, about 3 minutes, then flip and brown the other side, about 2 more minutes. Transfer to paper towels and continue frying the patties, adding more oil as necessary. Serve hot, sprinkled with a bit of sea salt.

indian potato fritters (aloo tikki)

VEGAN

MAKES 10 FRITTERS

40 MINUTES
(20 MINUTES
ACTIVE)

Aloo tikki are one of the classic street foods of India. In Delhi, you will find vendors setting up shop on any street corner to peddle these simple mashed-potato fritters. Each *aloo tikki walla*, or seller, has his own special technique and loyal customers who swear that this is the only one worth eating. I live for the day that America's street-food scene catches up to the rest of the world's!

In the meantime, here is my version of this dish. Crispy on the outside, creamy on the inside, these little guys are just two bites of pure goodness. Try them with Banana Raita (page 337) for an incredible combination of tastes.

1 pound russet or Yukon Gold potatoes (about 4 medium Yukon Golds)
½ cup peas, defrosted if frozen
2 tablespoons Homemade Bread Crumbs (page 345) or panko bread crumbs
1 teaspoon salt
1 teaspoon ground turmeric
½ teaspoon cayenne pepper
¼ teaspoon freshly ground black pepper
2 teaspoons minced fresh ginger
2 teaspoons coriander seeds
2 teaspoons cumin seeds
Vegetable oil, for shallow frying
Flaky sea salt (such as Maldon)

1   Place the potatoes in large pot of cold salted water. Bring to a boil, cook until tender, drain, cool thoroughly, and peel.

2   Lightly mash the potatoes (a potato ricer is ideal for this). Lightly mash the peas and mix them into the potatoes. Add the bread crumbs, salt, turmeric, cayenne pepper, black pepper, and ginger.

3   In a small skillet, toast the coriander and cumin seeds over medium-low heat just until fragrant, about 1 minute. Grind the spices in a mortar and pestle or spice grinder and add to the potato mixture. Mix everything thoroughly (using your hands is the easiest way to do this).

4   Fill a large skillet with oil to a depth of about ⅛ inch and heat over medium-high heat. Moisten your hands. Form patties by taking golf ball–size pieces of the potato mixture and patting them flat into 2½-inch rounds about ¾ inch thick. Press fairly firmly so they don't fall apart when frying. Fry the patties until golden brown, about 2 minutes on each side. Transfer to paper towels and finish with flaky sea salt.

blue-potato tarts

I love to make these tarts using a variety of potato that is blue all the way through. The presentation really shows off this beautiful vegetable. You can of course use other varieties. It is nice if they are small enough to arrange whole slices on these rectangular tarts.

If you happen to have truffle salt, you can use it throughout this recipe to add an extra dimension of flavor; it will still be perfectly delicious if you use regular kosher salt. (Of course, if you have an actual black truffle on hand, you can shave it into the cream and on top of the finished dish, and then invite me for dinner.)

6 small purple potatoes (each about 3 inches long)
1 tablespoon extra-virgin olive oil, plus additional for brushing
Truffle salt or kosher salt
1 sprig fresh rosemary
2 tablespoons water
1 recipe Basic Pastry Dough, chilled (page 351)
¼ cup heavy cream
½ cup fresh chèvre (goat cheese)
1 garlic clove, minced
1 tablespoon aged balsamic vinegar or thick balsamic reduction (see page 72)
1 tablespoon minced fresh flatleaf parsley leaves, for garnish

1 Preheat the oven to 400°F.

2 Slice the potatoes into very thin, even slices, between $\frac{1}{16}$ inch and $\frac{1}{8}$ inch thick. A mandoline is ideal for this job; you can also use the slicing blade on a food processor. In a small baking dish with a cover, toss the potatoes with 1 tablespoon olive oil and ¼ teaspoon truffle salt. Add the sprig of rosemary and the water. Cover and bake until the potatoes are fully tender but not falling apart, about 15 minutes. Remove the lid and allow to cool.

3 Line a baking sheet with parchment paper or a silicone mat. Roll out the pastry crust into two 4 x 12-inch rectangles and transfer to the baking sheet. Use your hands to form a low raised edge all the way around the rectangles. Prick the dough all over with a fork. Bake until golden brown, 10 to 15 minutes. Remove and let cool for 10 minutes.

▼ ▼ ▼

4 Whisk together the cream, chèvre, garlic, and ¼ teaspoon truffle salt. Brush the tart crusts with olive oil and then spread the chèvre mixture evenly over the crusts. Lay the potato slices over the tarts neatly, overlapping so about ⅛ inch of each potato is revealed. (You'll have more than you need; this allows for a few slices to break.) Brush the potatoes with more olive oil and sprinkle on a bit more salt.

5 Bake to heat through, about 10 minutes. Remove from the oven, allow to cool slightly, then drizzle with the aged balsamic vinegar and garnish with the parsley. Cut each tart into 5 slices and serve immediately.

BALSAMIC REDUCTION. If you don't have thick, aged balsamic vinegar on hand, you can make your own substitute in just a couple of minutes. It won't have the complexity of the real thing, but it is delicious in its own way (and a whole lot less expensive). Put 1 tablespoon of sugar in your smallest saucepan and place it over medium-high heat. Cook, without stirring, until the sugar melts and turns golden brown, about 3 minutes. Remove from the heat and carefully add 6 tablespoons of thin grocery-store balsamic vinegar. Return to high heat and whisk to dissolve the caramel into the vinegar. Cook until the liquid is reduced to about 1 tablespoon. You can test by dipping a spoon in it and allowing it to cool for a few seconds. If it is syrupy, it is done. Transfer to a small bowl and allow to cool before drizzling on the potato tart.

risotto balls (arancini di riso)

Arancini means "little oranges" in Italian, but these guys aren't quite as healthful as a piece of citrus. They are actually balls of risotto, stuffed with cheese, rolled in bread crumbs and deep-fried. What's not to like?

In Sicily, where they originate, arancini can be filled with all sorts of things, ranging from a slow-cooked ragu to ham or even mushrooms. Traditionally, they are served with a basic tomato sauce for dipping, though a drizzle of good aged balsamic vinegar is also delicious.

Although arancini are traditionally street food, you could serve them as a passed appetizer at a party or a fairly filling first course. And although they are a bit labor-intensive, you can prepare everything the day before so all you have to do at showtime is the actual rolling in bread crumbs and frying.

4 cups clear vegetable broth (Seitenbacher broth mix is excellent)
2 tablespoons extra-virgin olive oil
½ cup finely diced onion
1¼ cups Arborio or other risotto rice
¼ cup dry white wine or dry vermouth
¼ cup freshly grated Parmesan
Kosher salt
3 large eggs
4 ounces scamorza, smoked mozzarella, or other flavorful, meltable Italian
  cheese, cut into cubes a little bigger than ½ inch
Vegetable oil, for deep-frying
1½ cups finely ground Homemade Bread Crumbs (page 345)
Flaky sea salt (such as Maldon)
1½ cups basic tomato sauce (your favorite homemade or prepared), warmed

1 Pour the broth into a saucepan and bring it to a simmer.

2 Heat a medium saucepan over medium-high heat. Add the olive oil and onion and cook, stirring, until the onion softens but doesn't brown, 1 to 2 minutes. Add the rice and cook, stirring, until it turns translucent, about 1 minute. Add the wine and cook for 30 seconds.

3 Begin to add the broth. Initially, add just enough to cover the rice. Reduce to a simmer. Stir occasionally—you don't need to stir it as much as you would if you were serving this as regular risotto. Add broth occasionally, as you see it dip below the level of the rice. You probably won't need all of it. Stop when the rice is al dente—tender to bite but with a tiny hint of resistance in the center. Don't add so much liquid that the rice is soupy. Stir in the Parmesan. Taste and add salt if needed.

▼ ▼ ▼

4 Allow the rice to cool to room temperature. You can spread it out on a baking sheet if you want that to happen faster. Beat 1 egg lightly and stir it into the rice.

5 With dampened hands, form the rice into 12 balls about 1½ inches in diameter. Poke a hole into each of the balls, insert a cube of cheese, then re-form the rice around the cheese. If you like, you can now store these pre-formed balls in a single layer in the refrigerator for a day. Wrap them well so they don't dry out.

6 When you are ready to finish cooking, heat 3 inches of oil in a deep saucepan to 360°F. (You can use a deep pot on the stove or a dedicated deep-fryer appliance.) Beat the remaining 2 eggs in a shallow bowl and place the bread crumbs in another shallow bowl. (Hint: Don't put all the bread crumbs in the bowl at once; that way, if you have some left they will be uncontaminated to save for later.) Dip each ball first in the beaten eggs, then in the bread crumbs, rolling to coat them. Fry the balls in small batches so the oil doesn't cool down too much, which would make them greasy. Cook, turning occasionally, until deep brown.

7 Remove the balls to plates covered in paper towels. Season with flaky sea salt. Allow them to cool a bit before serving and warn your guests about the molten cheese in the middle, so they don't burn their mouths. (These guys really hold the heat, especially in the center.) Serve with a bowl of the tomato sauce for dipping.

soups

garlic miso broth

VEGAN

MAKES 4 SMALL
OR 2 LARGE
SERVINGS

15 MINUTES

Every culture has a soup to which it attributes magical healing powers. I find this broth incredibly restorative when I'm coming back from a cold—but it's also what I turn to when I just want something quick and deeply warming. If you want to make it into something more substantial, add a few deep-fried puffs of tofu (available at Asian groceries) or thinly sliced vegetables. Personally, I prefer the austere but fortifying broth on its own.

I always have a couple of kinds of miso in the refrigerator. Sealed airtight, miso keeps for a very long time and is standing by when I want it for soup or to add deep flavor to a sauce.

A whole head of garlic sounds like a lot, but because it is simmered (rather than sautéed), the flavor mellows rapidly into a sweetness that blends easily with the flavor of miso. I really like to taste the garlic, so I keep the amount of miso on the low side, but you could also boost it up to 2 or even 3 tablespoons.

4 cups water, plus an additional few tablespoons
1 head garlic (about 10 cloves), peeled and thinly sliced
1 tablespoon red miso
1 teaspoon high-quality tamari or shoyu
1 teaspoon toasted sesame oil
Kosher salt
16 deep-fried tofu puffs (optional), at room temperature
1 tablespoon thinly sliced scallion

1   Pour the 4 cups water into a saucepan and bring to a simmer. Add the garlic and simmer for 10 minutes.

2   Whisk the miso, tamari, and sesame oil with a few tablespoons of water until it forms a pourable paste. Remove the garlic broth from the heat and whisk in the miso paste.

3   Strain the soup to remove the garlic and any undissolved bits of miso. Return to the pot and reheat but do not boil. Taste and add salt or more tamari if needed.

4   Ladle into serving bowls. Add the tofu puffs, if using, sprinkle on a few scallion slices, and serve immediately.

roasted maitake mushrooms
in smoky tea broth

VEGAN

SERVES 4

30 MINUTES

Maitakes, also known as hen-of-the-woods (not to be confused with chicken-of-the-woods, which is completely different!), are a wild mushroom well worth seeking out at farmers' markets or gourmet grocers. Maitakes are rather expensive, and their dramatic ruffled appearance and rich flavor are unusual, so when I use them, I like to make them the focus of a dish.

If you have never had lapsang souchong tea, you are in for a treat. It is intensely smoky, unlike any other tea I've had. That smokiness makes it a perfect broth base to show off the earthiness of roasted maitakes.

You could cut the maitake up into bite-size pieces, but this dish is more dramatic when the mushroom is served in larger pieces—which also keeps it from getting soggy. Give guests a knife so they can cut the maitake at the last moment.

½ cup finely diced bok choy stems
1 tablespoon water
1 pound fresh maitake mushroom(s)
3 tablespoons vegetable oil
½ teaspoon kosher salt
2 teaspoons lapsang souchong tea
2 cups boiling water
1 tablespoon tamari
Toasted sesame oil
Flaky sea salt (such as Maldon)
2 teaspoons finely sliced scallion, white and light green parts only

1 Preheat the oven to 450°F using convection, or 475°F without convection. Warm four shallow soup bowls.

2 Place the bok choy in a small bowl with the 1 tablespoon water and microwave on High for 1 minute. (Alternatively, you can steam the bok choy or blanch it in boiling water.) Reserve.

3 Divide the mushroom into 4 portions (leaving the pieces as large as possible) and place on a rimmed baking sheet. Toss with the vegetable oil, coating the mushroom as evenly as possible, and sprinkle with the kosher salt. Roast until fragrant, starting to brown, and becoming tender, about 20 minutes.

▼ ▼ ▼

4 While the mushroom is roasting, place the lapsang souchong tea in a small, heatproof bowl and cover with the boiling water; allow to steep for 5 minutes. Strain. Add the tamari. Taste and season with a bit of salt if needed. The broth should be smoky and mildly salty, with a distinct note of soy.

5 When the mushrooms are ready, place one portion in each bowl. Place the bok choy around the maitake. Reheat the broth in the microwave and divide among the bowls. Top each bowl with a drizzle of toasted sesame oil, a pinch of flaky sea salt, and the scallions. Serve piping hot.

TALKING WITH MY BLOG READERS. I learned a lot from conversations with the readers who made this soup when I sent it out for additional testing. The original version called for a garnish of lime zest, but not a single person chose to use it. And I had also listed some other ingredients as optional. Looking back, I see that I was just making this simple dish too complicated. Sometimes the best way to strengthen a dish is to edit it down so a single, clear idea shines through.

BUYING AND STORING DRIED HERBS AND SPICES. Buying most dried herbs and spices in prepackaged jars at the grocery store is a huge waste of money. You will find much better prices in the bulk section of natural foods stores or ethnic markets, and you can buy as much or as little as you need. Try to find a store with a lot of turnover, to ensure that the herbs haven't been sitting around too long. When you buy in bulk, you can also take a tiny pinch and give it a rub and a sniff to make sure the aromas are lively.

When you get your herbs and spices home, store them in tightly closed small jars, preferably in a drawer or cabinet. You want to minimize their exposure to light, heat, oxygen, and moisture. If you must store them on an open shelf, dark glass bottles will minimize light damage.

Most herbs and spices are at their best only for a few months after purchase. If in doubt, rub a pinch between your fingers, and smell and taste. If you don't get bright, full flavors, put them in the compost and get a new batch. If they aren't too flat, just a little weak, you can still use them. But add a little more than the recipe calls for.

cucumber and dill soup (tarator)

GLUTEN-FREE

MAKES 8 CUPS,
SERVING 6 TO 8

20 MINUTES,
PLUS 1 HOUR TO
CHILL

The recipe for this refreshing, yogurt-based soup comes from my wife's cousin Sabi, an Israeli whose family emigrated from Bulgaria, where the soup is known as *tarator*. Our family elaborates it with mint and chives in addition to the traditional dill. It is perfect for a hot summer day when you don't want to heat up the kitchen.

Sabi's recipe calls for 4 cloves of garlic, but I find that 1 or 2 are just about right. If you are making it a day in advance, remember that the garlic will grow in strength.

I prefer the traditional method, where the cucumbers are chopped by hand, while my wife likes them peeled and pureed in the food processor. Try it both ways and decide for yourself!

3 medium cucumbers or 2 large English cucumbers
2 tablespoons rice vinegar or other mild-flavored vinegar
¼ cup extra-virgin olive oil
1 tablespoon kosher salt
½ teaspoon freshly ground black pepper
1 or 2 garlic cloves, minced (see headnote)
¼ cup finely chopped fresh chives or scallions, white and light green parts only
½ cup loosely packed fresh mint leaves, finely chopped
1 bunch fresh dill, stems removed, finely chopped (reserve 1 tablespoon for garnish)
4 cups (1 quart) low-fat yogurt
2 cups (1 pint) low-fat sour cream, plus additional if needed

1 Peel the cucumbers only if the skin is tough. Cut the cucumbers in half lengthwise and remove the seeds with a spoon. Very finely dice the cucumbers (the cubes should be about ⅛ inch in size). The easiest way to do this is to cut it into long strips, then cut those in half lengthwise, then cut across. You may need to go back over the whole pile with your knife, as when mincing herbs. (For a different style of soup, or if there isn't time to chop the cucumbers by hand, peel them and puree in a food processor.) Put the cucumbers in a large bowl, which can be the bowl you ultimately use to serve the soup.

2 Add the vinegar, olive oil, salt, pepper, garlic, chives, mint, and dill and stir well.

3 Stir in the yogurt and sour cream. Taste and adjust the seasoning.

4 Refrigerate for at least 1 hour. Chill your serving bowls as well.

5 Check the soup texture. If it is very thick, stir in a little cold water. If it is too thin, you can add a little more sour cream. Taste and adjust the seasoning again. To serve, ladle into serving bowls and garnish with the reserved dill.

cool tomato and buttermilk soup

GLUTEN-FREE

SERVES 4

10 MINUTES

This refreshingly tart, beautifully pink soup lends itself to improvisation. You could make a vegan version using part vegan sour cream and part soy (or rice or hemp) milk. A little bit of lemon zest added to the puree is great. You could garnish with cherry tomato halves or diced cucumber instead of additional confit, or use a different herb, such as tiny leaves of oregano or thyme.

Taste your buttermilk first and be sure you like the flavor and texture. If it is too thick or too sour, dilute it with up to $^2/_3$ cup milk.

2½ cups cold buttermilk
36 Tomato Confit halves (page 343; use the optional thyme and tarragon)
1 teaspoon kosher salt
Finely chopped fresh chives
Extra-virgin olive oil
Flaky sea salt (such as Maldon)

1   Chill four small bowls.
2   In a blender or with an immersion blender, puree the buttermilk, 32 of the tomato confit halves, and the kosher salt. Run the blender for at least 1 minute to make the puree as smooth as possible. Pass through your finest-mesh strainer. Stir in more buttermilk to adjust the texture if needed, then taste and adjust the seasoning. You can refrigerate the soup, covered, until serving time.
3   Finely chop the remaining 4 tomato confit halves.
4   Divide the soup among the bowls. Top each one with some chopped confit, chives, a drizzle of olive oil, and a few flakes of salt, and serve.

celery soup with fregola sarda or israeli couscous

Gentle and comforting, this soup is like something your grandmother might have made. It looks right served in those shallow soup plates of hers that you don't use often enough. Serve it with Brussels Sprout Gratin (page 248) for a perfect comfort-food dinner.

The broth starts with just water, so that you can really taste the celery. The garnish includes both thinly sliced raw celery and celery leaves to emphasize the flavor and add just a hint of crunch.

Fregola sarda is a small, round, toasted pasta from Sardinia with a delightful nutty flavor. If you can't find it, you can substitute Israeli couscous, but pan-toast it first—I explain how below. (Don't confuse the tiny-grained Moroccan couscous, which just doesn't work in this soup, with the larger Israeli couscous.) Another option is pearled barley, but it will require more cooking time.

½ cup *fregola sarda* or Israeli couscous
2 tablespoons extra-virgin olive oil
½ cup finely diced white onion
1 teaspoon kosher salt
2 large celery ribs, finely diced
4 cups water
Juice of half a lemon
1 tablespoon shoyu
¼ cup grated Parmesan or Grana Padano
¼ cup very thinly sliced inner celery rib
Big handful celery leaves
Freshly ground black pepper

1 Warm four soup bowls in a low (200°F) oven. Place a medium saucepan (at least 2 quarts) over medium heat. If using *fregola sarda*, skip to step 2. If using Israeli couscous, dry-toast it in the pot, stirring occasionally until light brown.

2 Add the olive oil, onion, kosher salt, and diced celery. Cook until the vegetables have softened somewhat, about 4 minutes. Add the *fregola sarda*. Add the water and bring to a simmer, then lower the heat. Cook until the pasta is just al dente, 10 to 12 minutes (or check package directions).

3 Turn off the heat and stir in the lemon juice and shoyu. Taste and adjust the seasoning.

4 Divide the soup among the bowls. Top with a sprinkle of grated cheese, the sliced celery, celery leaves, and a grind of black pepper. Serve immediately.

butternut squash soup
with maple pumpkin seeds

VEGAN
GLUTEN-FREE
SERVES 4 TO 6
45 MINUTES

Butternut squash is a classic flavor of fall. I emphasize the autumnal connection by pairing it with pumpkin seeds glazed with maple syrup and a drizzle of pomegranate molasses. A bit of orange zest adds the final bright note that brings it all together.

For maximum flavor, I like to brown the squash. If you want to retain a brighter color, brown it less and simmer it more. The glazed pumpkin seeds are also terrific in salads or anywhere you want a little crunch. The same method works fine for other nuts, especially walnuts.

Pureed soups are all about achieving a velvety smooth texture. When you blend this soup, allow the blender to run for at least 2 minutes, and then pass the results through a very fine-mesh sieve or chinois.

¼ cup extra-virgin olive oil
1 small onion, finely diced
2 celery ribs, finely diced
2 leaves fresh sage, thinly sliced
Kosher salt
3 garlic cloves, minced
1½ to 2 pounds butternut squash, peeled, seeded, and cut into ½-inch cubes
2 cups vegetable broth
1 cup plain soy milk (or whole milk, if you don't need this to be vegan),
  plus additional as needed
1 cup raw green (hulled) pumpkin seeds
1 teaspoon sugar
2 teaspoons maple syrup
Flaky sea salt (such as Maldon)
4 teaspoons pomegranate molasses
1 orange

1 Heat the olive oil in a medium saucepan (at least 2 quarts) over medium heat. Add the onion, celery, sage, and a big pinch of kosher salt and cook, stirring occasionally, until the vegetables have softened, about 4 minutes. Add the garlic and cook 1 more minute.

2 Add the butternut squash and ½ teaspoon kosher salt and cook, stirring frequently, until the squash is lightly browned and mostly tender, about 10 minutes. Add the broth and soy milk, bring to a simmer, reduce the heat to medium-low, and continue to cook until the squash is fully tender, about 15 minutes more.

▼ ▼ ▼

3 Meanwhile, put the pumpkin seeds and sugar in a small skillet over medium heat. Toast, stirring frequently, until the seeds are starting to brown and the sugar is melted, about 3 minutes. Add the maple syrup and a big pinch of flaky sea salt and stir and cook for 1 minute more. Scrape the seeds onto a silicone mat or parchment paper and allow to cool in clusters.

4 Warm your soup bowls in a low (200°F) oven. Remove the soup from the heat and very carefully and thoroughly puree with a blender (working in batches) or stick blender. (See below for safety tips on pureeing hot soups.) Strain back into the saucepan through a fine-mesh sieve and add a little more soy milk if needed to reach a nice soup texture. Warm the soup over medium-low heat to bring it back to serving temperature. Taste and adjust the seasoning.

5 To serve, ladle the soup into the warmed bowls. Top with a drizzle of the pomegranate molasses and a small handful of the pumpkin seed clusters, broken up if needed. Zest the orange directly over the soup so that the essential oils are released, allowing a few strands of zest to fall on each bowl. Finish with a few more grains of flaky sea salt and serve immediately.

PUREEING HOT SOUPS. The safest way to puree a hot soup may be to use a stick blender. Remove the soup pot from the heat, put the stick blender in, well under the surface, and whiz, moving the blender around in the pot.

You can also puree hot soup in a blender, but you have to be very careful! I've seen some pretty scary—and very messy—incidents in professional kitchens when people didn't take proper precautions.

Let the soup cool for a few minutes. Fill the blender less than half full—never more than that. Always leave the lid vent open and use a folded dishtowel to cover the top loosely, so that steam can escape. Always start on the lowest speed. Once the soup is blending, you can increase the speed.

Of course, always follow the manufacturer's safety recommendations when using any appliance.

tomato-chickpea soup

VEGAN

GLUTEN-FREE
OPTION

SERVES 4

30 MINUTES

This soup—basically a very fresh minestrone—was born of simple necessity. I had a pile of crudités left from a party and a family that needed a quick, hot dinner after we cleaned up from the festivities.

You can certainly substitute other vegetables for cauliflower and green beans. Just be sure to cut them small enough to cook through but retain just a bit of bite in 10 minutes. Fennel would be especially welcome.

In general, I'm a big believer in *mise en place*, the practice of preparing all ingredients before you start to cook. But this recipe is actually so simple that you can start sautéing each vegetable while chopping the next.

¼ cup extra-virgin olive oil, plus additional for garnish
1 small white onion, finely diced
2 garlic cloves, thinly sliced
1 teaspoon kosher salt
2 small carrots, cut into ⅛-inch-thick half-moons
2 celery ribs, finely diced, leaves reserved for garnish
1 handful green beans, ends trimmed and cut into ¾-inch lengths
1½ cups very small cauliflower florets
1 (28-ounce) can whole peeled tomatoes
1 (15-ounce) can chickpeas, rinsed and drained
1 tablespoon tamari or shoyu (gluten-free if required)
Juice of half a lemon
2 cups clear vegetable broth (such as Seitenbacher broth mix;
   check your brand if gluten-free required)
½ teaspoon dried basil
1 teaspoon dried thyme
Flatleaf parsley leaves, for garnish (optional)

1 Heat the olive oil in a medium saucepan (at least 3 quarts) over medium-high heat. Add the onion, garlic, and salt and sauté for 1 minute. Add the carrots and celery and sauté for 2 minutes. Add the green beans and cauliflower and sauté for 2 minutes more.
2 Add the juice from the tomatoes. Coarsely chop the tomatoes and add them to the pan.
3 Add the chickpeas, tamari, lemon juice, broth, basil, and thyme. Bring to a simmer; reduce the heat and simmer for 10 minutes. Taste and adjust the seasoning.
4 Serve, garnished with a drizzle of olive oil and the reserved celery leaves, or use parsley, if you prefer.

red lentil and kabocha squash soup with harissa oil

VEGAN

GLUTEN-FREE

SERVES 4 TO 6

40 MINUTES
(15 MINUTES
ACTIVE)

This is a great soup to serve when there are kids at the table, because it is quite mild if you leave the harissa oil off their portions. With the garnish, the flavors come alive, and you'll want to mop up every bit with a good artisanal bread or toasted pita.

Red lentils are nice for soups and purees because they basically dissolve when cooked, leaving a silky smooth texture. Don't try to make this recipe with green or black lentils!

If you don't have kabocha squash, you can make this with a cooking pumpkin (such as a sugar pie pumpkin) or butternut or acorn squash. You won't need a whole squash, so it is also a good way to use leftovers from an earlier meal. If using previously cooked squash, simply heat it through in step 1.

¼ cup extra-virgin olive oil
1½ cups peeled, seeded, and cubed kabocha squash
6 garlic cloves, minced
1 teaspoon coriander seeds
½ teaspoon hot red pepper flakes
1½ cups red lentils
2 teaspoons kosher salt
6 cups water
Juice of half a lemon (optional)
Fresh cilantro leaves, for garnish
Quick Harissa Oil (page 349), for drizzling

1 Heat the olive oil in a 3-quart saucepan over medium-high heat. Add the kabocha squash and cook, stirring occasionally, until lightly browned, about 3 minutes.

2 Reduce the heat to medium. Add the garlic, coriander seeds, and hot red pepper flakes and cook, stirring, for 30 seconds. Do not let the spices burn.

3 Warm your soup bowls in a low (200°F) oven. Add the red lentils, salt, and water to the saucepan. Bring to a boil, lower the heat to maintain a simmer, and cook until the lentils have mostly fallen apart, about 30 minutes. Carefully puree, very thoroughly, with a blender or immersion blender. (See page 89 for safety tips on pureeing hot soups.) Taste and adjust the seasoning, and stir in the lemon juice, if using.

4 Divide the soup among the warmed bowls. Garnish with the cilantro leaves and a generous drizzle of the harissa oil, and serve immediately.

white bean and kale soup

VEGAN OPTION

GLUTEN-FREE OPTION

MAKES 10 CUPS, SERVING 6

1½ HOURS, USING PRES-SURE COOKER (20 MINUTES ACTIVE)

The bean cooking liquid is an integral part of the broth for this warming soup. I give you three options for building more umami on that base: a Parmesan rind (which I save in the freezer when it becomes too hard to grate), dried porcini mushrooms, or vegetarian broth powder. Feel free to use two of these choices if you like!

If you have a pressure cooker, you can make this entire soup in it, including cooking the beans. If not, you can do it just as well on the stovetop; you just need to plan further ahead so you can soak and cook the beans.

¼ cup extra-virgin olive oil, plus additional for garnish
1 medium onion, finely diced
1 whole head garlic, peeled and minced
1 carrot, finely diced
1 teaspoon kosher salt
2 bay leaves
1 teaspoon minced fresh rosemary leaves
One or more of the following: 1 Parmesan rind or ¾ ounce dried porcini mushrooms or 2 tablespoons vegetable broth powder (gluten-free if needed)
2 cups dried white beans, such as cannellini or navy, rinsed and picked over
7 cups water
1 bunch dinosaur (lacinato) kale, stems stripped and discarded, leaves cut into ribbons
Juice of 1 lemon

PRESSURE COOKER METHOD

1 In the pressure cooker base, but without pressure, heat the olive oil over medium-high heat. Sauté the onion, garlic, carrot, and salt until the onion is translucent, about 4 minutes.

2 Add the bay leaves, rosemary, and your choice(s) of the Parmesan rind, dried porcini, and/or broth powder. Add the beans and water. Bring up to high pressure and cook for 40 minutes, then allow the pressure to release naturally. Open the lid.

3 Remove the bay leaves and Parmesan rind, if using.

4 Add the kale and lemon juice and simmer for 10 minutes, until the kale is tender. Taste and adjust the seasoning, then serve, garnished with a generous drizzle of extra-virgin olive oil.

▼ ▼ ▼

STOVETOP METHOD

1 Cover the beans with several inches of water and soak overnight. Drain the beans and place in a large saucepan. Cover with water by at least 2 inches and bring to a boil. Reduce the heat and simmer the beans until tender, 1½ to 2 hours. Drain the beans, reserving the bean broth.

2 In a large saucepan, heat the olive oil over medium-high heat. Sauté the onion, garlic, carrot, and salt until the onion is translucent, about 4 minutes.

3 Add 4 cups of the bean broth, the bay leaves, rosemary, and your choice(s) of the Parmesan rind, dried porcini, and/or broth powder. Bring to a simmer and cook for 30 minutes.

4 Remove the bay leaves and Parmesan rind, if using.

5 Add the beans, kale, and lemon juice and simmer for 10 minutes, until the kale is tender. Taste and adjust the seasoning, then serve, garnished with a generous drizzle of olive oil.

DON'T STICK TO THE RECIPE. A shockingly large number of home cooks treat recipes as if they were written in stone. If that describes you, let me explicitly invite you to change the recipes you see in this book. Unless I've specifically mentioned that a certain ingredient shouldn't be substituted or a particular method changed, you should by all means experiment.

Go ahead and make the Tomato-Chickpea Soup (page 90) with white beans instead of chickpeas. Want to make the Golden Beet Tartare (page 114) using Indian spices? Try it! You think the Tea-Smoked Lychees (page 34) sound good, but you don't have access to fresh lychees? Maybe it would be tasty with cherimoya or rambutan or even peeled grapes. Like the sound of the Grilled Tofu and Pepper Tacos (page 144), but you're allergic to soy? Make them with seitan instead.

Of course, you'll want to be a little more careful with baking recipes. But even there, as long as you don't greatly alter the basic ratios of flours, fats, and liquids, you've got plenty of room to wiggle.

If you have been cooking for a while, you have a pretty good idea what works in the kitchen. Just trust your instincts, taste the food frequently, and enjoy the freedom to be creative. You'll be a better cook for it, even if once in a great while you end up ordering pizza!

black bean soup with orange-jalapeño salsa

VEGAN OPTION

GLUTEN-FREE
OPTION

SERVES 6

30 MINUTES

I developed this black bean soup so that it would satisfy those who prefer mild dishes (including kids) as well as those of us who prefer a bolder spice. The soup is very straightforward, and on the side, we have a bright and intense orange and jalapeño salsa. You may also pass grated cheddar cheese for those who would prefer to think of it as vegetarian chili.

I find that home-cooked beans are far better than canned. They just seem to have more flavor and a better texture. On the other hand, canned beans sure are convenient if you haven't thought ahead to soak and boil a batch. Just be sure to rinse them well. Alternatively, get a pressure cooker and you can decide to make beans in the late afternoon and have them beautifully cooked for dinner that night.

You can puree the soup with a stick blender, blender, or potato masher.

6 cups cooked black beans, cooking liquid reserved, or 4 (15-ounce) cans
    black beans, rinsed and drained
2 bay leaves
Vegetable broth powder (gluten-free if you need it; optional)
3 tablespoons extra-virgin olive oil
1 white onion, diced
1 yellow bell pepper, seeded and diced
4 garlic cloves, minced
Kosher salt
1 tablespoon dried oregano
1 teaspoon ground cumin
1 teaspoon (or more) smoked paprika (optional)

FOR THE SALSA
6 fresh mandarin oranges (or fewer, larger oranges)
¼ cup finely diced red onion
1 jalapeño pepper (or more to taste), thinly sliced
¼ teaspoon kosher salt
1 handful fresh cilantro leaves

TO SERVE
Mexican crema or sour cream (to make this dish vegan, use vegan sour cream
    or avocado slices)

▼ ▼ ▼

1 Place the beans and bay leaves in a 6-quart pot. Add enough reserved cooking liquid or water (with a little vegetable broth powder, if you wish) to barely cover the beans. Bring to a simmer.

2 Heat the olive oil in a skillet over medium-high heat. Add the onion, bell pepper, garlic, and a big pinch of salt, and sauté until the vegetables are starting to brown, about 5 minutes. Add the oregano, cumin, and smoked paprika, if using, and cook for 1 minute more. Remove from the heat.

3 Pluck the bay leaves out of the beans. Stir the onion mixture into the simmering beans.

4 Remove the soup from the heat and lightly puree. (See page 89 for safety tips on pureeing hot soups.) I like it about 75 percent pureed, with some significant texture left.

5 Return the soup to the heat. Add more water as needed to produce a soup that's moderately thick, but thinner than a stew. Taste and adjust the seasoning. It will almost certainly need salt unless you used pre-salted canned beans. You may also find you want more cumin or smoked paprika. Simmer for at least 10 to 15 minutes to allow the flavors to develop.

6 *For the salsa:* Cut the oranges into supremes (see page 125) and then cut those into cubes. Mix with the red onion, jalapeño pepper, and ¼ teaspoon kosher salt. Taste and adjust the seasoning. Immediately before serving, stir in the cilantro.

7 To serve, ladle the soup into bowls and either top with approximately 3 tablespoons of the salsa and some crema, or pass the salsa and crema at the table.

COOKING DRIED BEANS. Home-cooked beans have much better flavor and texture than canned beans, and they are more economical as well. Always rinse dried beans thoroughly and sort through them carefully, removing any that are discolored or broken, as well as any stray sticks or pebbles. Never add salt until they are fully cooked, as that can toughen the skins.

Stovetop method: Cover the beans with several inches of water and soak overnight. (If you don't have time to soak beans overnight, you can get decent results by bringing them to a boil, turning off the heat, and leaving them covered for 1 to 2 hours.)

Drain the beans and place them in a large saucepan. Cover with water by at least 2 inches and bring to a boil. Reduce the heat and simmer the beans until tender. Depending on the type of bean and how old they are, this can take anywhere from 1 to 2 hours. Drain the beans, reserving the liquid if needed for the dish you are making.

Pressure cooker method: With a pressure cooker, there is no need to presoak beans. Consult your manufacturer's manual for exact instructions and timing, but generally speaking you should use no more than 1 pound (about 2 cups) of beans, cover them with 8 cups of water, and add a couple tablespoons of oil. The large amount of water and the oil reduce the chance of foam from the beans clogging the pressure cooker vent. Cook on high pressure for 30 to 40 minutes, depending on the type of bean, then allow the pressure to release naturally. If you are in a hurry, add about 4 minutes to the cooking time and carefully do a quick pressure release. Drain the beans, reserving the liquid if needed for the dish you are making.

red pozole with beans (pozole rojo de frijol)

VEGAN OPTION

GLUTEN-FREE

SERVES 4 AS A
ONE-POT MEAL
OR 8 AS A FIRST
COURSE

40 MINUTES

Pozole is a hearty Mexican soup or thin stew that dates back to pre-Columbian times. It makes a terrific one-pot meal on a cold day. The broth is mildly spicy and sour, a perfect companion for the hearty beans and hominy corn.

There are more variations of *pozole rojo* than you can count, but as long as it has hominy and some kind of red chile in it, you are in the ballpark. Much of the fun comes with the accompaniments, which you can put out on a big platter, letting diners choose for themselves.

For simplicity, I call for canned hominy and beans. With these shortcuts, *pozole* can be a weeknight supper. If you want a more leisurely and even better soup, you can cook them both from scratch. Hominy corn is available dried, and to use it, you have to soak it overnight and boil it for several hours, very much as you would dried beans. (If you go this route, use ⅔ cup dried pinto beans and 1 cup dried hominy.)

1 or 2 (or more, if you like a lot of heat) dried chiles de árbol, ancho chiles, or guajillo chiles, rinsed and stemmed
2 tablespoons vegetable oil
1 medium onion, diced
4 garlic cloves, minced
¾ cup canned diced tomatoes (those "fire roasted" ones would be good if you have them), plus additional as needed
1 tablespoon dried Mexican oregano or 1½ teaspoons European oregano
6 cups mild, clear vegetable broth or water
Kosher salt
1 (15-ounce) can pinto beans, rinsed and drained
2 (15-ounce) cans hominy, rinsed and drained
Juice of 2 limes, plus additional as needed
Some or all of the following for garnish: avocado slices, fresh cilantro, crumbled cotija cheese, lime wedges, tortilla chips, shredded cabbage or lettuce, sliced onions, and sliced radishes

1 Soak the chiles in just enough boiling water to cover for 20 minutes or so, then puree in a mini food processor with the soaking liquid.

2 Heat the oil in a large soup pot over medium heat. Add the onion and garlic and cook until the onions are somewhat softened, about 2 minutes.

3 Add the tomatoes, oregano, and vegetable broth and bring to a simmer. Add 2 teaspoons salt if you are using water.

4 Add the pinto beans and hominy and bring back to a simmer. Allow to simmer for 10 minutes.

5 Add half the pureed chiles and all the lime juice and stir. Taste and adjust the seasoning, adding salt and more lime juice or tomatoes as needed to produce a piquant broth. Add more of the pureed chiles to reach your preferred heat level and pass the rest as a condiment.

6 Serve it forth, with a good selection of garnishes.

spicy corn and potato stew

VEGAN

GLUTEN-FREE

SERVES 4

30 MINUTES

If your New England corn chowder packed up and moved to New Mexico, it might turn into this spicy (but not too hot) stew. Plenty of garlic, chili powder, oregano, and lime juice make this irresistible.

The recipe calls for New Mexico chile powder, which is made from a specific, individual variety of pepper. I find that this powder has much more character than the generic chili powder mixtures. It is relatively easy to find at any grocery that has a supply of Mexican ingredients. Pick up the Mexican oregano while you are there too; it has a sweeter, more resinous flavor than the familiar European oreganos. In a pinch, you can use any kind of chili powder that you have available or grind dried chiles of your choosing.

I like to make a stock with the corncobs, but if you are pressed for time, you can also just use water.

4 cups fresh corn kernels (shaved from 5 or 6 cobs), cobs reserved
3 tablespoons vegetable oil
4 cups diced (in approximately ⅜-inch cubes) waxy potatoes, such as red-skinned
6 garlic cloves, minced
¼ cup minced shallots
2 tablespoons New Mexico chile powder (see headnote)
1 teaspoon ground cumin
2 tablespoons dried Mexican oregano (if substituting European oregano, reduce by half)
Pinch of ground cinnamon
1 teaspoon kosher salt
2 limes
1 handful fresh cilantro leaves, for garnish

1 If you are making a corn stock, put the corncobs in a saucepan with enough water to cover, and bring to a boil; reduce the heat and simmer for 10 minutes. Remove the corncobs and strain the resulting lightly flavored broth.

2 Heat 1½ tablespoons of the vegetable oil in a 3-quart saucepan over medium-high heat. Add the corn and sauté, stirring occasionally, until it blisters and darkens in spots, about 5 minutes. Spoon the corn into a bowl.

3 Place the potatoes and the remaining 1½ tablespoons oil in the pan. Lower the heat to medium. Cook, stirring occasionally, until the potatoes are almost tender. Add the garlic, shallots, chile powder, cumin, oregano, cinnamon, salt, and the juice of 1 lime, and cook for about 2 more minutes, until very fragrant.

▼ ▼ ▼

4 Return the corn to the pan, along with 2½ cups of the corncob broth or water. (Add more liquid if you prefer it a little soupier.) Bring to a simmer. Taste and adjust the seasonings, adding more salt, chile powder, or lime juice as desired. Simmer for a few more minutes to allow the flavors to meld and the potatoes to finish cooking; they should be fully tender but not falling apart.

5 To finish, divide the soup among four bowls. Quarter the remaining lime and squeeze the juice from one quarter into each serving. Garnish with cilantro and serve immediately.

salads

green mango salad

VEGAN

GLUTEN-FREE

SERVES 4

20 MINUTES

Green mango salad is addictive. It hits all those sweet, tangy and fresh notes that wake up your palate at the beginning of a meal or refresh it after a bite of spicy curry. My wife and I have been known to select Vietnamese restaurants purely on the strength of their mango salad and to use the leftover dressing to flavor our noodles when vegetarian house sauce isn't available.

This salad works best with slightly underripe mangoes. You want them to be firm but not rock hard. The easiest way to cut them is with a mandoline, which also makes for a neater presentation. You can do it with a knife, too; it just takes a little more time.

I've experimented with different ways to make the dressing without fish sauce. Often, a little soy sauce works as an umami-rich substitute, but in this case, I like a bit of toasted sesame oil instead; not traditional, but I think it works very well. This dressing is rather sweet. You should adjust it to balance the particular mangoes you are working with.

4 tablespoons palm sugar *or* 2 tablespoons granulated sugar and 2 tablespoons light brown sugar
⅓ cup fresh lime juice
2 teaspoons grated fresh ginger
1 teaspoon kosher salt
1 tablespoon toasted sesame oil
2 underripe mangoes, peeled and cut into 2 x ¼ x ¼-inch batons
Half a small red onion, cut into very thin rings and soaked briefly in cold water
1 small green chile (Thai bird, jalapeño, or serrano), stemmed, seeded, and thinly sliced (optional)
1 tablespoon toasted sesame seeds
1 handful fresh cilantro or mint leaves, or a mixture

1 If using palm sugar, crush it first in a mortar and pestle (it may help to microwave it a bit or moisten it first). Combine the sugar, lime juice, ginger, salt, and sesame oil in a small container with a lid. Shake well to dissolve the sugar. Taste and adjust the balance of flavors. The dressing should be fairly sweet.

2 Just before serving, combine the dressing with the mango, red onion, green chile, most of the sesame seeds, and most of the herbs. Toss well to coat with the dressing.

3 Garnish with the remaining sesame seeds and herbs and serve.

thai tofu salad

VEGAN

GLUTEN-FREE
OPTION

SERVES 4

20 MINUTES

Thai salads (*yams*) are tremendously refreshing, full of the bright flavors of herbs, citrus, and chile peppers, balanced with salt and sweetness from either fruit or palm sugar. They are great with a beer or as part of a complete meal with rice and a curry or noodle dish.

The traditional way to eat these salads is to use Thai sticky rice to pick them up or wrap them in lettuce or cabbage leaves.

Once you understand their basic aesthetic, you can readily improvise your own yams. Feel free to include just about any tropical fruit, raw or lightly cooked vegetables, or roasted peanuts. Go ahead and adjust the heat level to your liking, and add or subtract from the dressing. For example, you could replace the cilantro in this recipe with Thai basil; you could add garlic, or fresh ginger, or lemongrass . . . you get the idea!

The most typical Thai choice would be bird chiles. They are tiny and wicked hot. If you don't have them, serranos or even jalapeños would be a good alternative. Remove the seeds and ribs if you want it mild, or use them if you want maximum kick. It is a good idea to wear food-safe rubber gloves when working with hot peppers, to avoid getting the irritating oils on your skin.

FOR THE DRESSING
1 tablespoon soy sauce (use a wheat-free version for gluten-free)
6 tablespoons fresh lime juice (from about 3 limes)
1 teaspoon sugar (preferably palm sugar)
**1 to 3 Thai bird chiles or serrano chiles, seeds and ribs removed (see headnote)
   and very thinly sliced**
1/2 cup thinly sliced shallots (preferably the large red variety)
Kosher salt

FOR THE SALAD
1/4 cup vegetable oil
1 pound extra-firm tofu, cut into 3/8-inch-thick slabs
Kosher salt
Freshly ground black pepper
1 cup diced seedless English cucumber
4 scallions, white and light green parts, cut into bite-size lengths
1/2 cup lightly packed fresh cilantro leaves, plus additional for garnish
2 tablespoons minced fresh mint leaves

▼ ▼ ▼

1 *For the dressing:* Combine the soy sauce, lime juice, sugar, chiles, and shallots in a salad bowl. Taste and add salt as needed, and adjust other components to get a good balance of flavors. It should be very intense; it will seem much milder when tossed with the salad.

2 *For the salad:* Heat the oil in a large skillet (preferably cast iron) over medium-high heat. Pat the tofu dry. Add tofu to the skillet in a single layer and fry until quite brown on one side, 3 to 5 minutes. Flip and brown the other side. Transfer to paper towels and season with salt and pepper.

3 After the tofu has cooled, cut it into ⅛-inch-thick slices.

4 Add the tofu, cucumber, scallions, cilantro, and mint to the bowl with the dressing. Toss well.

5 Garnish with a few leaves of cilantro and serve.

classic chopped salad

VEGAN OPTION

GLUTEN-FREE

SERVES 4

30 MINUTES

Chopped salad is exactly what it sounds like: a salad whose ingredients have all been cut down to a fairly uniform size, around $\frac{1}{2}$-inch pieces. It works well as a side dish, and it shines as one of the all-time great entrée salads when you want a lighter meal. It is easy to eat because there's nothing to take apart with a knife, which makes it particularly good for a dinner party.

The classic leaf for chopped salad is romaine lettuce hearts. You can use some of the darker outside leaves as well, but the ribs provide the structure that keeps the salad in cubes with some airspace, instead of collapsing. A fantastic way to cut romaine is to make some lengthwise cuts, leaving the base intact, before cutting across the leaves at $\frac{1}{2}$-inch intervals. Making three of these lengthwise cuts is great for a normal salad, but for a chopped salad try five.

As with any green salad, the lettuce must be scrupulously, absolutely dry.

Beyond the romaine, you can choose just about any other salad ingredients that play well together. I've suggested one grouping below, but feel free to make up your own. I particularly like to include rather large amounts of fresh herbs such as mint.

If it is more convenient, you can make part of this salad several hours in advance. Bell peppers, cucumbers, olives, chickpeas, and so forth can all be cubed and refrigerated until game time. The lettuce can be washed, cut, and spun dry about an hour ahead of dinner and put back in the fridge to chill and remove the last bit of moisture in a low-humidity environment. Just don't weight it down with the other ingredients or, heaven forbid, dress it until the last minute.

3 romaine lettuce hearts, cut as described in headnote
$\frac{2}{3}$ cup cooked chickpeas, coarsely chopped
Half an English cucumber, diced
$\frac{1}{2}$ cup pitted kalamata olives, coarsely chopped
$\frac{1}{4}$ cup minced sweet onion, such as Maui or Vidalia
$\frac{1}{2}$ cup finely diced jarred roasted red pepper
2 scallions, white and light green parts only, cut into $\frac{1}{4}$-inch lengths
$\frac{1}{2}$ cup feta, crumbled (omit for vegan)
1 large handful fresh mint leaves, torn
Dressing of your choice; Lemon-Mustard Vinaigrette (page 327) works very well

1   Layer the lettuce, chickpeas, cucumber, olives, onion, roasted pepper, scallions, feta, and mint in a large salad bowl.

2   Immediately before serving, add dressing to taste. Toss and serve.

middle eastern bread salad (fattoush)

VEGAN

SERVES 4

15 MINUTES

Fattoush is a classic way to use up leftover pita bread. Much like Italian panzanella, the dish features slightly stale bread tossed with tomatoes, vegetables, and herbs. If you happen to have purslane (a tart, edible succulent), it is excellent in this salad.

Tangy, deep-red sumac is used throughout the Middle East as a final garnish on everything from hummus to kebabs, as much for color as flavor. If you can't find it, the salad will still be delicious, but it is well worth searching out in Middle Eastern markets or online.

Feel free to add other fresh herbs, black olives, a handful of chickpeas, feta cheese, or a dollop of thick yogurt if that suits your mood.

1 pita bread, toasted until well browned, cut or broken into ½-inch squares
2 medium-size ripe tomatoes, diced
Half a cucumber, peeled if the skin is tough, diced
2 tablespoons minced red onion
1 generous handful fresh cilantro leaves
1 generous handful fresh mint leaves
1 tablespoon extra-virgin olive oil
1 tablespoon fresh lemon juice
¼ teaspoon kosher salt, or to taste
Freshly ground black pepper
Ground sumac, for garnish

1 Within a few minutes of serving, so the pita doesn't beome soggy, combine the pita, tomatoes, cucumber, onion, cilantro, mint, olive oil, lemon juice, salt, and several grinds of black pepper. Taste and adjust the seasoning; you may need more olive oil, lemon juice, salt, or pepper.

2 Garnish with a big pinch of the sumac and serve.

golden beet tartare

VEGAN OPTION

GLUTEN-FREE
OPTION

SERVES 4

1 HOUR
(20 MINUTES
ACTIVE)

If your only experience with beets is the canned version, you haven't really had beets. I can't tell you how many people I've converted to shameless beet-loving over the years. I'm a certified beet evangelist (which makes it legal for me to marry root vegetables in most states).

Of course this dish is really a beet salad, but it uses some of the complementary flavors often associated with beef tartare. The visual resemblance would be stronger with red beets, but I'm not really trying to mimic a meat dish here, just riffing off of it. I didn't think it needed beef tartare's raw egg on top, but I did put rosemary mayo on the toast for a little fattiness. Sieved hard-cooked egg would be nice, too. I didn't add anything acidic, but if you want a little citrus juice in there, it is okay with me.

You can serve this as an appetizer or as a side salad with a grilled entrée.

¼ cup mayonnaise (vegan mayo if you prefer)
2 teaspoons very finely minced fresh rosemary leaves
1¼ teaspoons flaky sea salt (such as Maldon)
2 large golden beets (about 1½ pounds total), tops trimmed and discarded
   or saved for another use
Kosher salt
¼ cup peeled, seeded, and finely diced cucumber
¼ cup finely diced red onion
1 tablespoon capers, drained
2 tablespoons extra-virgin olive oil
1 teaspoon fresh lemon juice
1 tablespoon minced fresh chives
Freshly ground black pepper
4 slices artisanal bread, such as *pain au levain*, toasted or grilled and cut into
   1-inch-wide fingers (omit or substitute a gluten-free bread if needed)

1 Combine the mayonnaise, rosemary, and ¼ teaspoon of the sea salt. Cover and refrigerate while you prepare the beets.

2 Put the beets in a saucepan, cover with water, add a big pinch of kosher salt, and bring to a boil. Reduce the heat and cook at an active simmer until the beets are tender, 20 to 40 minutes (depending on size). Drain, then place beets in a bowl of ice water for a few minutes to cool. Peel and finely dice the beets to make 1½ cups of diced beets. The beet pieces should be no larger than ⅛ inch. The easiest way to do this is slice off the sides, tops, and bottoms to make cubes, then cut first into uniform slices (using a mandoline if you have one), then batons (sticks), then dice. You'll have some extra stuff you can snack on or save for another purpose. If you take your time and do a nice, neat dice, this dish will look beautiful.

3 Combine the beets, cucumber, onion, capers, olive oil, lemon juice, and remaining 1 teaspoon sea salt. Taste and adjust the seasoning.

4 To plate, arrange a mound of beet salad on each of four plates, or use a ring mold to make perfect circles of salad. Top with the chives, a few grinds of black pepper, and a few more flakes of salt.

5 Spread the rosemary mayo on the toast and serve.

FINDING GREAT INGREDIENTS. In U.S. cities, we are lucky to live in a golden age of access to great ingredients. Even at conventional groceries, there is an expanded (if, on occasion, somewhat dreary) selection of organic produce and usually an aisle or two of ethnic ingredients. Go to an upscale grocer like Whole Foods and you can lay your hands on local cucumbers, Meyer lemons, cheeses from remote Alpine caves, and 20 types of heirloom rice.

This incredible bounty makes it all too easy to ignore other beautiful foods that require a bit of initiative to track down. But if you do go to the trouble to find them, you'll be supporting small businesses and the local economy.

Farmers' markets and CSAs are terrific sources of fresh fruits and vegetables. Nothing compares to their just-picked strawberries, heirloom tomatoes, garlic scapes, or zucchini blossoms at the peak of the season. And don't forget that some markets are open year-round, offering cool-season favorites like kale and apples.

Mexican, Korean, Indian, and Middle Eastern markets, to name a few, offer an unbelievable selection of foods in their niches, far beyond what you would find at an all-purpose grocer. Bring a sense of adventure, read lots of labels, and come home with some inexpensive thrills. You may have to work around a language barrier, but most stores have employees who are passionate about their food and will be happy to offer advice and expertise.

Certain products like tofu, tortillas, fresh pasta, fresh cheeses, and kimchi are often available from local artisans who focus on a single product. Freshly made tofu, or corn tortillas that are still warm from production, are incomparably better than those that have been stored for a month at the grocery. As the world becomes more diverse, you can often find these artisans in medium-size towns where you wouldn't have imagined them 10 years ago.

Don't forget the Internet as a source for fantastic ingredients. Especially if you don't live in an urban area, try retailers such as Chef Shop (chefshop.com), Le Sanctuaire (le-sanctuaire.com), and World Spice Merchants (worldspice.com), which all have passionately curated selections and can ship anywhere.

grilled eggplant salad

VEGAN

GLUTEN-FREE

SERVES 4 TO 6

1 HOUR
(20 MINUTES
ACTIVE)

When I've fired up my charcoal grill to make a meal, I like to use the residual heat to roast vegetables slowly for use the next day. This is a terrific method for eggplant, which can then be turned into a smoky baba ghanouj or this eggplant salad with bright Thai flavors.

Of course if you don't feel like grilling, you can use the oven instead, although the flavor won't be as complex.

My favorite variety of eggplant is the smallish, dense, dark purple pear-shaped type that I find at farmers' markets toward the end of summer. The flesh is incredibly creamy and sweet. And when you pick one up, it will seem to weigh twice as much as you'd expect. If you can't find them, the thinner Asian varieties will work well, too—just expect a shorter cooking time.

2 medium eggplants (see headnote)
3 tablespoons fresh lime juice
1 tablespoon mirin
1 tablespoon palm sugar or brown sugar
1 teaspoon toasted sesame oil
2 teaspoons finely grated fresh ginger
1/2 teaspoon kosher salt
2 tablespoons finely diced red onion
2 tablespoons finely diced scallion, white and light green parts only
1/4 cup loosely packed fresh mint leaves, coarsely chopped
1/4 cup thinly sliced mild red chile pepper (or red bell pepper)
1 tablespoon paper-thin slices jalapeño pepper

1 Set the eggplants over the dying embers of a charcoal grill, cover, and slowly roast the eggplants, turning occasionally, until they are completely tender and slumping, about 45 minutes. Alternatively, place the eggplants on a baking sheet and roast them in a 375°F oven for about 45 minutes.

2 Meanwhile, whisk together the lime juice, mirin, sugar, sesame oil, ginger, and salt. Taste and adjust the seasoning for a good balance of sweet, sour, and salty.

3 When the eggplants are cool enough to handle, slice them into 1/2-inch-thick slabs, optionally leaving the stem end attached for presentation.

4 When you are ready to serve, spoon the sauce over the eggplants generously. Top heavily with the red onion, scallion, mint, red pepper, and jalapeño pepper, finish with a few more grains of salt, and serve at room temperature.

ten-minute chickpea salad with feta and basil

GLUTEN-FREE

SERVES 3 AS AN
ENTRÉE OR 8 AS
A SIDE DISH

10 MINUTES

This hearty salad was born out of desperation, when I arrived home at 5:30 and our annual block party potluck was due to start at 6:00. I needed to entertain two crazy kids while I cooked, so I knew I would have to put something together that didn't require any complicated steps, but I wasn't about to settle for bland! Easy potluck recipes are a dime a dozen, but the challenge here was to deliver one with big flavors.

I raided the pantry and refrigerator and created this chickpea salad with Mediterranean flavors. As you toss it, the crumbled feta dissolves a little bit and makes a creamy dressing.

You could easily add or substitute other herbs (tarragon, dill, or mint would be nice), as well as olives, blanched green beans, or artichoke hearts. My wife makes a delicious variation with a few cups of prepared Israeli couscous added. (Israeli couscous is large pearls, not the tiny grains of traditional couscous.)

This recipe shows why it is such a good idea to keep your pantry stocked with things like cans of chickpeas, roasted peppers, and good olive oil. When you don't have time to do much cooking, you can still get something great on the table.

2 (15-ounce) cans chickpeas, rinsed and drained
Half a red onion, finely diced
Half an English cucumber, finely diced
1 jar roasted red or yellow peppers, coarsely chopped
8 ounces feta, crumbled
1 garlic clove, crushed and minced
1 handful fresh basil leaves, torn
3 tablespoons fresh lemon juice
¼ cup extra-virgin olive oil
Kosher salt
Freshly ground black pepper

1 Combine the chickpeas, onion, cucumber, roasted peppers, feta, garlic, basil, lemon juice, and olive oil in a salad bowl. Toss well.

2 Taste and add salt and pepper as needed. Depending on how salty your feta is, you might not need any salt.

3 Serve right away, or refrigerate for up to a few hours.

WHEN THINGS GO RANCID. Some people are especially sensitive to certain smells. For some reason, I'm exquisitely aware of the musty smell of rancid fat. Fat goes rancid when it is broken down by water, oxygen, or bacteria. Rancid fat doesn't just smell and taste bad. It is bad for you, because it is full of free radicals, which put oxidative stress on your body.

Whole grains, whole-grain flour, nuts, and seeds are particularly vulnerable to going rancid. To avoid long storage, buy them in small quantities, preferably from retailers that turn over their inventory rapidly. Keep these ingredients well sealed in a cool, dry place, and always give them a deep sniff before using. If they smell even a little off, they belong in the compost.

persimmon, parsley, and olive salad

VEGAN

GLUTEN-FREE

SERVES 4

10 MINUTES

The two common varieties of persimmon are Fuyus, which are rather squat, and Hachiyas, which are more oblong. Fuyus are eaten crisp, while Hachiyas are inedibly astringent until they are as soft as pudding. So for this salad, you will only want to use Fuyu persimmons.

In North America, persimmons are generally available in late fall to early winter. The flavor is moderately sweet and flowery, with a slight tang and muskiness, somewhat similar to mango. You generally have to peel the fruit unless the skin is unusually tender.

It might seem strange to use parsley as the "lettuce" in a salad, but I think you will like it. This isn't the sort of thing you eat in huge quantities; it is more of an accompaniment to cleanse the palate.

You can prepare all of the ingredients in advance, but don't dress the salad until the last minute or the parsley will wilt. A little thinly sliced red onion or scallion may be added. This salad is also great with blood oranges instead of persimmon.

Leaves from 1 bunch fresh flatleaf parsley, cleaned and thoroughly dried
2 Fuyu persimmons, peeled if the skin is tough, cut in medium dice
1 cup flavorful black olives, such as kalamata or alfonso, pitted
2 tablespoons extra-virgin olive oil
2 teaspoons sherry vinegar
Kosher salt (may not be needed if the olives are quite salty)
Freshly ground black pepper

1 Toss the parsley, persimmons, and olives together in a salad bowl.

2 Drizzle in the olive oil and toss to coat lightly, then add the vinegar and toss again. Taste and add salt (if needed) and pepper. Mound on a platter or distribute among four salad plates and serve.

pear and gouda salad

This salad takes advantage of the easy and unusual Cryo-Pickled Onions (page 339). The onions go in the salad, and the pickling liquid is used to make the vinaigrette. (You'll have to make the onions at least a day in advance of serving the salad.)

Buy the best aged Gouda you can afford for this salad. The good stuff is at least one year old and has a slightly crystalline texture and pronounced nutty flavor.

For a more elegant presentation, refrigerate four salad plates and serve this as a composed salad instead of in a family-style bowl.

2 tablespoons pickling liquid from Cryo-Pickled Onions (page 339)
5 tablespoons extra-virgin olive oil
¼ teaspoon kosher salt
1 head romaine lettuce, mostly hearts, sliced
⅓ cup green pumpkin seeds (pepitas), skillet-toasted if raw
2 ounces aged Gouda, thinly sliced with a cheese plane or vegetable peeler
1 ripe pear, peeled and sliced into 16 pieces just before serving so it doesn't brown
⅓ cup Cryo-Pickled Onions (page 339)

1 Whisk together the pickling liquid, olive oil, and salt. Don't worry if the vinaigrette doesn't completely emulsify. Taste and adjust the seasoning.

2 Put the lettuce, toasted pumpkin seeds, Gouda, pear slices, and pickled onions in a salad bowl.

3 Give the dressing one last whisk and dress the salad. Start with half the dressing and add more as needed so that the leaves are nicely coated but not drenched; serve at once.

potato and green bean salad with arugula pesto

GLUTEN-FREE

SERVES 4

1 HOUR (15 MIN-
UTES ACTIVE)

This potato salad will really grab attention on a buffet table. The arugula pesto is a bright emerald green that holds its color much better than basil-based pesto. You should still make the sauce as close to serving time as possible because the fresh flavors begin to dissipate, emphasizing the bitter aspect of the arugula. The mint adds a subtle bright note that makes all the difference.

It is always best to start potatoes in cold water. That gives the interior a chance to cook before the outside has gone to mush.

FOR THE VEGETABLES
1 pound small, waxy potatoes, such as red-skinned
2 tablespoons kosher salt
8 ounces green beans, trimmed and halved

FOR THE ARUGULA PESTO
2 ounces baby arugula (about 3 cups loosely packed leaves)
¼ cup loosely packed fresh mint leaves
3 tablespoons extra-virgin olive oil
1 or 2 garlic cloves, coarsely chopped (use the larger amount if you are a garlic lover)
¼ teaspoon kosher salt
1 ounce Grana Padano or Parmigiano-Reggiano, grated (about ¼ cup)

TO COMPLETE THE SALAD
Freshly ground black pepper
½ cup toasted walnut pieces (optional)

1 *For the vegetables:* Place the potatoes in a large pot of cold water with the salt. Bring to a boil over high heat, then lower the heat to maintain a vigorous simmer. When the potatoes are fork-tender, 10 to 15 minutes (depending on size), transfer them to a bowl with a slotted spoon. Add the green beans to the water and boil for 2½ minutes. Transfer the green beans to a separate bowl. Rinse both vegetables in cold water until cool; drain well. Cut the potatoes in half if they are much larger than bite-size. Set aside.

2 *For the arugula pesto:* Combine the arugula, mint, olive oil, garlic, salt, and cheese in a mini food processor. Process until the mixture forms a fairly smooth paste with some texture left. Alternatively, you can use an immersion blender, or a regular blender if you make a double batch. Taste and adjust the seasoning.

3 *To complete the salad:* Toss the potatoes and green beans with the arugula pesto, several grinds of black pepper, and the walnut pieces, if using. Taste, add more salt if needed, and serve.

shaved artichoke salad with blood oranges

VEGAN OPTION
GLUTEN-FREE
SERVES 4
15 MINUTES

Artichokes are almost always served cooked, but they can be delicious raw as well. They have a pleasant, slightly astringent taste. You could toss them with a lemony vinaigrette and garnish with shards of Parmigiano-Reggiano for a nice treatment, but do try this recipe, with a mayonnaise-based dressing that yields a salad reminiscent of celery root rémoulade.

To prevent the artichoke from browning, prepare the dressing first so that you can toss the shaved artichoke in it immediately. It is possible to make this salad with a knife, but a mandoline will give you thinner, more even slices.

Blood oranges are in season in the winter months. If you can't find them, any other orange will work as well; you'll only be missing the visual interest of the bright red segments.

Ras el hanout, which literally means "head of the market," is a North African mixture of a dozen or more spices. You can find it at good Middle Eastern markets or online at worldspice.com.

2 blood oranges
¼ cup mayonnaise or vegan mayonnaise
1 teaspoon sherry vinegar
¼ teaspoon kosher salt
¼ teaspoon *ras el hanout* (optional)
2 large globe artichokes, preferably with 3-inch stems
2 teaspoons minced fresh chives
Flaky sea salt (such as Maldon)
Freshly ground black pepper

1 Chill four small plates. Working over a small bowl, cut the oranges into supremes (see page 125). Squeeze the peel and membranes to extract all the juice. Reserve 1 tablespoon of the juice and drink the rest. Reserve the supremes.

2 Whisk the reserved 1 tablespoon orange juice with the mayonnaise, sherry vinegar, kosher salt and *ras el hanout*, if using, in a large bowl. Taste and adjust the seasoning.

3 Trim a tiny bit off one artichoke stem. Peel the stem. Pull off all of the leaves (which you can steam and serve separately if you like). Use a spoon to remove the hairy choke. Quickly peel and pare around the outside of the artichoke bottom. You should be left with a peeled stem attached to a nicely trimmed heart, with all the leaves and choke gone. Working quickly, cut the artichoke into very thin slices with a mandoline and toss with the dressing. Repeat with the other artichoke.

4 To serve, pile a small mound of the dressed artichoke on each plate. Try to keep it centered and as high and fluffy as possible for a nice presentation. Top with the orange supremes, chives, flaky sea salt, and a few grinds of black pepper and serve.

jicama, radish, and orange salad

VEGAN
GLUTEN-FREE
SERVES 4
15 MINUTES

When I serve a filling entrée, I like to have a brightly flavored, refreshing salad. It offers a nice contrast, makes the meal a little lighter, and cuts the fattiness of the main dish. Here is a simple salad, dressed only with fresh orange juice, that goes beautifully with Mexican and other Latin American meals. You can work on it while your entrée finishes cooking; it's also a great task to give to a friendly volunteer. Don't forget to pass them a *cerveza*!

If you've never had jicama (pronounced HEE-come-uh), you are in for a treat. The texture is crisp like an apple, and the flavor is a little sweet. They are surprisingly easy to find in typical grocery stores, and of course you can find them at Mexican markets.

Half a jicama, peeled and cut into 2 x ¼ x ¼-inch batons
1 big handful radishes, trimmed and cut into quarters
4 Valencia oranges, cut into supremes (see below), juice reserved
¼ teaspoon kosher salt
Freshly ground black pepper
1 handful fresh cilantro leaves, torn, for garnish

1 Combine the jicama, radishes, and orange supremes in a salad bowl with the salt and several hearty grinds of black pepper.
2 Add ¼ cup reserved orange juice and toss lightly.
3 Taste and adjust the seasoning. Garnish with the cilantro leaves and serve.

CUTTING CITRUS SUPREMES. A supreme (pronounced soo-PREHM) is nothing more than a citrus segment that is free of any membrane or white pith. Supremes are beautiful to look at, and the taste is more intense than a regular segment. They aren't difficult to make, but it takes a little practice to learn the knife technique. (Please attempt this only if you feel comfortable! If you are concerned about injuring yourself, just use intact peeled segments instead.)

First, slice off ½ inch from the top and bottom of the fruit. Set the fruit, one cut side down, on your cutting board, and use a sharp knife to cut off the of the peel and pith, cutting from top to bottom and following the fruit's contour. Trim off any bits of pith that remain.

Hold the peeled fruit in your hand over a bowl (to catch the juices). Take your knife and slice in on both sides of a segment, as close as possible to the membrane. If the segment doesn't fall right out, a little twist of the knife at the end of the second cut should remove it. Rotate the fruit to the next segment and repeat.

When you are done, you will have extracted all of the segments, which are now sitting in a little puddle of juice. Squeeze the peel and membrane pieces to extract the rest of the juice.

watermelon radish and watercress salad

GLUTEN-FREE

SERVES 4

10 MINUTES

This delicious salad is driven purely by its beautiful ingredients; all you have to do is take a little care to arrange them nicely.

Watermelon radishes are green on the outside, but when sliced you see that they are intensely red in the middle, looking much like tiny watermelons. If you have a mandoline, use it here: It is excellent for slicing them thinly and evenly.

If you have difficulty finding watercress, check the refrigerated produce section of upscale markets. They often carry hydroponic watercress, making this peppery green, once strictly seasonal, available year-round. Look for bright, fresh leaves with no signs of wilting. The tart cress makes a great foil for the sweet figs and pomegranate seeds (or more technically, arils).

1 large watermelon radish, very thinly sliced
Extra-virgin olive oil
4 handfuls watercress, rinsed and dried
1 lemon
4 ripe fresh figs, halved
¼ cup pomegranate seeds
16 shavings Parmigiano-Reggiano or other hard aged cheese
12 toasted walnut halves
Flaky sea salt (such as Maldon)

1 Arrange a circle of watermelon radish slices on each of four chilled plates. Drizzle with a little olive oil.

2 Toss the watercress with a bit of the olive oil and a squeeze of lemon juice. Place a fluffy handful on each plate. This is the critical step to making the salad look nice—aim to make a tall, high mound in the center, and don't let it spread out.

3 Add 2 fig halves, 1 tablespoon pomegranate seeds, 4 cheese shavings, and 3 toasted walnut halves to each plate. Sprinkle with flaky sea salt and serve immediately.

latin american green lentil salad

VEGAN OPTION

GLUTEN-FREE

SERVES 4 AS AN
ENTRÉE OR 8 AS
A SIDE DISH

45 MINUTES
(20 MINUTES
ACTIVE)

Lentil salad went through some bad times in the 1980s and '90s. It was usually flaccid, overdressed, and filled with canned vegetables. But there was always the shadow of a good, simple, rustic dish there.

I like to make this with French lentils, otherwise known as green lentils. The best ones are from the area of Le Puy. They are a little smaller and plumper than common brown lentils, and they hold their shape even when tender, instead of pureeing themselves into lentil soup. Another option is the black "Beluga" lentil.

Once you have cooked lentils in hand, a salad is a simple thing. You can pick any combination of cooked and raw vegetables that go well together, fresh herbs that complement them, and a straightforward dressing of citrus juice and olive oil. For a Greek variation, for example, you could use lemon instead of lime and feta instead of *queso fresco*, and add thyme and oregano.

1½ cups French green lentils (*lentilles du Puy A.O.C.* are the best)
1 cup tiny waxy potatoes, such as red-skinned, cut into ½-inch cubes
   if larger than bite-size
3 tablespoons extra-virgin olive oil, plus additional for the potatoes
Kosher salt
Half a medium cucumber, peeled, seeded, and diced
6 radishes, thinly sliced
Half a small red onion, finely diced
1 big handful fresh mint leaves (chopped if large; reserve a few for garnish)
1 big handful fresh parsley leaves (reserve a few for garnish)
Juice of 1 lime
½ cup crumbled *queso fresco*
Freshly ground black pepper
1 avocado, sliced

1 Preheat the oven to 400°F.
2 Rinse the lentils and pick them over for stones and debris. Place them in a saucepan, cover with plenty of water, and boil until tender but not falling apart, about 25 minutes, adding more water if needed. Drain the lentils and spread them out on a baking sheet to cool.
3 Put the potatoes on a rimmed baking sheet and toss with a drizzle of olive oil and salt. Slide the pan into the oven and roast until the potatoes are tender and browned, about 15 minutes.
4 Combine the lentils, potatoes, cucumber, radishes, onion, mint, and parsley in a salad bowl. Add the lime juice, 3 tablespoons olive oil, and 1 teaspoon salt, and toss well.
5 Taste and adjust the balance of acidity and salt as needed; add more olive oil or lime juice if it needs a little more dressing.
6 To serve, top with the *queso fresco*, the reserved mint and parsley, a nice grind of black pepper, and the avocado.

warm frisée salad with brown butter vinaigrette

GLUTEN-FREE

SERVES 4

15 MINUTES

Warm salads seem a little more filling than typical cold salads, and a bit special, too. They are nice in cool weather, especially if you aren't serving a soup to take the chill out of the air. Classic non-vegetarian warm salads often include bacon and its rendered fat. I came up with this version that uses brown butter and caramelized turnips to create some of that rich flavor and texture.

To turn this salad into a light meal, top it with a poached or fried egg and serve it with slices of toasted artisanal bread. Toasted walnut or pecan halves and shavings of Parmigiano-Reggiano are also delicious additions.

Be careful not to let the butter burn. You want it to brown lightly and develop a nutty aroma, while becoming infused with the flavors of turnip and mushroom. At the first sign of overcooking, lower the heat to medium-low or even low.

4 tablespoons (½ stick) unsalted butter
2 turnips (about 3 inches in diameter), peeled and cut into ¼-inch half-moons
 (about 20 half-moons total)
Flaky sea salt (such as Maldon)
4 large button or crimini mushrooms, cut into ¼-inch slices
1 garlic clove, minced
1 head frisée, core removed, rinsed and thoroughly dried
2 tablespoons champagne vinegar or sherry vinegar
½ cup toasted hazelnuts
Freshly ground black pepper

1 Melt the butter in a large skillet over medium heat. Line 2 plates with paper towels. Add the turnips to the skillet in a single layer and cook until lightly browned on one side. If the butter starts to smoke or burn, lower the heat. Flip the turnips and cook until browned on the bottom and tender when poked with a toothpick. Using a slotted spatula or spoon, transfer the turnips to the paper towels and season with a sprinkle of flaky sea salt.

2 Cook the mushrooms in the same way as the turnips, and again transfer to paper towels and season with salt.

3 Add the garlic to the butter and cook for 30 seconds. Turn off the heat. Add the frisée, champagne vinegar, and ¼ teaspoon salt. Toss the frisée in the butter just long enough for it to begin to wilt slightly, about 30 seconds.

4 Using tongs, remove the frisée, gently shaking off any excess butter. Divide among four salad plates. Divide the turnips, mushrooms, and hazelnuts among the plates. Season each salad with some hearty grinds of black pepper and serve immediately.

main-course
sandwiches and tacos

crispy quesadilla with pecorino and roasted garlic onion jam

GLUTEN-FREE

MAKES 1
QUESADILLA
(MULTIPLY AS
NEEDED)

10 MINUTES

Pretty much everyone loves a quesadilla. Whether you are feeding mild Monterey Jack to a 3-year-old or Taleggio and grilled figs to a sophisticated foodie, a tortilla and melted cheese is quick to make and irresistible. Let me tell you about a simple trick that will take your quesadillas from tasty but floppy to crispy and delicious: Brush both sides of the quesadilla with a bit of oil before putting it on the pan or griddle on medium-high heat, and then let it cook for plenty of time on each side.

I told you it was simple! It doesn't need to be a lot of oil, but the difference is amazing. When you cook a quesadilla dry, the shell simply heats up and dries out a bit, which is okay. But when you brush on a bit of oil and let it cook awhile, the tortilla gets crispy on the outside, with a little chew left, and tastes like a perfect fresh tortilla chip.

To get your creative juices flowing, here's a tasty quesadilla I like to make, filled with young pecorino cheese, red onions, and Stonewall Kitchen Roasted Garlic Onion Jam (available at gourmet grocers or from amazon.com). You should substitute ingredients wildly and make whatever sounds good to you!

To turn this into a meal, serve two quesadillas with refried beans, Non-Traditional *Arroz Verde* (page 265), and a salad.

¼ cup grated young pecorino (semisoft; optionally flavored with peppercorns)
2 (6-inch) soft corn tortillas
A few thin slices of red onion
1 tablespoon Stonewall Kitchen Roasted Garlic Onion Jam
2 teaspoons vegetable oil

1 Heat a cast-iron skillet, flat griddle, or other heavy frying pan over medium heat.

2 Sprinkle the cheese on one tortilla and top it with the onion.

3 Spread the jam on the other tortilla and cover the first one, jam side down.

4 Brush one side with the oil and put the quesadilla in the skillet, oiled side down. Brush the other side with oil.

5 Cook for several minutes on each side, until the quesadilla develops beautiful crispy brown spots. Be patient and get it really well done for maximum flavor.

6 When the quesadilla is done on both sides, transfer it to a cutting board and carefully cut it into quarters with decisive presses of a sharp knife. Serve while still hot and crispy.

superfrico grilled cheese

MAKES 1 SAND-
WICH (MULTIPLY
AS NEEDED)

10 MINUTES

Everyone knows the best part of a grilled cheese sandwich (not to mention lasa-gna, gratin, mac & cheese, and the like) are the bits where the cheese gets brown and crispy. So one night I said to myself, why can't grilled cheese be more crispy? What happens if I just make a *frico* (cheese crisp) right there in the skillet and weld it to my already delicious grilled cheese? Would this not be a fine addition to a superb late-night supper?

The answer was a resounding yes—so much so that I don't make grilled cheese any other way now. It only takes a minute or two more than a standard sandwich, but the extra dimension of texture takes it to a whole new level.

1 tablespoon unsalted butter, plus additional as needed
2 thin slices artisanal sourdough bread (or other bread of your choice)
½ cup grated provolone (or other cheese of your choice)
3 tablespoons grated cheddar mixed with 2 teaspoons grated Parmigiano-Reggiano

1 Melt the butter in a cast-iron skillet over medium or slightly higher heat.

2 Place the slices of bread in the skillet. Flip over the bread slices to lightly moisten both sides with the melted butter.

3 Top one slice of bread with the provolone and cover with the other slice of bread. Press down firmly with a heavy-duty spatula or a smaller skillet. Cook, flipping a couple of times and pressing down occasionally, until golden brown on both sides, about 6 minutes total.

4 When the basic grilled cheese is done, remove it from the pan. Lower the heat to medium if necessary. If the pan seems very dry, melt a touch more butter in it. Sprinkle the mixed cheddar and Parmigiano into the still-hot skillet, in a shape roughly the same as the sandwich but a little larger.

5 Now watch closely as the cheese melts. You'll see the fat start to cook out and the cheese begin to brown and crisp. When it has just begun to brown, put the sandwich back in the pan, on top of the melted cheese, and press down to weld the *frico* to the bread.

6 Let cook for 1 minute more, then, using a thin spatula, lift out the sandwich, flip it over onto a plate, cut it in half, and serve. If there are any crispy bits left in the skillet, retrieve them and place on top of the sandwich.

iraqi-jewish eggplant sandwich (sabich)

VEGAN OPTION

GLUTEN-FREE
OPTION

MAKES 4
SANDWICHES

30 MINUTES

Sabich is a popular Sabbath food for Iraqi Jews, who, when they emigrated to Israel and set up a community in Ramat Gan, brought the sandwich with them. It has since gained widespread popularity, and of course, in typical Israeli fashion, there are 100 variations and 200 opinions about which one is best.

There is something about the creaminess of the egg and the fried goodness of the eggplant that works really well together. And the garnishes of Israeli salad (tomatoes and cucumbers with a bit of lemon juice), hummus, onions, pickles, parsley, and *amba* give your mouth the full workout of sweet, spicy, sour, herbaceous, smooth, and crispy.

Amba is a pickled mango condiment. You may be able to find it at a Middle Eastern grocery, or check the Internet for a recipe and make your own. If you can't find it or make it, use a little harissa or other hot sauce instead.

2 plum tomatoes, finely diced
Half an English cucumber, finely diced
Juice of 1 lemon
Kosher salt
¼ cup vegetable oil
1 large eggplant, peeled and cut into generous ¼-inch slices
4 large eggs, hard-cooked, peeled, and sliced (omit for vegan)
2 cups hummus (store-bought or make your own)
1 cup pre-seasoned tahini (sesame paste, also known as tehina or tahina) *or*
   1 cup plain tahini seasoned with 1 clove minced garlic and lemon juice to taste
½ cup loosely packed fresh flatleaf parsley leaves
Half a small white onion, minced
½ cup thinly sliced or diced dill pickle
***Amba* (pickled mango; see headnote for substitutions)**
4 pita breads (omit and serve as a salad for gluten-free)

1 In a small bowl, make a simple salad of the tomatoes, cucumber, and lemon juice, adding salt to taste.
2 Put the vegetable oil in a large skillet over medium-high heat. Fry the eggplant in batches until completely tender, turning to brown on both sides, about 7 minutes total; drain on paper towels and sprinkle with salt. (You can also grill the eggplant instead of frying for a different, lighter taste.) Transfer to a serving dish.
3 While the eggplant is frying, put the eggs, hummus, tahini, parsley, onion, dill pickle, and *amba* in small bowls so diners can build sandwiches to their own specifications.
4 Toast or grill the pita bread.
5 Serve it forth, preferably with a cold beer, and encourage everyone to make a gigantic sandwich.

KNIVES. Nothing slows down most home cooks more than the absence of sharp knives and a working knowledge of how to use them. If it takes you 10 minutes to disassemble a head of broccoli or slice a couple of onions, you may find it hard to get motivated to take on more complex recipes. If the results look more like they were hit with a lawnmower than crafted with a precision tool, your food won't cook very evenly or look as appetizing as it might.

Every cook should have a decent chef's knife, at least 6 inches long but preferably 8 inches. Your knife needs to be made of a high-quality steel that will hold an edge, and it has to feel good in your hand. Go to a well-stocked kitchenware or cutlery store and hold a few until you find the right knife for your particular hand.

You'll need to keep your knife sharp with regular passes on a sharpening steel and an occasional professional sharpening. There are also excellent motor-driven knife sharpeners that can be purchased for use at home. While a bit expensive, they will return the investment over time.

Okay, you've got a good knife with a sharp edge. Now what? Learn how to hold food safely with your other hand, tucking your fingertips under while guiding the blade with your knuckles. Learn, too, how to hold the knife itself with a proper overhand grip, with no index finger extending along the blade.

I learned a lot of the basic knife skills from Edward Espe Brown's *Tassajara Cooking* (Shambala, 1986), back when I was cooking weekly dinners for a crowded college co-op. While it is possible, with lots of trial and error, to learn from a book or video, I think the best way is to spend a little time with a competent instructor. Ask around for a local cooking school or store that offers short classes on basic knife skills. If that's not available, find a friend with good knife skills to show you the ropes. However you learn, focus first on making safe and consistent cuts. Increased speed will come naturally once you build the right foundation.

kouftikes de prasa sandwiches

MAKES 4
SANDWICHES

2½ HOURS
(30 MINUTES
ACTIVE)

All over the Middle East and even in India, a *kofta* is a little meatball or patty. There are a few vegetarian versions, too. These *kouftikes de prasa* are made of leeks bound together with bread crumbs and eggs. The Sephardic side of my family looks forward to them for our Rosh Hashanah feast.

I up the ante by serving them in pita sandwiches with spicy pickled cabbage flavored with preserved lemon (available in Middle Eastern markets and gourmet groceries) and harissa. This transforms them from an appetizer into an entrée with street-food flair.

The cabbage needs to sit for a couple of hours to soften. You can even toss it together the day before and let it marinate in the refrigerator overnight. In a pinch, just use plain shredded lettuce instead, and serve hot sauce on the side.

FOR THE SPICY CABBAGE
2 cups finely shredded red cabbage
½ teaspoon kosher salt
¼ cup white vinegar
Half a preserved lemon, finely chopped
2 teaspoons harissa or Thai-style chile sauce (such as sriracha)

FOR THE LEEK PATTIES
2 large leeks, white and light green parts only (about 12 ounces)
2 tablespoons extra-virgin olive oil
¾ teaspoon kosher salt
4 large eggs, beaten
½ cup Homemade Bread Crumbs (page 345)
½ teaspoon ground cumin
¼ teaspoon Aleppo pepper or cayenne
Pinch of ground cinnamon
Vegetable oil, for shallow frying
Flaky sea salt (such as Maldon)

TO FINISH THE SANDWICHES
4 pita breads, lightly toasted or grilled
20 thin half-moons of cucumber
½ cup thick Greek yogurt or *labneh*
Ground sumac
A handful fresh mint or cilantro leaves, torn

▼ ▼ ▼

1   *For the spicy cabbage:* Thoroughly toss together the cabbage, salt, vinegar, preserved lemon, and harissa. Cover and refrigerate for at least 2 hours, or up to 24 hours. Allow to return to room temperature before serving.

2   *For the leek patties:* Cut the leeks in half lengthwise and then into ¼-inch-wide half-moons. Wash in 3 changes of water and dry thoroughly (a salad spinner works well for this).

3   Heat the olive oil in a large skillet over medium-high heat. Add the leeks and sauté until tender and starting to shrivel, about 5 minutes. Transfer to a mixing bowl. (You can use the same skillet to fry the leek patties in a moment.)

4   Thoroughly mix the leeks, salt, eggs, bread crumbs, cumin, Aleppo pepper, and cinnamon.

5   Heat about ⅛ inch vegetable oil in the skillet over medium-high heat. When the oil is shimmering, drop in ¼ cup leek batter with a measuring cup and use the back of the cup to smooth the patty into a circle about 4 inches in diameter. Repeat with remaining batter, making 8 patties total (fry them in two batches if necessary, adding a bit more oil as needed). Fry each patty until golden brown, about 3 minutes per side. Transfer to paper towels and season with flaky sea salt.

6   *To finish the sandwiches:* Place 2 leek patties on a pita. Top with a handful of the spicy cabbage, 5 cucumber slices, and 2 tablespoons Greek yogurt. Sprinkle a little sumac on the yogurt and scatter a few mint leaves over the whole sandwich. Repeat with remaining ingredients. Fold the pita over to eat as a sandwich. Serve immediately.

caribbean lentil-stuffed flatbread (dal poori roti)

You might be surprised to find this recipe in a main-course section, but they are quite filling. It takes only a small side-dish curry and a little rice to make a complete meal. Most people will only need one of these hearty breads, so for a smaller group, you may want to cut the recipe in half.

Variations on *dal poori roti* are made on many of the Caribbean islands, but you can tell by the name and style that they originated with Indian immigrants. The name can seem confusing because in Indian terminology, a poori and a roti are two different types of bread.

I like to use about 50 percent whole-wheat pastry flour when I make the dough. Not only is it more nutritious than white flour, it also adds a more complex flavor. Pastry flour is lower in gluten, which helps keep the bread tender.

These breads are best when steaming hot; otherwise, the filling can be dry. They reheat beautifully in the microwave if you've made them ahead.

FOR THE DOUGH
4 cups all-purpose flour
3½ cups whole-wheat pastry flour
2 tablespoons baking powder
2 teaspoons kosher salt
6 tablespoons (¾ stick) unsalted butter, melted
2½ cups warm water, plus additional as needed

FOR THE FILLING
3 tablespoons vegetable oil
Half a medium-size onion, diced
2 garlic cloves, minced
2 teaspoons kosher salt
1½ cups yellow split peas, sorted and rinsed
6 cups water
1 teaspoon ground turmeric
2 teaspoons ground cumin
½ teaspoon cayenne pepper

TO COOK THE BREADS
Unsalted butter

▼ ▼ ▼

1   *For the dough:* Whisk the flours, baking powder, and salt together in a large bowl. Add the melted butter and 2½ cups of warm water and stir until a shaggy mass forms. You may need to add up to ½ cup additional warm water. The goal is a soft, pliable dough that isn't too sticky. Transfer to a floured work surface and knead until smooth, about 5 minutes. Form the dough into a ball, rub with a little oil, wrap in plastic wrap, and set aside to rest for about 1 hour. (Another option is to use a stand mixer. Use the paddle attachment for the initial mixing, then switch to the dough hook for the 5 minutes of kneading.) Make the filling while the dough rests.

2   *For the filling:* Heat 1 tablespoon oil in a large saucepan over medium-high heat. Add the onion, garlic, and 1 teaspoon salt and sauté until the onion is translucent, about 2 minutes. Add the split peas and 6 cups water. Bring to a boil, then reduce the heat and simmer until the peas are easily crushed between your fingers—tender enough to eat but not turning into soup, about 25 minutes.

3   Drain the peas and transfer them to a food processor. Add the remaining 2 tablespoons oil, the turmeric, cumin, cayenne, and the remaining 1 teaspoon of salt. Pulse until the peas are coarsely pureed, retaining a bit of texture. Taste and adjust the seasoning. You may also need to add a couple tablespoons of water. The right texture is one that is stiff enough to form a ball, without being bone-dry. If it is too wet, it will make the roti soggy.

4   When the dough is done with its initial rest, divide it into 12 pieces (if using a scale, they will be about 135 grams each). Form into balls, place on a lightly floured board or baking sheet, cover with plastic wrap, and allow to rest for an additional 30 minutes.

5   *To cook the breads:* Heat a large, heavy skillet (at least 12 inches in diameter) or griddle over medium heat. Take one ball of dough and, on a lightly floured work surface or a silicone board, roll it out to a 5-inch circle. Place 3 tablespoons of the filling in the center. Pull the edges of dough up around the filling toward the center and pinch to seal completely. Flatten with your hand and then roll out to a 10-inch circle less than ¼ inch thick. If you can't roll them out this thin, or a little dal breaks through, they will still taste fantastic. (You can start cooking the bread while continuing to form the rest of the breads.)

6   Melt a little butter in the skillet and put in the first bread. Cook until lightly browned on the first side, about 1½ minutes, pushing down on the edges occasionally. You don't want it to brown so much that it is crispy; the bread should remain soft. Turn and cook the other side until lightly browned, about 1½ minutes more. Repeat with remaining breads, stacking them on a plate and covering them to keep them warm. Serve immediately or reheat if made in advance.

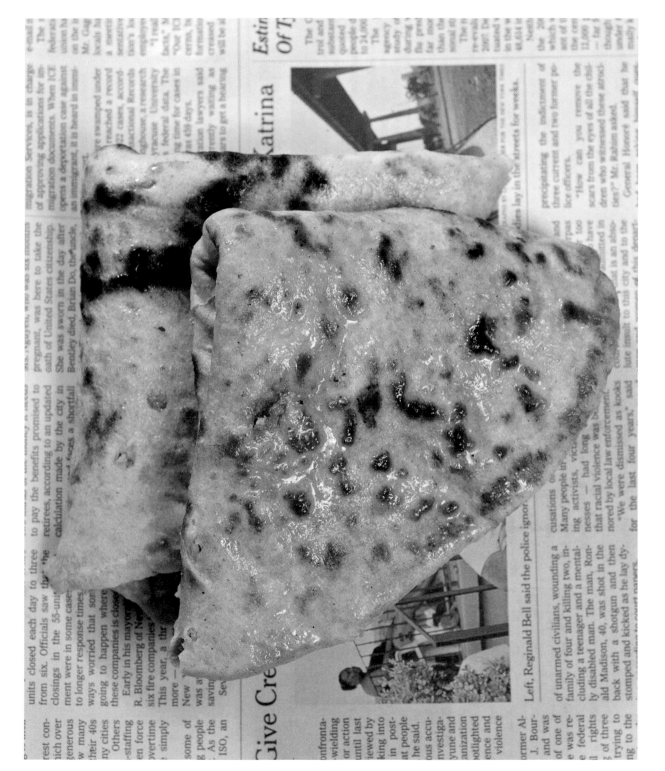

shiitake tacos with asian pear slaw

VEGAN

GLUTEN-FREE

MAKES 8 TACOS

30 MINUTES

I love to make up taco combinations using a substantial component like shiitake mushrooms, contrasted with a bright fresh slaw. Serve these up with big plates of refried beans, Mexican rice (or the Non-Traditional *Arroz Verde* on page 265), and homemade guacamole for a feast that is only a bit more work than ordinary "taco night" but a lot more interesting.

The technique of dry-roasting the jalapeño peppers and garlic for these tacos is common in Mexican cuisine. It is a quick way of both mellowing and concentrating the flavors. I highly recommend wearing disposable rubber gloves when seeding and chopping the jalapeños, to avoid the risk of having your hands burn later or, worse, transferring the capsaicin to your eyes.

The bok choy in this recipe is the full-grown vegetable, usually 10 to 12 inches long, with dark green leaves; don't substitute baby bok choy.

You can take this same Asian pear slaw and use it as a condiment for other dishes. Add a little toasted sesame oil if you are serving it as part of an Asian meal.

FOR THE FILLING
4 jalapeño peppers
6 garlic cloves (not peeled)
3 tablespoons vegetable oil
1 white onion, diced
1 pound fresh shiitake mushrooms, stems removed and quartered
Two-thirds of a head of bok choy, carefully washed and cut into 1-inch slices
1 teaspoon kosher salt
½ teaspoon ground cumin
Ground cinnamon

FOR THE SLAW
Juice of 1 lime
1 Asian pear
⅓ cup thinly sliced red onion
A handful fresh cilantro leaves
¼ teaspoon kosher salt

TO SERVE
16 (6-inch) soft corn tortillas

1   *For the filling:* Place a large skillet (preferably cast iron) over medium-high heat. Without adding any oil, dry-roast the jalapeños and unpeeled garlic cloves until blistered and charred, about 8 minutes, turning a couple of times. When the jalapeños are cool enough to handle, remove and discard the stems. Remove the seeds and ribs if you want a milder dish, then cut the peppers into thin slices. Remove the skin from the garlic cloves and roughly chop.

2   Return the skillet to high heat. Add the oil and, when it is shimmering, add the white onion. Sauté until moderately browned, about 5 minutes. Add the shiitakes and sauté until the shiitakes begin to soften, about 3 minutes. Add the roasted jalapeños, roasted garlic, bok choy, salt, cumin, and a pinch of cinnamon. Cook, stirring occasionally, until the leaves of the bok choy have wilted and the stems are mostly tender but still have a bit of a bite, about 6 minutes. Taste and adjust the seasoning.

3   *For the slaw:* Put the lime juice into a small bowl. Peel, quarter, and core the Asian pear. Using a mandoline or a knife, julienne the Asian pear, tossing with the lime juice as soon as it's cut so it doesn't brown. Add the red onion, cilantro, and salt.

4   *To serve:* Wrap the corn tortillas in a damp, clean dishtowel and microwave until soft and steaming, about 2 minutes. Make 8 stacks of 2 tortillas each. Top each pair of tortillas with a big spoonful of the filling, and a smaller spoonful of the slaw. Serve immediately.

grilled tofu and pepper tacos

VEGAN

GLUTEN-FREE

MAKES 12
SMALL OR 8
MEDIUM TACOS

30 MINUTES

I've found that the secret to delicious Mexican vegetarian food is to amp up the flavors and use lots of contrasting textures. These tacos—filled with grilled tofu and sautéed peppers, all basted with tangy *achiote* paste—have serious street-food flavor. They are meant to be eaten in just two or three bites. Pick 'em up, lean over your plate, and get on in there, or you'll be wearing some very tasty juices. Add Grilled Pineapple Salsa (page 334) for an awesome combination, or use the salsa of your choice.

The easiest way to cook with *achiote* (annatto) is to buy it as a paste, which comes as a slightly moist little brick. It isn't always easy to find the whole *achiote* seeds, and when you do, you have the added step of grinding the seeds, which are extremely hard. The El Yucateco brand of paste is nice because it doesn't have (or need) any synthetic food coloring added.

1½ ounces (about 4 teaspoons) *achiote* paste (also called annatto)
½ cup vegetable oil
1 teaspoon ground cumin
2 teaspoons Tapatío or other hot sauce
1 teaspoon kosher salt
10 ounces extra-firm tofu, cut into ⅓-inch slabs and patted dry
1 medium zucchini, cut lengthwise into ⅓-inch slabs
1 medium onion, thinly sliced
4 garlic cloves, thinly sliced
2 red bell peppers, cut into ¼-inch strips
1 yellow bell pepper, cut into ¼-inch strips
Fresh lemon or lime juice (optional)

TO SERVE
24 (4-inch) or 16 (6-inch) soft corn tortillas
Guacamole
Grilled Pineapple Salsa (page 334) or other salsa of your choice

1 Break up the *achiote* paste in a small bowl with a fork and mash in the oil, a little at a time, until it forms a lumpy paste. Mix in the cumin, hot sauce, and salt.

2 Heat a grill or grill pan over medium heat. Brush the tofu with the *achiote* oil on one side and grill, oiled side down, until well marked. Brush the other side, flip, and grill until well marked. Repeat with the zucchini, brushing the slabs with *achiote* oil and grilling until well marked and tender, about 3 minutes per side. Allow the tofu and zucchini to cool and then cut both into ⅓-inch dice.

3 Heat a skillet over medium-high heat. Add 2 tablespoons *achiote* oil. Add the onion, garlic, and bell peppers and sauté until very soft.

4 Add the tofu and zucchini to the pepper mixture. Taste and adjust the seasoning. It may need more salt, a little lime or lemon juice, or more heat.

5 *To serve:* Wrap the tortillas in a damp, clean dishtowel and microwave until soft and warm, about 2 minutes.

6 Make stacks of 2 tortillas each. Top with a moderate scoop of the filling and a spoonful of guacamole and salsa. Pass more hot sauce for those who want it.

TORTILLAS FOR TACOS. A good corn tortilla, when steamed, should be pliable enough to roll into a cylinder without cracking. Try to find a local place that makes tortillas. They will be dramatically better than the grocery-store brands. Searching online for *tortillerias* in your area may turn up some options. If that doesn't work, try asking a Mexican friend or at a Mexican grocery or restaurant.

The standard corn tortilla is 6 inches in diameter, which is suitable for tacos and quesadillas. Some brands also make a 7- or 8-inch version, but I find these less useful. You may also find 4-inch corn tortillas, which are great for street-food-style tacos that are easy to pick up and finish off in a couple of bites.

The best way to heat corn tortillas is to wrap them in a clean, damp dishtowel and microwave for 30 seconds at a time until they are soft, hot, and pliable, usually about 2 minutes total.

indian fry bread tacos

Navajo fry bread, and the Indian tacos made with it, have a sad past. They originated in Native American internment camps set up by the U.S. government in the 1860s, as a way to use the very limited rations provided. Today, fry bread and Indian tacos are a proud part of the culture, served at virtually every powwow with good reason—besides the history, they are delicious. (Although "Native American" is usually considered the more diplomatic term, it is never applied to this dish. The folks who make them and eat them universally refer to them as "Indian tacos.")

Fry bread is so much more filling than a corn tortilla that a single one, loaded up with flavorful toppings, makes a whole meal. If you have any dough left over, fry it up and served with confectioners' sugar or honey for a treat.

Don't knead the dough any more than is absolutely necessary to bring it together, because you want it to remain tender. For the same reason, fry it only until lightly golden brown. You aren't looking for a crisp shell here.

FOR THE FRY BREAD
3 cups all-purpose flour
1 teaspoon salt
1 tablespoon baking powder
1 cup milk, plus additional as needed
Vegetable oil, for frying

FOR THE SQUASH AND CORN TOPPING
4 poblano chile peppers
2 tablespoons vegetable oil
Half an onion, finely diced
3 garlic cloves, minced
1 pound yellow summer squash or zucchini (about 3 medium), cut into bite-size cubes
¾ teaspoon kosher salt
Kernels from 2 ears corn, or 2 cups frozen corn, defrosted
2 teaspoons dried oregano (preferably Mexican)

TO SERVE
3 cups tender cooked pinto beans (homemade or canned)
1 cup grated cheddar
½ cup minced white onion
1 cup halved cherry tomatoes
2 cups shredded iceberg lettuce
1½ cups guacamole
Thick salsa of your choice (smoky chipotle versions are good)

▼ ▼ ▼

1 *For the fry bread:* Whisk together the flour, salt, and baking powder in a large bowl. Add the milk and mix with a fork until you have a shaggy mass, adding a little more milk if needed. You want a dough that is fairly sticky, just barely firm enough to roll out. Turn the dough out onto a lightly floured surface and, with floured hands, knead for just a few seconds to make a big ball. Rub the dough lightly with oil, cover, and set aside until you are ready to fry.

2 *For the squash and corn topping:* Roast the poblano peppers on a grill, under the broiler, or carefully with tongs over an open flame until blackened and blistered all over. Set aside in a covered bowl until cool. Wearing rubber gloves, remove the skin, stem, and seeds, then cut the pepper into ¼-inch strips. (Mexican cooks call these rajas.)

3 Heat the oil in a large skillet over medium-high heat. Add the onion and garlic and sauté for 1 minute, then add the summer squash and salt. Sauté, tossing occasionally, until browned, about 4 minutes; add the corn and sauté for 2 minutes; add the poblano strips and oregano and heat through. Taste and adjust the seasoning.

4 When ready to fry the breads (just before serving; they are best fresh), pour ¾ inch of vegetable oil into a large, heavy skillet. Heat over medium-high heat to 365°F degrees.

5 Divide the dough into quarters, shape into balls, and roll each one out into a circle about 9 inches in diameter. Fry one at a time until medium golden brown, flipping to cook both sides, about 2 minutes total. Be careful when flipping—if you just flop it over with a spatula it can cause a dangerous splash. I use a spatula and a spoon to control them, but you could also use tongs. Transfer cooked breads to paper towels to drain.

6 *To serve:* Put a fry bread on each plate, and top with generous portions of the topping, the beans, cheese, onion, tomatoes, lettuce, guacamole, and salsa. Serve immediately.

main-course
pasta and noodle dishes

soba noodles in shiitake-shoyu broth with spring vegetables

SERVES 4

45 MINUTES

I'm rarely jealous of meat eaters, but their Asian noodle soups do get my attention. I wanted to create a very full-flavored broth with lots of umami intensity. I make it with dried shiitakes, kombu seaweed, and the best soy sauce available.

Soba are Japanese noodles made from buckwheat flour. Soba are often served cold with a dipping sauce, but they are equally great in hot soup. The buckwheat flavor is distinctively nutty and earthy. It has a particular resonance for me because it reminds me of the kasha that my Eastern European Jewish family served. Funny how the same flavor can work successfully in such different contexts.

The toppings for this soup are a nice transition from winter to spring. The leeks and dried mushrooms are mainstays of the cold weather months; asparagus and eggs have always symbolized spring. A few scallions add a bright top note, and the soft tofu brings another texture and some protein. I'm not sure I can think of anything I'd rather eat on a rainy day. Of course, you can vary the toppings to suit your mood and the contents of your vegetable drawer, and the soup could be made with ramen or udon noodles and still be delicious.

Shoyu is the Japanese name for soy sauce. If you can find unpasteurized nama shoyu, it is to most other shoyu what Parmigiano-Reggiano is to the stuff in the green can. The flavor is more complex and caramelized and less salty, with no chemical edge. Because it is unpasteurized, it is also claimed by some to be a source for healthy digestive probiotic bacteria. Another great soy sauce is made by Bourbon Barrel Foods in Kentucky. They use traditional methods but age their sauce in old oak whiskey barrels.

2 cups dried shiitake mushrooms
1 piece kombu seaweed (6 to 8 inches long)
1/2-inch piece fresh ginger, peeled
4 garlic cloves, coarsely chopped
8 cups water
4 medium leeks, white parts only, tough outer layer discarded, halved lengthwise, and carefully cleaned
3 tablespoons shoyu (Japanese soy sauce; see headnote), plus additional as needed
4 large eggs
1 bunch thick asparagus, tough ends removed and lightly peeled
1 tablespoon vegetable oil
Kosher salt

▼ ▼ ▼

9 ounces soba noodles
12 ounces soft tofu, cut into ½-inch cubes
2 scallions, white and light green parts only, thinly sliced on the diagonal
Toasted sesame oil

1 Briefly rinse the dried shiitakes. Place them in a saucepan with the kombu, ginger, garlic, and water. Simmer over low heat for 20 minutes.

2 Add the leeks and simmer until they are tender, about 10 minutes more. Remove the leeks with a slotted spoon and reserve. Remove and discard the kombu. Strain the broth through a fine-mesh sieve, squeezing out as much broth from the mushrooms as possible. Discard the shiitake stems. Slice enough of the shiitake caps thinly to yield 1 cup for serving, and save the rest for another use.

3 Add the shoyu to the broth. Taste and add more if needed.

4 Put the eggs in a small saucepan and cover with cold water by ½ inch. Bring to a boil over high heat, then cover and remove from the heat. Set a timer for 8 minutes; when the timer rings, transfer the eggs to a bowl of cold water. Peel the cooled eggs and cut them in half lengthwise.

5 Heat a grill pan or large, heavy skillet over medium-high heat. Brush the asparagus with the vegetable oil and cook in a single layer, turning from time to time, until spears are tender and charred spots are appearing on all sides, about 8 minutes. Remove and season with salt.

6 Boil the soba noodles according to the package directions and drain.

7 Bring the broth back to a simmer.

8 Warm four large soup bowls in a low (200°F) oven. To serve, put about 1 cup of noodles in each of the warmed bowls. Top the noodles with the leeks, eggs, asparagus, sliced shiitake caps, tofu, and scallions. Take your time to make an attractive arrangement. Ladle in about 1½ cups of the broth. Drizzle in a few drops of sesame oil and serve it forth.

planning a meal: start with a base ingredient

Just as an omnivorous meal might be centered on a particular meat or fish, a vegetarian meal is often based on a grain or pasta—or, sometimes, a bean. The choice of that base ingredient will often suggest appropriate accompaniments. For example, if you want couscous, you'll probably be better off making a Moroccan tagine than a Thai curry!

Here are a few sample menus to get you thinking:

1 fresh pasta
Shaved Artichoke Salad with Blood Oranges, page 124
Pappardelle with Eggplant Ragu and Fresh Ricotta, page 172
Zabaglione with Roasted Plums, page 286

2 quinoa
Tomato-Chickpea Soup, page 90
Quinoa Cakes, page 193
Stir-Fried Corn with Lemongrass, page 253
Grilled Chinese Broccoli and Lemon, page 245

3 rice and lentils
Cucumber and Dill Soup (*Tarator*), page 83
Middle Eastern Rice and Lentil Pilaf (*Mujadara*), page 201
Oven-roasted cauliflower with Quick Harissa Oil, page 349

4 beans
Green salad with Lemon-Mustard Vinaigrette, page 327
Chili *Borracho*, page 213
Brown Butter Cornbread, page 273

5 polenta
White Bean and Kale Soup, page 94
Stuffed and Baked Polenta, page 235
Seckel Pears with Cinnamon Pastry Crumbs, page 290

See also Planning a Meal: Start with the Culture (page 183) and Planning a Meal: Start with What's Fresh (page 227).

spaghetti with garlic and oil (aglio e olio)

VEGAN OPTION

SERVES 3 OR 4

20 MINUTES

Other than tossing noodles with butter and cheese, making spaghetti *aglio e olio* is just about the simplest way to prepare pasta. You can have this ready two minutes after the pasta is done boiling, so it makes a perfect meal when the day gets away from you but you still want to eat something home-cooked.

While the dish is very simple to make, it can achieve perfection through attention to a few details. The clean and direct flavors of extra-virgin olive oil and garlic, spiked up with a few hot pepper flakes, are all it takes to make this dish outstanding. I often gild the lily with a handful of Parmigiano-Reggiano and fresh bread crumbs, but there are others who will insist this is sacrilege. The choice is yours.

1 pound spaghetti
4 tablespoons extra-virgin olive oil
8 garlic cloves (or to your taste), thinly sliced
Hot red pepper flakes
½ teaspoon kosher salt
¼ cup minced fresh flatleaf parsley leaves
½ cup Homemade Bread Crumbs (page 345; optional)
Freshly grated Parmigiano-Reggiano (optional)

1 Bring a large pot of well-salted water to a boil. Warm your serving bowls in a low (200°F) oven.

2 Add the spaghetti and cook for the minimum time specified on the package.

3 While the pasta is cooking, heat the oil in your largest skillet over medium heat. Add the garlic, a pinch (or more) of hot red pepper flakes, and salt and cook until the garlic is softened but not browned, about 3 minutes. Remove from the heat.

4 Test a strand of pasta, and if it is not yet al dente, let it cook for another minute. When the pasta is done, scoop out and reserve 1 cup of the cooking water. Drain the pasta.

5 Turn the heat under your skillet to medium-high, and add the pasta to the oil along with ½ cup of the pasta water. Toss thoroughly with tongs, adding more of the pasta water if it seems dry.

6 Divide the pasta among the serving bowls and garnish with the parsley and the bread crumbs and cheese, if using. Serve immediately.

rice vermicelli (bun)
with ginger-grapefruit sauce

When well made, *bun* (pronounced, roughly, boon) is just about one of the greatest foods ever invented. Thin Vietnamese rice noodles are topped with a variety of cooked and fresh ingredients, lots of herbs, and a sweet-and-savory sauce to make a light, healthy, and superbly delicious meal-in-a-bowl. It is salad and entrée in one amazing package.

You can make a terrific *bun* at home. You have the luxury of gathering great fresh ingredients, and you can make a sauce that is vegetarian by design (unlike those at your local Vietnamese joint), with big bright flavors, including fresh grapefruit juice. (Or for a vegetarian version of *nuoc cham*, see page 332).

The key to *bun* is all in the *mise en place*. You have quite a few ingredients that need preparation. Nothing complicated—it just takes a little time to get them all together, and you want to be organized for final assembly.

My choices for ingredients and sauce can be a starting point; you can add or subtract anything you like. As long as it fits within Vietnamese flavor profiles, it will still be a great dish. Other things I love to include are Thai basil, lemongrass (sautéed with the tofu), roasted peanuts, and papaya.

FOR THE SAUCE
3 grapefruits
Juice of 2 limes (grate and reserve the zest from 1 lime to finish the dish)
2 tablespoons sugar (use palm sugar, if you have it)
2 teaspoons soy sauce (use a wheat-free version for gluten-free)
1 tablespoon minced fresh ginger
Kosher salt

FOR THE BUN
8 ounces Vietnamese rice vermicelli noodles
1 cup julienned carrot (cut with a mandoline, if available)
1 cup julienned daikon (cut with a mandoline, if available)
2 tablespoons rice vinegar
1 tablespoon toasted sesame seeds
¼ cup vegetable oil
1 cup sliced shallot (cut rings about ⅛ inch thick)
Kosher salt
1 pound extra-firm tofu, cut into 2 x 2 x ⅓-inch squares
¼ cup sweet soy sauce or *kecap manis* (use a wheat-free version for gluten-free)

▼ ▼ ▼

TO ASSEMBLE
1 head romaine lettuce, cut into bite-size pieces
2 small hot chile peppers, thinly sliced
1 medium cucumber, seeded and diced
1 ripe mango, peeled and diced
3 scallions, white and light green parts only, thinly sliced
1 cup lightly packed fresh cilantro leaves
Grated zest of 1 lime
Sriracha, or similar thick Asian chile sauce

1 *For the sauce:* Cut the grapefruit into supremes (see page 125), working over a bowl to catch the juice and making sure to squeeze all the juice from membranes and peel. Strain the juice and reserve the supremes separately. Add the lime juice, sugar, soy sauce, ginger, and 1 teaspoon salt. Taste and adjust sugar and salt, remembering that it needs to be strongly flavored to play off of all the other ingredients.

2 *For the bun:* Bring a pot of water to a boil, remove from the heat, and add the rice noodles; let sit for 10 minutes. Check the texture; the noodles should be tender but not mushy. Soak a minute or two longer if necessary. Drain and reserve.

3 Combine the carrot, daikon, rice vinegar, and sesame seeds and set aside to pickle a bit.

4 Heat 2 tablespoons oil in a skillet over medium-high heat. Add the shallots and cook until dark brown. Transfer to paper towels and season liberally with salt. As they cool, the shallots will become crispy.

5 Heat the remaining 2 tablespoons oil in the skillet and cook the tofu, working in batches if needed, until brown on both sides. Return all the tofu to the skillet and drizzle with the sweet soy sauce; continue cooking for another 30 seconds to caramelize the sauce. Turn off the heat and leave the tofu in the skillet until you are ready to assemble the dish.

6 *To assemble:* Divide the lettuce among four large bowls. Top each with a big handful of the rice noodles. Then top with an attractive arrangement of the grapefruit supremes (you may end up with more grapefruit supremes than you need—these are a cook's treat), carrot-daikon salad, tofu, sliced chiles, cucumber, and mango, and finally the shallot rings, scallions, cilantro, and lime zest. You can either pour on the sauce yourself or divide it into individual bowls for your guests to add as they see fit. Offer the sriracha on the side.

A KITCHEN TOOL TO MAKE YOUR LIFE EASIER. A mandoline is one of the best things you can buy to streamline your cooking prep and improve the look of your dishes. You can buy high-end ones that run upward of $100, but most chefs use the simpler $20 model from Benriner, a Japanese brand. It makes quick work of creating uniform slices ranging in thickness from paper-thin up to about $1/4$ inch, and you can attach additional blades to cut juliennes of various widths.

fresh fettuccine with broccoli rabe in a light, lemony sauce

From May through October, there's a farmers' market just a couple of blocks from my house that's open on my day off. My regular ritual is to swing by in the afternoon, select what looks great, then figure out what to cook with my bounty. If I don't have another plan, I'll often pick up a pound of fresh pasta from one of the vendors to serve as the base for improvisation.

This dish came about one week when beautiful broccoli rabe was available. If you don't have broccoli rabe, you could make this dish with zucchini or summer squash. Fresh basil would be a delicious addition as well.

Fresh pasta doesn't generally pair well with the full-bodied tomato "gravy" you would serve with dried spaghetti. For this dish, I developed a much lighter broth of tomato juice, white wine, and lemon, all emulsified with butter, which coats the noodles without overwhelming their delicate flavor.

1 large bunch broccoli rabe (big enough that you can't quite get your hand around it), cut into bite-size pieces
4 tablespoons (½ stick) unsalted butter, plus additional as needed
4 garlic cloves, minced
Half a white onion, finely diced
Pinch of hot red pepper flakes
Kosher salt
1 (14.5-ounce) can diced tomatoes in juice (preferably San Marzano), drained, with juice reserved
¾ cup dry white wine or vermouth
Juice of half a lemon
1 pound fresh fettuccine (not dried)
1 cup freshly grated Parmigiano-Reggiano
Freshly ground black pepper
1 large handful fresh flatleaf parsley or basil leaves, coarsely chopped

1   Warm a serving platter or bowl in a low (200°F) oven. Fill a large bowl with ice water.
2   Bring a large pot of well-salted water to a boil. Boil the broccoli rabe until the stems are tender, about 3 minutes. Use a skimmer or slotted spoon to transfer the rabe to the ice water (to retain the color), and reserve the boiling water for cooking the pasta.

▼ ▼ ▼

3 Melt the butter in a large skillet over medium heat. Add the garlic, onion, hot red pepper flakes, and ½ teaspoon salt, and cook until the onions have softened, about 3 minutes. At this point, your house will be fragrant and diners may start wandering in with wild looks of anticipation in their eyes.

4 Whisk the butter and onions while drizzling in the juice from the tomatoes. You want the butter to emulsify, as in a *beurre blanc* (or in this case a *beurre rouge*). If it gives you any trouble, whisk in a little more cold butter. Then add the diced tomatoes, ½ cup of the wine, and the lemon juice. Bring to a slow simmer and cook until slightly reduced; it should coat the back of a spoon. Taste and adjust the seasoning; it probably needs more salt and possibly more lemon juice.

5 When you are nearly ready to serve, add the broccoli rabe to the sauce to reheat, and bring the water back to a boil. Cook the pasta. Fresh pasta usually takes about 3 minutes. When it is just al dente, immediately drain it and add it to the skillet with the remaining ¼ cup wine, ½ cup of the grated cheese, and a few grinds of black pepper. Toss together until the noodles are coated.

6 To serve, use tongs to arrange the noodles on the serving platter. Pour the rest of the sauce, which won't have mixed in too well, over the top, distributing the broccoli rabe and tomatoes. Top with the remaining ½ cup cheese, more black pepper, and the parsley, and eat immediately.

VERMOUTH. When I want to cook with white wine but don't feel like opening a bottle, I use dry vermouth, which I always have on hand. (Hey, martini time can strike without warning!) Vermouth is a fortified wine, meaning it has extra alcohol, so it will keep for at least a few months in the re-frigerator. It is subtly infused with herbs and spices that add an extra dimension to your cooking.

Sweet red vermouth can also be interesting; I particularly like it in pasta sauces with walnuts. But because it's sweet, it doesn't work as a one-to-one substitute for red wine.

basil gnudi with summer squash

Light and pillowy, *gnudi* are ricotta ravioli without the pasta. They pair well with a delicate sauce that allows your handiwork with the dumplings to shine through. This simple sauté of summer squash and cherry tomatoes flavored with white wine and garlic fits the bill.

I've flavored the *gnudi* heavily with fresh basil. Combined with the sweet dairy flavor of the ricotta and the tomatoes, they are reminiscent of a Caprese salad and make a beautiful light entrée.

The trick to this recipe is getting the right amount of flour into the dough; you want enough to hold the dumplings together but not so much that they get heavy, and that can vary depending on the ricotta and eggs. You may want to cook a test dumpling before shaping the rest of them. If it falls apart, stir in another tablespoon or so of flour.

FOR THE SAUCE
3 tablespoons unsalted butter
2 garlic cloves, minced
½ cup minced white onion
½ teaspoon kosher salt
1½ cups sliced summer squash (¼-inch-thick rounds)
1½ cups halved yellow cherry tomatoes
½ cup white wine or dry vermouth

FOR THE GNUDI AND GARNISH
1 pound ricotta, drained if necessary (see page 164)
¼ cup freshly grated Parmigiano-Reggiano
6 tablespoons all-purpose flour, plus additional for dredging
¾ cup packed fresh basil leaves, finely chopped (reserve a few small leaves for garnish)
Kosher salt
1 large egg plus 2 large egg yolks

TO SERVE
8 squash or zucchini blossoms, separated into single petals (optional)
½ cup white wine or dry vermouth
2 tablespoons cold unsalted butter, cut into 6 pieces
Flaky sea salt (such as Maldon)
Freshly ground black pepper

▼ ▼ ▼

1   *For the sauce:* Melt the butter in a large sauté pan over medium heat. Add the garlic, onion, and salt, and cook for 2 minutes. Add the squash, and cook for 3 minutes. Add the cherry tomatoes, and cook for 1 minute. Add the wine, and reduce the heat to low. Simmer for 5 minutes. Taste and adjust salt, if needed. Turn off the heat, cover the skillet, and reserve the sauce on the back of the stove.

2   *For the gnudi and garnish:* Bring a large pot of salted water to a boil.

3   In a medium-size bowl, using a wooden spoon, beat together the ricotta, Parmigiano-Reggiano, 6 tablespoons flour, and chopped basil leaves. Season with salt to taste. Beat in the egg and egg yolks.

4   To form the *gnudi*, fill a shallow bowl with flour for dredging and have ready a baking sheet sprinkled heavily with flour. Flour your hands as well. Grab about 1 heaping tablespoon of dough, quickly roll it into a ball (it will be quite sticky), roll it around in the flour, and transfer it to the baking sheet. Repeat with the remaining dough. Sprinkle the tops of the *gnudi* with more flour. At this point, you can either complete the dish, or wrap with the baking sheet plastic and refrigerate the *gnudi* for up to 4 hours.

5   To cook the *gnudi*, gently add half of the batch to the boiling water and simmer until they rise to the top and stay there for about 1 minute, about 5 minutes total time. (You may have to give them a very gentle nudge off the bottom.) Transfer with a slotted spoon to a plate while you cook the second batch. After the first batch has cooled a bit, test one to make sure it is done to your liking.

6   *To serve:* Warm four pasta bowls in a low (200°F) oven. Warm the sauce over low heat. Add the *gnudi* and the zucchini blossoms, if using, to the sauce and raise the heat slightly. Cook for 1 minute. Divide the *gnudi* and vegetables and some of the sauce among the bowls. Add the wine to the pan, raise the heat to medium, and simmer, stirring and scraping any browned bits from the bottom of the pan. Whisk in the butter, cook until slightly thickened, 1 minute or so, and spoon the sauce over the four bowls. Garnish with the small basil leaves, a few grains of salt, and a grind of black pepper, and serve immediately.

DRAINING RICOTTA. If your ricotta seems watery, line a colander with cheesecloth and set it on a plate. Dump the ricotta into the colander and let it drain in the refrigerator for a few hours.

Calabro is by far the best widely available brand of ricotta in the U.S. and is well worth seeking out; it won't need draining.

peppery absorption-cooked red-wine capellini

VEGAN

SERVES 4

30 MINUTES

Cooking pasta by the absorption method instead of the usual technique may seem a bit scary to those of us who grew up with noodle orthodoxy. Actually, it is a great way to cook pasta, and it can be a big time-saver. You don't have to wait for water to boil, and, if you design your sauce and condiment to be built in with the pasta, you don't have two pots to clean at the end.

For this recipe, I toast the capellini in the oven first. This is characteristic of how noodles are handled in Spain and Mexico (where the pasta is called *fideos*) and the Middle East. I enjoy the additional browned flavors. You can do this while prepping and sautéing your vegetables.

Because the tomatoes and zucchini cook along with the noodles, I call for less initial liquid than you will see in most absorption-cooked pasta recipes. Instead, you'll check along the way and add more as needed. Be sure to reserve some of the tomatoes for garnish. I love to include an ingredient in both cooked and raw forms in the same dish to experience its full range of flavors.

This dish is quite assertive, with substantial quantities of red wine, black pepper, smoked paprika, and garlic. It isn't one I would necessarily recommend serving to young children or those who prefer milder tastes.

1 pound capellini
3 tablespoons extra-virgin olive oil
Half a large white onion, thinly sliced
6 garlic cloves, minced
Kosher salt
1½ pounds zucchini, diced
1 bunch asparagus, trimmed and cut into ½-inch lengths
1½ cups halved cherry tomatoes
1 tablespoon smoked paprika
1 teaspoon freshly ground black pepper
¼ teaspoon cayenne pepper
2 tablespoons fresh oregano leaves
1 teaspoon minced fresh rosemary
1¼ cups red wine (I use an inexpensive Spanish Tempranillo),
**   plus additional as needed**
1¼ cups water, plus additional as needed
Minced fresh flatleaf parsley leaves, for garnish

▼ ▼ ▼

1 Preheat the oven to 375°F. Break the capellini into approximately 3-inch lengths. Spread the pasta on a baking sheet, slide it into the oven, and toast, tossing occasionally with tongs, until golden brown, about 12 minutes.

2 Meanwhile, heat the olive oil in a large pot (at least 5½ quarts) with a lid over medium heat. Add the onion, garlic, and a pinch of salt and cook, allowing them only to soften and grow aromatic but not brown, about 5 minutes. Increase the heat to medium-high and add the zucchini and another pinch of salt. Sauté until the zucchini is well browned, about 5 more minutes.

3 Place the noodles on top of the zucchini mixture. Layer the asparagus and 1 cup of the cherry tomatoes on top of that and sprinkle in the smoked paprika, black pepper, cayenne pepper, oregano, and rosemary. Pour the red wine and water over the top. Toss as best you can with tongs; it will be hard at first because the noodles are stiff. Return the heat to medium and cover the pot.

4 Every 3 minutes, remove the lid and toss the pasta. The total cooking time will be 8 to 12 minutes. Toward the end, taste a noodle each time you remove the lid to see if it is done. If not, and there isn't any moisture left on the bottom of the pot, add a bit more wine or water, about ⅓ cup.

5 When the noodles are done to your liking, taste and make any final adjustments to the seasoning. Transfer to serving bowls. Garnish with the remaining ½ cup cherry tomatoes, the parsley, and another grind of black pepper. Serve immediately.

TALKING WITH MY BLOG READERS. One of the great things about being a blogger is having an audience of readers who cook the recipes I post and provide feedback. I love reading everyone's input, and I think this quote from Sandy has to be one of my favorites: "This dish is downright sexy. The bold flavors and spicy aromas combined with the rich, dark colors and the smooth spice of the cappellini just make it a manly dish. If I could bottle the scent and spray it on my boyfriend, I would! Haha . . . I loved that it was rich and light at the same time."

loaded otsu noodles

VEGAN

SERVES 4

30 MINUTES

Cold Chinese sesame noodles often include peanut butter in the sauce. Otsu, on the other hand, is a Japanese version that's actually based on sesame paste. I make a lively sauce with sweet and regular soy sauce, ginger, citrus, and spices, and load up the noodles up with tofu, eggplant, and cucumbers. The result is a cold dish that is a huge hit with kids as well as adults and is easy to make ahead for summer barbecues.

See page 222 for information about long pepper, which adds an amazing floral kick to the sauce. You'll also find suggestions there for substitutions if you don't have the long pepper.

FOR THE SAUCE
¼ cup toasted sesame paste (tahini)
2 tablespoons tamari or other soy sauce
1 tablespoon sweet soy sauce (*kecap manis*) or 2 teaspoons sugar
2 teaspoons rice vinegar
Juice and grated zest from half a lemon (or yuzu or lime)
1-inch piece fresh ginger, peeled and grated
1 teaspoon or more sriracha or similar thick Asian chile sauce, or ½ teaspoon
   cayenne pepper
Freshly ground black pepper
1 piece long pepper (optional), crushed in a mortar and pestle

FOR THE NOODLES
9 ounces plain buckwheat soba (Japanese noodles)
1 heavy eggplant (about 1½ pounds), sliced into ½-inch rounds
¼ cup vegetable oil
8 ounces extra-firm tofu
⅓ cup toasted sesame seeds
1 English cucumber, cut into ½-inch cubes
Half a head of iceberg lettuce for serving, leaves pulled apart
2 scallions, white and light green parts only, thinly sliced
Flaky sea salt (such as Maldon)
Freshly ground black pepper

1   *For the sauce:* Combine the tahini, tamari, sweet soy sauce, vinegar, lemon juice and zest, ginger, sriracha, pepper, and long pepper, if using, in a small bowl and whisk until smooth (or you can use a mini food processor). Let the sauce rest so the flavors can develop while you make the noodles and vegetables.

2 *For the noodles:* Prepare the noodles according to the package directions, typically by boiling about 4 minutes. Don't let them overcook. Rinse in cool water and drain.

3 Heat a grill pan over medium-high heat or preheat the broiler. Brush the eggplant with 2 tablespoons of the vegetable oil and grill or broil until deep brown on both sides and thoroughly tender. Let cool, then slice the rounds into approximately 1 x 2-inch pieces.

4 Heat the remaining 2 tablespoons oil in a skillet over high heat. Slice the tofu into approximately 2 x 1 x ¾-inch rectangles, dry thoroughly with a paper towel, and sauté in a single layer until nicely browned on both sides, about 5 minutes total.

5 Taste and adjust the sauce. Does it need more salt? More citrus? More heat? Is it too thick? You want a fairly liquid texture, not pasty, and it should be highly flavored. If it's too thick but has plenty of flavor, use a little cool water to thin it out.

6 In a large bowl, toss together the noodles, sauce (reserving 2 tablespoons), sesame seeds (reserving 1 tablespoon), cucumber, eggplant, and tofu.

7 To serve, line a bowl or platter with the iceberg lettuce and mound the noodles on top. It can be hard to get the vegetables to mix in, so you may need to distribute them a bit with your tongs. Top with (in order): the reserved sauce, the scallions, the remaining sesame seeds, a couple pinches of salt, and a grind of black pepper.

linguine with mushrooms

Living in Seattle, we get some of the best and freshest wild mushrooms in the country at our markets. The bounty of morels, chanterelles, porcini, maitake, and dozens of other varieties is astonishing. Because of that, I sometimes forget how delicious cultivated button mushrooms can be, but this recipe puts them to great use.

This dish is super simple to make. The critical step is in the final minute of cooking. Be sure to add enough of the pasta cooking water to deglaze the pan and develop a bit of sauce. If you serve this dry (or "tight," as chefs say), it will be bland and chewy. There should be a little shine. You never need to worry about diluting your sauce with pasta water; the cooking water is seasoned with salt and has some body from the starch shed by the noodles, so in small quantities, it won't make your sauces watery.

3 tablespoons unsalted butter (use olive oil for vegan)
Half a white onion, finely diced
4 garlic cloves, thinly sliced
Kosher salt
1½ pounds white or brown button mushrooms, sliced a scant ¼ inch thick
½ cup white wine or dry vermouth
1 pound linguine
Parmigiano-Reggiano, grated or cut with a vegetable peeler (omit for vegan)
Freshly ground black pepper
1 handful fresh flatleaf parsley leaves, minced or left whole

1. Bring a very large pot of well-salted water to a full, rolling boil. Warm your serving bowl or bowls in a low (200°F) oven.

2. Melt 2 tablespoons of the butter in a very large skillet (preferably not nonstick) over medium-high heat. Add the onion, garlic, and a pinch of salt and sauté for 2 minutes. Add the sliced mushrooms and ¼ teaspoon salt. Cook, turning occasionally, until the mushrooms release their moisture and then start to brown. Add the white wine to the pan and scrape the bottom with your spatula. Taste a mushroom and adjust the seasoning if needed. Reduce the heat to low.

3. When the mushrooms are nearly done, boil the linguine according to the package directions, being sure to leave it al dente. Reserve 2 cups of the cooking water. Drain the linguine.

4. Add the remaining 1 tablespoon butter to the mushrooms and stir. Add the linguine to the mushrooms and mix thoroughly, again scraping up the browned bits from the bottom of the pan. Add the pasta water a little at a time until the pasta is quite lightly sauced, with just a little sheen. You probably won't need all of the pasta water.

5. Serve the pasta family-style in a big bowl or in individual bowls. Be sure to get all those delicious mushrooms onto the pasta. Finish with cheese, black pepper, and lots of parsley.

pappardelle with eggplant ragu and fresh ricotta

SERVES 3 OR 4

30 MINUTES

Fresh pastas are most often paired with delicate sauces. But a counterexample is a rich, flavorful ragu served over wide noodles like pappardelle. Eggplant makes a terrific vegetarian ragu, accented by bell peppers and fresh ricotta. You can also turn this into a spicy ragu by using Fresno peppers instead of red bells.

The crucial step in making this dish exceptionally delicious is to cook the pasta al dente so that its elastic bite contrasts with the melting texture of the eggplant and ricotta.

Be sure to gather all of the garnishes in advance, so that when the pasta is finished you can apply them quickly and get the hot bowls right to the table.

⅓ cup extra-virgin olive oil
1 red onion, finely diced
6 garlic cloves, thinly sliced
2 large eggplants (about 3 pounds total), peeled and cut into 1-inch cubes
½ teaspoon hot red pepper flakes
1½ teaspoons kosher salt
1 red bell pepper or, for a spicy version, 3 Fresno chiles, seeded and thinly sliced
1 cup dry red wine
1 pound fresh pappardelle or other fresh pasta (preferably wide, flat noodles)
1½ cups ricotta (Calabro is an excellent brand), at room temperature,
    drained if necessary (see page 164)
Minced fresh flatleaf parsley or mint leaves
Freshly grated Parmigiano-Reggiano
Grated zest of 1 orange
Freshly ground black pepper

1 Bring a large pot of salted water to a boil. Warm your serving bowls in a low (200°F) oven.
2 Heat the olive oil in your largest skillet over medium-high heat. When the oil is hot, add the onion and garlic and sauté for 1 minute; don't allow the garlic to burn. Add the eggplant, hot red pepper flakes, and salt. Lower the heat to medium. Cook, stirring occasionally, until the eggplant is nearly tender, about 8 minutes. You can add a little more oil if you need to, but don't get carried away, as the eggplant will just keep soaking it up. If there is a lot of sticking, lower the heat and add some of the red wine.
3 Add the red bell pepper and cook for 2 more minutes. Add the red wine, scraping up any browned bits stuck to the bottom of the skillet, and continue to cook until the eggplant is fully tender, about 2 more minutes. Reduce the heat to very low. Taste and adjust the seasoning.

4 Boil the pasta according to package directions. For fresh pappardelle, this will usually take 3 to 5 minutes. Scoop out 1 cup of the pasta water and reserve. Drain the pasta and toss with the simmering eggplant ragu, mixing in some or all of the pasta water as needed to achieve a light glaze on the noodles; don't let it turn into a soupy sauce.

5 Divide the pasta among the serving bowls. Divide the ricotta as well, placing 5 or 6 tablespoon-size dabs on each serving. Top with the parsley or mint, grated cheese, orange zest, and black pepper, and serve immediately.

sicilian spaghetti with pan-roasted cauliflower

VEGAN OPTION

SERVES 3 OR 4

30 MINUTES

The classic Sicilian flavors in this dish (orange zest, raisins, capers, pine nuts, red pepper flakes, and fennel) might sound a little outlandish if you've never tasted them all together. Don't be deterred; the combination is astonishingly good. Done properly, each bite is a little surprise that might be sweet, spicy, salty, toasty, herbaceous, or all of the above!

I particularly love the orange zest in the final garnish. It becomes fragrant from the heat of the pasta, making it irresistible.

If you get all of your ingredients ready in advance, you can boil the pasta while you are pan-frying the cauliflower, and everything will be ready at the same time.

1 head cauliflower, broken into large florets
¼ cup extra-virgin olive oil, plus additional for drizzling
4 garlic cloves, thinly sliced
1 teaspoon fennel seeds
½ teaspoon hot red pepper flakes
Kosher salt
Zest and juice of 1 orange
Juice of half a lemon
3 tablespoons capers
¼ cup raisins, plumped in hot water and drained
1 pound spaghetti
⅓ cup pine nuts, toasted
Freshly ground black pepper
Fresh flatleaf parsley leaves, for garnish
Freshly grated Parmesan, for garnish (omit for vegan)

1 Bring a very large pot of well-salted water to a rolling boil and warm your serving bowls in a low (200°F) oven. Add the cauliflower, boil for 5 minutes, then tranfer to a colander with a slotted spoon and allow it to drain for a few minutes (leave the boiling water on the stove to use for the spaghetti). The cauliflower will not be fully tender at this point.

2 Heat a large skillet (preferably cast iron) over high heat. When it is hot, add the olive oil, garlic, fennel seeds, and red pepper flakes. Cook for about 20 seconds and then add the drained cauliflower and about ¾ teaspoon salt, and toss to coat with the oil. Cook, tossing occasionally, until the cauliflower is tender and developing deep brown caramelized spots. Keep the heat high and don't toss the cauliflower too often, so that the surfaces on the bottom of the pan brown. When it is nearly done, mix in the orange juice, half of the orange zest, the lemon juice, capers, and raisins. Turn off the heat.

▼ ▼ ▼

3 Cook the pasta until al dente; drain immediately, reserving 1 cup of the pasta water, and toss the spaghetti with a little olive oil.

4 Add the pasta to the cauliflower mixture, set over medium heat, and toss everything together; tongs work well for this. If the dish seems a little dry, add a ladle or two of the pasta water. Raise the heat to high and cook for about 1 more minute. Taste and adjust the seasoning.

5 To serve, divide the pasta among the serving bowls. The cauliflower will not mix in well, so you will probably need to distribute it with tongs. Garnish with a drizzle of extra-virgin olive oil, the remaining orange zest, the pine nuts, black pepper, parsley, and Parmesan.

chiang mai curry noodles (khao soi)

Khao soi is an iconic dish from the Chiang Mai region of northern Thailand, though its roots are thought to be Burmese or Chinese Muslim. It inspires cultlike devotion among initiates and you can't find it often enough at Thai restaurants in America, which is why I think it is well worth making at home. Fresh, soft egg noodles are served in a spicy coconut-milk broth redolent of homemade curry paste. Pickled cabbage or mustard greens, lime juice, and crispy fried noodles provide a balance of textures and flavors that cut the richness of the coconut.

The amount of fried tofu to use depends on the variety you find at your local Asian market. My favorite kind has a deep-fried skin but is still pretty dense inside. If yours is like that, you'll want about 1½ pounds. If you find instead the type that is light and pillowy all the way through, use only about 12 ounces, since it is a much larger volume for the amount of sauce. The dish should essentially be a soup with, say, eight bites of tofu on top of the noodles, not just tofu glazed with sauce!

My version isn't completely authentic; I skip making a second chili sauce (*nam prik pao*) that is used as a garnish and simply pass more of the curry paste for those who like more heat.

FOR THE CURRY PASTE
5 large, whole dried red chiles (such as pasilla, ancho, or New Mexico),
    stemmed but not seeded
½ cup diced shallot
2 teaspoons grated fresh ginger
1 garlic clove, sliced
½ teaspoon coriander seeds
1 teaspoon ground turmeric
2 teaspoons garam masala or other Indian spice mix of your choice
¼ cup water

FOR THE CRISPY NOODLES
Vegetable oil, for frying
1 big handful of the noodles you will be using for the main dish

FOR THE SAUCE
3 (13.6-ounce) cans coconut milk
½ cup light soy sauce
2 tablespoons sugar
¾ to 1½ pounds packaged fried tofu (see headnote)
Kosher salt
1 cup water

▼ ▼ ▼

FOR THE PICKLED VEGETABLE
1 cup Chinese pickled mustard greens *or* 1 cup Sichuan pickled vegetable
   (see headnote page 186) *or* 1 cup sliced napa cabbage (⅛ inch thick) tossed with
   ¼ cup white vinegar and ½ teaspoon kosher salt

TO COMPLETE THE DISH
1 pound fresh flat (about ⅛ inch wide) or spaghetti-shaped Asian egg noodles,
   minus a handful fried up for garnish
4 Key limes, halved, or 2 regular limes, quartered
Fresh cilantro leaves
½ cup thinly sliced shallot

1 *For the curry paste:* Place a medium skillet over medium heat. Put the chiles in the pan and
   dry-toast them for 2 minutes. Add the shallot, ginger, and garlic and continue to cook, tossing once or twice, until the chiles are very fragrant but not burning. Add the coriander seeds,
   turmeric, and garam masala, toss to combine, and remove from the heat. Let cool slightly, then
   puree in a mini food processor (or with a mortar and pestle), adding about ¼ cup of water (or
   more as needed) to form a coarse paste.

2 *For the crispy noodles:* In a very small saucepan, heat ½ inch of vegetable oil over medium-
   high heat. Throw in one noodle, and when it sizzles, add half of the noodles that you have set
   aside for crisping. Cook, turning frequently with tongs, until golden brown and crispy. Transfer
   to paper towels and repeat with the rest of the noodles to be crisped.

3 Bring a large pot of salted water to a boil and warm four serving bowls in a low (200°F) oven.

4 *For the sauce:* While the pot of water heats, pour 1 can of the coconut milk into a large saucepan (at least 4 quarts), place it over medium heat, and simmer until it begins to separate. Stir
   in about half of the curry paste, along with the soy sauce and sugar, and continue cooking until
   the sauce becomes thick enough to coat a spoon, about 10 minutes. Add the fried tofu and
   simmer for 10 more minutes. Taste and adjust seasoning, adding more salt if desired. If you like
   it hotter, stir in more of the chili paste. Add the remaining 2 cans of coconut milk and the water,
   and bring back to a simmer.

5 *To complete the dish:* Drain and squeeze most of the liquid out of the pickled vegetable. Boil
   the noodles according to the package directions; cook until they are tender but still have a bit of
   bite. Drain and divide among the serving bowls. Top each serving of noodles with one-quarter
   of the sauce and tofu, a squeeze of lime juice, a handful of the pickled vegetable, one-quarter
   of the crispy noodles, and a few cilantro leaves. Serve immediately, passing the thinly sliced
   shallot, remaining limes, and curry paste at the table.

main courses
from the stovetop

chirashi sushi

Chirashi ("scattered") sushi is presented in a bowl instead of rolled up in nori sheets, so it is a lot simpler to make. Don't be intimidated by the list of toppings below. This is a fairly elaborate version, but you can absolutely simplify it. You could make this with nothing but avocado and fried tofu, and it would still be delicious.

My strategy is to get the rice cooking and then simply make as many toppings as I have time for. Feel free to substitute others that fit into the Japanese theme. Pickled daikon, sweet omelet (tamago), a few tempura green beans, or asparagus would all be very welcome.

FOR THE SUSHI RICE
2 cups Japanese rice
6 tablespoons rice vinegar
3 tablespoons sugar
4 teaspoons kosher salt

FOR THE COOKED TOPPINGS
1 medium or 2 small Japanese eggplants
3 tablespoons vegetable oil
1/3 cup water
Kosher salt
1 cup beech mushrooms or small button mushrooms
8 shiitake mushroom caps
1 pound extra-firm tofu, cut into eight 1½ x 3 x ½-inch pieces

TO SERVE THE SUSHI
1 cucumber
1 tablespon rice vinegar
Kosher salt
1 handful *kaiware* radish sprouts
4 shiso leaves
Half a ripe avocado, thinly sliced
Pickled ginger
2 teaspoons umeboshi plum paste (or 4 pickled umeboshi plums, pitted and mashed)
Wasabi paste

▼ ▼ ▼

1 *For the sushi rice:* Cook the rice using a rice cooker or according to package directions. Whisk together the rice vinegar, sugar, and salt.

2 When the rice is done, turn it out into a large, shallow wooden bowl (such as a salad bowl) and sprinkle on the vinegar mixture. With one hand, fan the rice with a magazine or something similar; at the same time, with your other hand, gently cut and fold the rice with a paddle. Do not stir the rice or it will become mushy. Keep cutting, folding, and fanning until the liquid is absorbed and the rice has nearly cooled to room temperature, about 5 minutes.

3 *For the cooked toppings:* Cut the eggplant in half lengthwise. If using medium eggplant, cut it again in half lengthwise. Score the skin side of each eggplant in a fine diamond pattern, making cuts about ¼ inch apart.

4 Heat a large skillet over medium-high heat and add 1 tablespoon of the oil. Add the eggplant, flesh side down, and cook until starting to brown, about 3 minutes. Flip and cook for 2 minutes. Add the water; cover the pan and continue cooking until thoroughly tender, 3 to 5 minutes more. Remove the eggplant and season with salt.

5 Wipe out the skillet, add 1 tablespoon of the oil, and increase the heat to high. Stir-fry the beech mushrooms for 1 minute, then transfer them to a plate with a slotted spoon. Repeat with the shiitake mushroom caps (adding a bit more oil if needed), cooking for about 2 minutes.

6 Return the skillet to high heat, add the remaining 1 tablespoon of oil, and cook the tofu in a single layer until golden brown, about 2 minutes on each side. Remove and season with salt.

7 *To serve:* Peel the cucumber, then use the peeler to shave it into long, thin sheets, avoiding the seeds. Toss the cucumber with the rice vinegar and a pinch of salt.

8 Divide the sushi rice among four bowls. Carefully arrange portions of the eggplant, beech mushrooms, shiitakes, cucumber, sprouts, shiso, avocado, ginger, and plum paste around the rice. Finish with the wasabi, making sure that it's visible so that it isn't eaten accidentally all at once.

planning a meal: start with the culture

If you want to eat miso soup, garlicky spaghetti, and Vietnamese mango salad for dinner and finish up with a nice crème caramel for dessert, don't let me stop you! That said, groups of complementary foods and flavor profiles within particular cuisines have developed over the centuries for good reasons. When we respect those combinations, we stand on the shoulders of giants and greatly improve our chances of making a delicious meal. Here are some sample menus to get you started:

1 a north indian feast
Basmati rice
Indian Potato Fritters (*Aloo Tikki*), page 70
Chana Masala with Mushrooms, page 209
Five-Minute Indian-Style Cabbage, page 250
Banana Raita, page 337, or Onion Chutney, page 340

2 a mexican meal with a hearty soup
Red *Pozole* with Beans (*Pozole Rojo de Frijol*), page 100
Jicama, Radish, and Orange Salad, page 125
Spectacular Chocolate-Espresso Brownies, page 292 (but omit the espresso
   and add ½ teaspoon each of cinnamon and ancho chile powder)

3 thai tastes at home
Jasmine rice
Thai Tofu Salad, page 109
Red Curry Delicata Squash, page 190

4 southern italian flavors with a hint of north africa
Persimmon, Parsley, and Olive Salad, page 120
Sicilian Spaghetti with Pan-Roasted Cauliflower, page 175
Sesame-Orange Sablé Cookies, page 289, served with vin santo or grappa

5 modern vietnamese fare
Green Mango Salad, page 106
Chanterelle *Banh Mi* Bites, page 61
Rice Vermicelli (*Bun*) with Ginger-Grapefruit Sauce, page 156

See also Planning a Meal: Start with a Base Ingredient (page 153) and Planning a Meal: Start with What's Fresh (page 227).

crispy vietnamese crêpes (banh xeo)

VEGAN

GLUTEN-FREE

SERVES 6 AS A
MAIN COURSE
OR 12 AS AN
APPETIZER

45 MINUTES

The first time I had *banh xeo*, I was actually giddy. The combination of textures and flavors is absolutely mind-blowing.

This vegan crêpe is crispy on the outside, soft on the inside, flavored with mushrooms and onions, and filled with a big pile of bean sprouts. You tear off a piece and wrap it with lettuce and fresh herbs, then dip it in vegetarian *nuoc cham*, with its complex combination of savory, sweet, spicy, and salty flavors.

One crêpe with all of the fixings is most of a light meal, or you could cut it in half to make appetizer portions.

Don't be discouraged if your first one turns out ugly! It might take a couple of tries before you are making perfect exemplars. As long as you cook them until they're crispy, even the unlovely ones will be delicious. One key to success is to cut the mushrooms, tofu, and onions very small and thin so they don't break up the surface of the crêpe too much.

FOR THE CRÊPES
1 cup rice flour (not sweet rice flour, which is used for making desserts)
1½ cups coconut milk
2 scallions, white and light green parts only, thinly sliced
1 teaspoon ground turmeric
1 teaspoon kosher salt
½ cup water, plus additional as needed
6 tablespoons vegetable oil
12 shiitake or crimini mushroom caps, finely diced
6 ounces extra-firm tofu, finely diced
6 tablespoons finely diced red onion
4½ cups mung bean sprouts
Kosher salt

TO SERVE
1 head red or green leaf lettuce, separated into leaves, rinsed, and patted dry
1 bunch fresh cilantro, thin stems on, rinsed and dried
1 bunch fresh mint, thins stems on, rinsed and dried
1 bunch fresh Thai (holy) basil, thin stems on, rinsed and dried
2 cups Vegetarian *Nuoc Cham* (page 332)

1   *For the crêpes:* Whisk together the rice flour, coconut milk, scallions, turmeric, salt, and ½ cup water. Whisk in additional water (starting with about ½ cup) as needed to give the mixture a pourable consistency. The batter needs to be thin enough to spread around the pan before it sets. (After you make the first one, if you have trouble it getting to spread, add more water.)

2   Heat 1 tablespoon of the oil in a 10-inch nonstick skillet with sloping sides and a lid (which can be makeshift; it doesn't have to fit tight) over medium-high heat. Add one-sixth of the mushrooms, tofu, and red onion. Sauté until browning nicely, about 2 minutes.

3   Remove the pan from the heat. Spread the vegetables and tofu out in a single, sparse layer. Pour ⅓ cup of the crêpe batter over and around the vegetables and immediately swirl the pan to distribute the batter over the whole surface. The batter won't cover the vegetables, just surround them. Return to the heat. Place ¾ cup of the bean sprouts in a big pile over half of the crêpe. Cover the pan and let cook until the bean sprouts have started to soften, about 90 seconds.

4   Remove the lid and continue to cook until the edges of the crêpe are getting crispy and brown. Peek underneath, lifting the edge with a silicone spatula, to make sure it is browning there as well. When done, slide it onto a plate and fold the bare half over the bean sprouts. Sprinkle with a little extra salt. Repeat for the remaining crêpes.

5   *To serve:* Arrange a big pile of the lettuce and herbs either on a platter or on individual plates. Set out individual bowls of the Vegetarian *Nuoc Cham*.

sichuan dry-fried green beans and tofu

VEGAN

GLUTEN-FREE
OPTION

SERVES 2 WITH
RICE AS A MEAL,
OR 4 AS PART
OF A LARGER
SPREAD

25 MINUTES

If you have ever ordered dry-fried green beans at a good Chinese restaurant, you know how delicious they can be, but I bet you don't know what's in them! The dish is typically full of yummy brown stuff, and for years, I wondered just what it was. I knew there was garlic and ginger in there, but I didn't think that could account for all of it.

It turns out the answer is Sichuan preserved vegetable, which is a pickled mustard tuber that you find canned at a good Asian grocery. It is better to buy the chunk style and chop it yourself; if you buy it pre-shredded, you'll want to rinse off some of the salt. The taste is somewhat like that of kimchi, and I find it rather addictive. On page 338 you'll find another way to use this treasure, to make an Indian Sichuan pickle.

I've added tofu and a few mushrooms to the traditional green bean dish, which makes it into a one-dish supper for two or a hearty part of a larger dinner for four.

Don't be scared off by the quantity of oil in this recipe, and please don't stint on it when frying the green beans. Most of it is drained off before the dish is completed.

6 tablespoons vegetable oil
1 pound firm or extra-firm tofu, thoroughly patted dry, cut into ¾-inch cubes
**1 pound green beans, trimmed and cut in half if long, rinsed and thoroughly dried
   (to avoid spattering)**
1 cup thinly sliced white mushrooms or shiitake mushrooms caps
⅓ cup finely chopped Sichuan preserved vegetable
1-inch piece fresh ginger, finely chopped or grated
4 garlic cloves, minced
2 tablespoons soy sauce (use a wheat-free version for gluten-free)
1 teaspoon toasted sesame oil
2 teaspoons sugar
¼ teaspoon kosher salt

1 Heat a wok or large skillet over the highest heat. Pour in 2 tablespoons of the oil, and when it is shimmering, add the tofu and stir-fry until golden brown, about 4 minutes. Transfer the tofu to a plate with a slotted spoon.

2 In the same pan, heat the remaining 4 tablespoons oil and, when the oil is shimmering, add the green beans. Cook, stirring occasionally, until the green beans are somewhat shriveled and developing black spots in many places. Depending on the heat of your stove, this may take anywhere from 4 to 10 minutes. Add the mushrooms and stir-fry for 1 minute more. Turn off the heat and drain the green beans and mushrooms in a colander, leaving about 1 tablespoon oil in the pan.

3 Return the pan to the heat. Cook the Sichuan preserved vegetable, ginger, and garlic for 30 seconds, until very fragrant. Return the green beans, mushrooms, and tofu to the pan and toss to combine.

4 Whisk together the soy sauce, sesame oil, sugar, and salt, and pour over the green beans. Toss to coat, cook for 30 seconds more, and serve immediately.

caramel-cooked tofu

GLUTEN-FREE
OPTION

SERVES 2 TO 4

20 MINUTES

The Vietnamese technique of caramel cooking is most often applied to chicken, but it works equally well to produce a deeply flavored tofu that is lacquered with a sweet, salty, and fragrant sauce. The traditional method requires you to make the caramel sauce separately, but Chef John of the blog Food Wishes came up with this simpler technique, which allows you to create the sauce right in the pan with your main ingredient.

Feel free to add a small amount of vegetable to this stir-fry. Sliced fresh bamboo shoots are excellent. For something that takes a few minutes, like broccoli, cook it separately first and then add it at the end. More tender items such as red bell peppers can be added at the same time as the white onion.

This recipe will serve two hungry adults with nothing but rice as an accompaniment, or more diners as part of a larger spread.

¼ **cup rice wine or dry sherry**
2 **teaspoons rice vinegar**
¼ **cup soy sauce (use a wheat-free version for gluten-free)**
1 **teaspoon toasted sesame oil**
2 **garlic cloves, minced**
1 **teaspoon minced fresh ginger**
½ **cup sugar**
1 **pound extra-firm tofu, patted thoroughly dry and cut into 2 x 2 x ⅓-inch pieces**
2 **tablespoons vegetable oil**
½ **cup thinly sliced white onion**
4 **to 8 dried small red chiles (optional)**
5 **scallions, white and light green parts only, thinly sliced**

1 Whisk together the rice wine, rice vinegar, soy sauce, sesame oil, garlic, ginger, and sugar until the sugar dissolves.

2 Heat the oil in a large, heavy skillet (preferably cast iron) over high heat. Lay the tofu squares in the skillet in a single layer (or as close to a single layer as possible). Fry until golden brown on one side, about 4 minutes.

3 Flip the tofu and immediately pour in the sauce; add the white onion and chiles, if using. The sauce will sputter and begin to caramelize. Keep a close eye on it, and move the tofu around a little bit to let the sauce get under it. Continue cooking until the sauce has thickened and becomes a fairly thick glaze coating the tofu, about 4 minutes more.

4 Serve immediately, topped with the scallions.

red curry delicata squash

VEGAN

GLUTEN-FREE

SERVES 4

30 MINUTES

You might not immediately think of putting winter squash in a Southeast Asian–style curry. I learned about it from tasting a terrific pumpkin curry at my local Thai place. I make my version with delicata squash, which is one of my favorite winter squash varieties. It is relatively easy to cut and peel, cooks quickly, and has a rich, sweet flavor.

If at all possible, you should use homemade Red Curry Paste (page 348), but a commercial paste will do in a pinch. Just be sure to check the ingredients if it is important to you that it be vegetarian or vegan.

This is a relatively dry curry; no coconut milk is added to produce a bowl of sauce, though it will have a small amount of liquid. Serve this with jasmine rice.

¼ cup vegetable oil
1 pound firm or extra-firm tofu, patted dry and cut into 2 x 2 x ½-inch squares
Kosher salt
1 tablespoon brown sugar
5 tablespoons Red Curry Paste (page 348 or use store-bought)
2 delicata squash (about 8 inches long), peeled, halved, seeded, and cut into
   ¼-inch (or so) half-moons
¼ cup water, plus additional as needed
1 cup broccoli florets cut very small
Freshly ground black pepper
1 handful fresh cilantro leaves and tender stems, for garnish

1   Place a big, heavy skillet or a wok over very high heat. (You'll need some sort of cover, but it doesn't have to be tight fitting.) When the skillet is hot, add 2 tablespoons of the oil and when it shimmers, add the tofu in a single layer. Cook on both sides until nicely browned, about 3 minutes on each side. Transfer with a slotted spoon or spatula to paper towels and season with a bit of salt.

2   Reduce the heat to medium-high. Add the remaining 2 tablespoons oil, the brown sugar, and the curry paste. Stir-fry, stirring constantly, for 1 minute. Add the squash and ½ teaspoon salt. Stir-fry for 1 minute, then add ¼ cup water and cover. Cook until the squash is tender, occasionally lifting the lid to stir, check doneness, and add a little water if needed. When it is nearly done, after about 7 minutes, add the broccoli. Re-cover and cook until the squash is fully tender, about 3 minutes more.

3   Stir in the tofu. Taste and adjust seasoning. If needed, add just a little more water to get a little bit of glossy sauce.

4   Spoon the curry into a bowl and garnish with a grind of black pepper and the cilantro.

quinoa cakes

GLUTEN-FREE

SERVES 4

20 MINUTES
IF YOU HAVE
QUINOA
ALREADY
COOKED AND
COOLED, 45
MINUTES
OTHERWISE

Long a staple grain in the Andes, quinoa, with its nutty flavor and high nutritional value, has become very popular in America.

These pan-fried quinoa cakes grain can serve as a foil for a wide variety of simply prepared vegetables, such as Stir-Fried Corn with Lemongrass (page 253). The cakes are not large, so plan on having a good quantity of vegetables. Add a sauce like Chimichurri (page 328) or Tomato Jam with Rosemary and Saffron (page 344) and you've got a wholesome and exciting meal.

When making quinoa, you should rinse the grain first to avoid any bitterness from the natural saponins (a soaplike chemical) in the seed coat. If you are making quinoa for another meal, make extra and refrigerate it, then make these cakes in a flash the next day. I make cakes like this with all manner of leftover grains, improvising flavorings and accompaniments based on whatever is threatening to overflow from the refrigerator.

1 cup uncooked quinoa (or 2 cups cooked and cooled)
2 cups water (if cooking quinoa)
½ teaspoon kosher salt
2 teaspoons smoked paprika
½ teaspoon ground cumin
½ teaspoon dried oregano or leaves from a couple stems fresh oregano, minced
2 or 3 large eggs, lightly beaten
Vegetable oil
Flaky sea salt (such as Maldon)
Freshly ground black pepper

1 If using uncooked quinoa, rinse the grain twice in cold water, then drain in a fine-mesh strainer. In a pot or rice cooker, combine the quinoa with 2 cups water. If using a pot, bring to a boil, reduce the heat to low, cover, and cook until the water is absorbed, 15 to 18 minutes. If using a rice cooker, simply use the regular white rice cycle. Allow the quinoa to cool. If you are in a hurry, spread the quinoa in a large, shallow dish and place, uncovered, in the refrigerator.

2 Combine the cooled quinoa, salt, paprika, cumin, oregano, and 2 eggs. You should have a "dough" that will form a moist ball. If the mixture is still dry and fluffy, add another egg.

3 Heat your largest skillet or, better yet, a flat griddle pan over medium-high heat. Lightly oil the skillet or griddle pan. Form ¼ cup of the quinoa mixture into a ball. Place it in the skillet and use a spatula to flatten it into a pancake about ¼ inch thick. Repeat to make 7 more pancakes, working in batches as necessary. Cook the quinoa cakes until golden brown on one side, 2 to 3 minutes, then flip and brown the other side, about 2 minutes more. Remove from the pan and season with flaky sea salt and pepper. Serve immediately.

crispy polenta cakes with white beans and morels

VEGAN

GLUTEN-FREE

SERVES 4

30 MINUTES
IF YOU HAVE
COLD POLENTA,
4 HOURS
(1 HOUR ACTIVE)
OTHERWISE

The key to this dish is to be bold and really fry the cakes until they are quite crispy and brown on the outside. The contrast of the crust with the soft interior is wonderful.

If you have had the foresight to make extra polenta, you can fry it up into cakes with a savory side of white beans and morel mushrooms in just half an hour. You can make these cakes with leftover polenta that has cheese or other flavorings in it as long as it has set up firm enough to form into a patty. If you don't have leftover polenta, you can make a fresh batch at lunchtime that will be plenty firm by dinner. In that case, you don't need to add anything other than salt.

These cakes are especially good with the Red Wine–Braised Cabbage on page 252.

6 cups water, plus additional as needed (if cooking polenta)
2 cups coarse cornmeal (or 6 cups cooked and chilled polenta)
Kosher salt
16 dried morel mushrooms
¼ cup plus 1 tablespoon extra-virgin olive oil
¼ teaspoon crumbled dried rosemary
1½ cups cooked white beans (such as cannellini) or 1 (15-ounce) can white beans,
    rinsed and drained
1 handful fresh flatleaf parsley leaves
Freshly ground black pepper
Flaky sea salt (such as Maldon)

1 If cooking the polenta, bring 6 cups water to a boil in a large saucepan. Whisk in the cornmeal and 1 tablespoon kosher salt. Return to a boil, reduce to a simmer, and cook, stirring occasionally, until mixture is thick and fairly smooth, about 30 minutes. You may need to add a little more water if it starts to pull away from the sides of the pan before it is fully cooked. When the polenta is done, transfer it to a heatproof bowl and refrigerate for at least 3 hours, until well chilled.

2 Put the dried morel mushrooms in a bowl and add just enough boiling water to cover them. Let sit for 15 minutes. Drain off and reserve the soaking liquid and strain through a very fine-mesh strainer. Halve any mushrooms that are larger than bite-size. Warm four dinner plates in a low (200°F) oven.

3 Heat 1 tablespoon olive oil in a medium-size skillet over medium-high heat. Cook the mushrooms with a big pinch of salt and the rosemary for 2 minutes. Add the beans, ½ cup of the reserved mushroom-soaking liquid, and ½ teaspoon salt and reduce the heat to maintain a simmer. Taste and adjust seasoning.

▼ ▼ ▼

4 Heat the ¼ cup olive oil in your largest skillet, preferably cast iron, over medium-high heat. Form a generous ½ cup of the chilled polenta into a patty about ⅜ inch thick. Repeat to make 3 more patties. Cook in the skillet until quite golden brown on one side, 3 to 4 minutes, then flip and brown the other side, about 3 minutes more. Repeat for a second batch of 4 patties.

5 To serve, divide the beans, some of the broth, and the morels among the plates. Top with 2 polenta cakes each and finish with a few leaves of parsley, black pepper, and a generous scattering of flaky sea salt.

DON'T FEAR HEAT. When I watch my friends cook at home, they often seem too intimidated to use the full power of their stoves. I've even seen folks who hesitate to turn the burner up all the way when they are trying to boil water. I want to tell them, "Don't worry, it isn't going to burn!"

High heat is often your friend. It creates rich, browned flavors and seared, crisp crusts that are so much more appetizing than mushy, half-steamed foods.

When cooking over high heat, it is essential to avoid crowding the pan. You will get the best results if the food is in a single, sparse layer so that the most surface area possible is in contact with direct heat.

The right heat level depends on your stove, your cookware, what you are cooking, how much of it there is, how it is cut, and what you are trying to accomplish. So the suggested stove settings—medium, medium-high, and so on—in this book (or any other cookbook) are just general guidelines.

Use your eyes, ears, and nose to pay attention to what is happening in the pan. If you are trying to brown some tofu and you don't hear any sizzle, turn up the heat. If you are trying to cook a thick pancake or patty through and the surface is dark brown after 30 seconds, turn it down. If you smell garlic or sesame seeds burning, you need to get them off the heat right away (and maybe start over). There is no substitute for using your senses in the kitchen!

corn and tomato confit risotto

GLUTEN-FREE

SERVES 4

30 MINUTES

Tomato confit is a fantastic way to extend summer to those months when the tomatoes aren't so spectacular. It lends its flavor to both the broth and the final garnish for this risotto, which is delicate but has a subtle intensity.

The goat cheese in the garnish isn't the typical fresh, soft chèvre, although you may substitute that in a pinch. The ideal cheese for this dish is semisoft, with a lacy texture and rounded flavor that complements the tomatoes and corn. I like Pondhopper from Oregon's Tumalo Farms. A goat Gouda is another fine option. As always, check with your cheesemonger and taste a few to find one you love.

30 Tomato Confit halves (page 343)
4 cups water
¼ cup extra-virgin olive oil
¼ cup minced onion
2 cups Arborio, Carnaroli, or other risotto rice
1 cup dry white wine
2 teaspoons kosher salt, plus additional as needed
Kernels from 1 large ear of corn or 1 cup frozen sweet corn, defrosted
½ cup freshly grated Parmigiano-Reggiano
6 ounces semisoft aged goat cheese, cut into small cubes
1 tablespoon fresh thyme leaves

1   Warm four serving bowls in a low (200°F) oven. Put 10 of the tomato halves plus any liquid you can pour off of the tomatoes into a blender with the water, and puree. Pour into a saucepan and bring this liquid to a bare simmer. Warm the remaining tomatoes gently in the microwave or a small saucepan and set aside.

2   Heat the olive oil in a large, heavy pot over medium heat. Add the onion and cook until softened but not browned, about 2 minutes. Add the rice and cook, stirring, until the rice turns slightly translucent, 1 to 2 minutes.

3   Add the wine and salt and cook, stirring, until the liquid is absorbed.

4   Add the tomato broth, one ladleful at a time, stirring very frequently. Continuous stirring isn't necessary. When the rice has absorbed most of the broth, add another ladleful. If you use up all the tomato broth before the rice is cooked, you can use a bit of simmering water.

5   After 16 minutes, begin to check a grain every minute. When there is a slight white pinhead that is a bit tough inside, add the corn. Add more salt if needed. Within 3 to 10 minutes, the rice should be tender but with just a hint of resistance to it, and it should be surrounded by creamy, starchy goodness. Take it off of the heat right away and stir in the Parmigiano.

6   Ladle into serving bowls. Top each serving with 5 of the reserved tomato confit halves, the goat cheese, and the thyme leaves, and serve immediately.

bocoles with spicy sweet potatoes

VEGAN OPTION

GLUTEN-FREE

SERVES 6

40 MINUTES

Bocoles are little pan-fried cakes of masa and mashed black beans, typically served as an *antojito* (appetizer). I learned about them from Diana Kennedy's magnificent opus, *My Mexico* (Clarkson Potter, 1998). For my version, I've replaced the pork topping with spiced-up pan-fried sweet potatoes and increased the portion size to make them into a satisfying vegetarian entrée. My kids love them, too; the older one now calls them yummy cakes.

The cakes fry up with a crispy exterior and somewhat creamy interior. If you have had an Indian *dosa*, which is made from a lentil batter, the crust is kind of like that.

If you don't have refried black beans, just cook half a chopped onion and 2 minced garlic cloves in a couple tablespoons of oil, add cooked black beans and a little more oil, and mash them to a smooth puree, adding water as needed. Season to taste.

There is a lot of confusion about sweet potatoes and yams, which aren't even related. The sweet potatoes to use for this have a dark orange-brown skin and orange flesh. But you may well find them labeled yams in your grocery!

FOR THE SWEET POTATO FILLING
2 tablespoons vegetable oil
1 white onion, diced
4 garlic cloves, minced
2 medium sweet potatoes, peeled and finely diced
2 or more jalapeño peppers, seeded and minced
1 teaspoon ground cumin
2 teaspoons New Mexico chile powder (or your preferred chile powder)
¾ teaspoon kosher salt
Juice of 1 lime

FOR THE BOCOLES
2½ cups masa harina
1½ cups plus 2 tablespoons warm water, plus additional as needed
¼ teaspoon kosher salt
2 cups refried black beans (Ducal brand is good, or make your own)
2 teaspoons baking powder
Vegetable oil, for pan-frying

TO SERVE
Shredded romaine lettuce
Mexican crema or sour cream (omit or use vegan sour cream for vegan)
Pomegranate seeds (optional)
Jicama, Radish, and Orange Salad (page 125), guacamole, or salsa of your choice
Lime wedges

1 *For the sweet potato filling:* Heat the oil in a large skillet over medium heat. Add the onion and garlic and cook for 1 minute. Add the sweet potatoes, jalapeño, cumin, chile powder, and salt. Cook, stirring occasionally, until the sweet potatoes are fully tender, about 10 minutes. Mix in the lime juice. Taste and adjust seasoning; it will likely need more salt. Feel free to make the filling spicier if that suits you. (If not making the *bocoles* right away, transfer to a bowl, cover, and refrigerate. Reheat before serving.)

2 *For the bocoles:* Mix the masa harina with the warm water and salt. Beat with a wooden spoon until smooth. If the dough is very stiff and crumbly, beat in a few more tablespoons of warm water.

3 Add the refried beans and baking powder; use your hands to mix thoroughly. Taste and add more salt if needed. (The dough can be refrigerated overnight at this point.)

4 Heat ⅛ inch oil in a large skillet over medium-high heat. Make golf ball–size balls of the dough and pat them between your hands into patties about ¼ inch thick. Fry until brown on the outside and cooked through but still soft on the inside, about 3 minutes on each side, working in batches as needed. Drain briefly on paper towels.

5 *To serve: Bocoles* don't wait, so set them immediately on a bed of shredded lettuce, topped with a generous amount of the sweet potato filling and then with the crema and pomegranate seeds, if using. Pass the salad, guacamole, or salsa and the lime wedges.

TALKING WITH MY BLOG READERS. You may wonder about the very small amounts of cinnamon and cumin in this dish. To my taste, *mujadara* is meant to be more earthy than heavily spiced, so I like the spices as very subtle accents. Some of my blog readers agree, while others prefer to use much more. The choice is yours.

For that matter, the same applies to any recipe. Like any author, I write recipes to my own taste and that of my friends and family. You should always feel empowered to taste and make adjustments to suit your own preferences. A recipe is a guideline, not a formula that must be followed to the letter.

middle eastern rice and lentil pilaf (mujadara)

Nutritious, satisfying, inexpensive, and easy to make, *mujadara* is simply a mixture of rice and perfectly cooked lentils, spiked with a big dose of caramelized onions and a bit of cumin and cinnamon. It is a hearty one-dish meal when served with nothing more than Greek yogurt and maybe a cucumber salad, or it can be part of a larger Middle Eastern feast. It is best served close to room temperature, not piping hot.

While the onions are caramelizing, you can cook the rice and lentils. If you don't have time to caramelize the onions slowly, a hotter and faster fry can also give you delicious results, with a sweet brown surface and a little remaining crunch.

Many folks cook the rice and lentils together, but I find that doesn't give enough control over their relative textures. *Mujadara* is best when the lentils are tender but not falling apart.

¼ cup vegetable oil
3 pounds white onions, sliced moderately thin
3 teaspoons kosher salt
½ cup white wine, dry vermouth, or water
6 cups cooked long-grain white or brown rice
3 cups cooked brown or green lentils (not red lentils or French lentils),
   tender but not falling apart
¼ teaspoon ground cinnamon
¼ teaspoon ground cumin
Freshly ground black pepper
1 small handful fresh flatleaf parsley leaves, coarsely chopped at the last minute
Flaky sea salt (such as Maldon)

1 Heat the oil in your largest skillet over medium-low heat. Add the onions and 2 teaspoons salt and cook, stirring occasionally, until very soft, about 45 minutes. Turn the heat to medium-high and continue cooking, stirring often, until the onions are deeply browned and sweet, another 20 minutes or more. (If you are pressed for time, you can cook the onions on medium-high heat, stirring often, until deeply browned, about 15 minutes.) Pour in the white wine and stir and scrape to incorporate the flavorful browned bits in the bottom of the skillet.

2 When the onions are cooked, fold the rice, lentils, cinnamon, cumin, half of the onions, the remaining 1 teaspoon salt, and several grinds of black pepper together in a large bowl. Taste and adjust seasonings.

3 Form a mound of the rice and lentil mixture on a large serving platter. Top with the remaining caramelized onions, the parsley, a grind of pepper, and a few grains of flaky sea salt.

ethiopian ful medames

Ful medames (pronounced fool MUH-dahm-ez) is one of my favorite foods. A big bowl of fava beans with lots of olive oil and garlic, it is eaten throughout the Middle East, mopped up with fresh pita. It's filling, inexpensive, and nutritious.

The main characteristics of Ethiopian *ful medames* are that the beans are fully mashed, a little of the Ethiopian spice mix berbere is added for flavor, and the dish is served with big rolls of white bread (not injera, the Ethiopian flatbread you might expect). The rolls are crusty on the outside and fluffy and warm on the inside. You don't want a real artisanal baguette here. Something with a softer texture that lets you soak up the sauce is ideal. This is the only utensil you need—no forks, spoons, or knives are traditionally used.

Berbere is the best-known spice mixture from Ethiopia. It typically contains chiles, ginger, cardamom, cloves, coriander, allspice, fenugreek, rue, and ajwain, and is quite hot. In this dish, it provides the background flavor and a bit of heat. You can find it at Ethiopian groceries or online at worldspice.com.

I set out to make my own Ethiopian-style *ful* because this simple and tasty dish makes a great weeknight supper that my kids love as much as I do. If you use canned fava beans (or cook them yourself in advance), you can have it on the table in 20 minutes.

The beans themselves are a type of fava, but they aren't the ones that look like giant lima beans. They are rounder, like chickpeas but a lot darker. Any Middle Eastern or Ethiopian store will carry them, usually both canned and dry. Just ask for *ful*. The canned ones work fine in this dish—just be sure to rinse them well before using.

4 big crusty rolls
¼ cup olive oil, plus additional for drizzling
4 garlic cloves, minced
1 cup minced white onion
1 tablespoon berbere (or to taste)
6 cups canned *ful* (round fava beans), rinsed and drained
1 cup water, plus additional as necessary
Kosher salt
6 tablespoons thinly sliced scallions, white and light green parts only
6 tablespoons crumbled feta
½ cup finely diced tomato
1 finely diced jalapeño pepper
2 large eggs, hard-cooked and cut into ⅛-inch slices
1 teaspoon ground cumin

1 Toast the rolls lightly in a toaster oven or oven.

2 Heat ¼ cup of the olive oil a large skillet over medium-high heat. Add the garlic and onion and sauté until softened but not brown, 1 to 2 minutes. Add the berbere and sauté for 1 minute more. Add the *ful* and 1 cup of water, and bring to a simmer.

3 Remove from the heat and mash the *ful*, adding water as needed to reach the texture of thick Mexican refried beans. Add salt to taste. Return to the heat briefly, just to warm through.

4 To serve, divide the mashed beans among four shallow bowls and drizzle rather generously with more olive oil. Top with the scallions, feta, tomato, and jalapeño pepper. Top with the egg slices and sprinkle with the ground cumin. Serve immediately, with the rolls on the side.

spanish lentil and mushroom stew

Have you ever noticed that well-browned, thickly cut mushrooms provide a completely different eating experience from those that are thinly sliced and sautéed? The water doesn't get cooked out of them; the surface simply gets seared and the interior retains a chewy texture—delicious!

Here these thick, chewy mushrooms are paired with French green lentils, seasoned with olive oil, sherry vinegar, and smoked paprika for a Spanish accent. The lentils and mushrooms are garnished with a little salad of cherry tomatoes and basil. Especially with earthy, brown plates of food, I love to finish with something bright and fresh to add a little visual interest and lighten the flavors.

Served with a good baguette, this would make a nice light, healthy meal for four; smaller portions can be the first course of a more elaborate meal for six.

You can use *lentilles du Puy* or black Beluga lentils. Just don't use standard big green or brown lentils, as they will turn to mush.

5 tablespoons plus 2 teaspoons extra-virgin olive oil
1 small white onion, finely diced
3 garlic cloves, minced
Kosher salt
2 cups French green lentils, rinsed and picked over
4 cups water
1 pound crimini mushrooms, quartered lengthwise
1 teaspoon smoked paprika
1 tablespoon plus 2 teaspoons sherry vinegar
1 pint cherry tomatoes, halved
12 big basil leaves, rolled into a bundle and cut into thin strips (chiffonade)
Freshly ground black pepper

1 Heat 3 tablespoons of the olive oil in a large saucepan over medium-high heat. Add the onion, garlic, and a pinch of salt and sauté until softened, about 3 minutes. Add the lentils and water. Bring to a boil, reduce to a simmer, and cook, uncovered, until lentils are tender but not falling apart, about 20 minutes. Drain.

2 While the lentils are cooking, heat 2 tablespoons of the olive oil in your largest skillet over high heat. When the oil is shimmering, add the mushrooms in a single layer and sauté, turning occasionally, until well browned, about 5 minutes. If your skillet isn't big enough to hold the mushrooms in one layer, work in batches. Season the mushrooms with ¼ teaspoon salt.

3 Put the lentils in a mixing bowl and add the smoked paprika, 1 teaspoon salt, and 1 tablespoon of the sherry vinegar. Taste and adjust seasoning. I like an edge of vinegary sourness that's not too overpowering.

4 Toss the cherry tomatoes and basil with the remaining 2 teaspoons olive oil, remaining 2 teaspoons sherry vinegar, and ¼ teaspoon salt.
5 To serve, divide the lentils among bowls. Top with the mushrooms, and top the mushrooms
   with the tomato salad. Give the whole thing a grind of black pepper and another little dusting of
   smoked paprika if you like.

eggplant and okra stew

VEGAN

GLUTEN-FREE

SERVES 3 OR 4

40 MINUTES

This West African–style stew, redolent of ginger and black pepper, is great made with baby eggplants just a little bigger than golf balls. You may find them at a farmers' market in late summer or at a store that specializes in Thai or Indian ingredients. Otherwise, use a regular globe eggplant and just cut it into bite-size pieces.

For a richer variation, you can mix ½ cup of unsweetened peanut butter or sunflower butter into the broth and/or add ½ cup of shelled roasted peanuts. This version especially reminds of stews I used to eat at my favorite Nigerian restaurant in Providence, Rhode Island.

Serve this stew over a bowl of rice for a satisfying one-dish meal. I like a long-grain white rice, such as basmati, with this stew, but you can also use a short-grain rice or any type of brown rice if you prefer.

8 baby eggplants (each slightly larger than a golf ball) or 3 medium or
   1 large eggplant (about 1½ pounds total)
2 tablespoons vegetable oil
1 medium white onion, diced
4 garlic cloves, thinly sliced
Kosher salt
2 tablespoons grated fresh ginger
1 tablespoon ground coriander
1 tablespoon ground cumin
1 teaspoon hot red pepper flakes (or to taste)
1 summer squash, diced
1 pound okra, trimmed and cut into 1-inch lengths
1 (28-ounce) can peeled whole tomatoes with juice
Kernels from 2 ears of corn or 2 cups frozen corn, defrosted
3 cups cooked long-grain rice
Freshly ground black pepper
1 handful fresh flatleaf parsley leaves, torn

1 Preheat the oven to 400°F. Prick each eggplant several times with a fork. (If not using baby eggplants, cut the eggplant into bite-size pieces and toss with a bit of olive oil.) Roast on a baking sheet until completely tender, about 30 minutes.

2 While the eggplant cooks, heat the vegetable oil in a 4-quart or larger saucepan over medium-high heat. Add the onion and sauté until it becomes translucent, about 2 minutes. Add the garlic, 1 teaspoon salt, 1 tablespoon of the grated ginger, the coriander, cumin, and hot red pepper flakes. Cook and stir for 1 minute more.

▼ ▼ ▼

3 Add the summer squash, okra, and the tomatoes with their juice. Break up the tomatoes with a fork. Bring to a simmer, then reduce the heat and simmer gently until the vegetables are tender, about 15 minutes. Turn off the heat. When the eggplant is ready, add it to the saucepan and heat the stew back up to serving temperature. Taste and adjust salt and spices.

4 Just before serving, add the corn kernels and the remaining 1 tablespoon grated ginger and cook for 2 minutes. Transfer to a serving bowl or serve in individual bowls over rice; finish with several grinds of black pepper and the parsley, and bring to the table immediately.

MISE EN PLACE—OR NOT! There is a conventional piece of advice that chefs will always give: Get all of your ingredients prepared and organized first, before you start to cook. In a restaurant kitchen, this isn't just handy, it is mandatory, because there is no time to stop in the middle of service to chop more onions or search for that backup bottle of balsamic vinegar.

Indeed, you will cook cleaner, better, and happier if you first set up your board, tools, and compost bucket, break down all of your vegetables and put them in little bowls, line up all of the spices you will need, and generally get everything laid out before you ever turn on the stove or oven.

On the other hand, sometimes when cooking at home it's okay to bend the rules. If you generally are quick with your knife, it is perfectly possible to cut broccoli for a stir-fry while the tofu is already in the pan or to work on a sauce while your vegetables are roasting.

These decisions are personal and depend on circumstances. I might make a recipe one way on the weekend and a very different way, with a lot more shortcuts, after work on a Tuesday. When there are obvious opportunities to overlap steps, I suggest them in the recipes in this book. But you should make it a habit to read through all of the instructions before you start and decide for yourself exactly how you want to tackle them.

chana masala with mushrooms

VEGAN OPTION
GLUTEN-FREE
SERVES 2 TO 4
30 MINUTES

Chana masala (spicy chickpeas) is one of those 10 dishes you find at pretty much every Indian restaurant in America. It's easy to understand why: It is inexpensive, delicious, healthy, and satisfying. The mass-prepared versions are usually pretty good, but you can make the dish at home and enjoy fresher, more vibrant flavors.

If you have the ingredients on hand and use canned chickpeas, you can make this *chana masala* in just 30 minutes. I find that canned chickpeas are often under-cooked and a little crunchy, so if I go that route, the first thing I do is put them on to simmer while I prepare everything else. To do this, put them in a saucepan with water to cover, bring to a boil, and let simmer while you prep.

The mushrooms add a little textural counterpoint without being a main focus of the dish. You can certainly omit them or use a different vegetable to suit your needs.

There are a lot of spices in this recipe, so to stay organized and efficient, gather everything into three separate bowls before starting to cook the curry.

FOR THE SPICE MIXTURE
2 teaspoons black mustard seeds
1 teaspoon fennel seeds
1 teaspoon cumin seeds
1 teaspoon coriander seeds

FOR THE TOMATO MIXTURE
1 medium tomato, cored and finely diced, or $\frac{1}{2}$ cup canned diced tomato
2 garlic cloves, minced
Half a medium onion, finely diced

FOR THE CHICKPEA MIXTURE
1 (15-ounce) can chickpeas, rinsed and drained (see headnote if using canned
    chickpeas), or $1\frac{1}{2}$ cups home-cooked chickpeas (see page 99)
$\frac{2}{3}$ cup quartered or thickly sliced white mushrooms
1 small, hot red chile pepper, thinly sliced
1 tablespoon grated fresh turmeric or 2 teaspoons ground turmeric
$\frac{1}{4}$ teaspoon ground cinnamon
Pinch of ground cloves
$\frac{1}{4}$ teaspoon cayenne pepper
2 tablespoons fresh lemon juice
1 teaspoon kosher salt

▼ ▼ ▼

TO COMPLETE THE DISH
3 tablespoons vegetable oil (or clarified butter or ghee if available)
1 teaspoon black mustard seeds
1 handful fresh cilantro leaves, for garnish

1   *For the spice mixture:* Combine the mustard, fennel, cumin, and coriander seeds in a small bowl.

2   *For the tomato mixture:* Combine the tomato, garlic, and onion in a medium bowl.

3   *For the chickpea mixture:* Combine the chickpeas (if you're using canned chickpeas and they've been simmering, drain them) with the mushrooms, chile, turmeric, cinnamon, cloves, cayenne, lemon juice, and salt in a medium bowl.

4   *To complete the dish:* Heat 2 tablespoons of the vegetable oil in a large skillet over medium-high heat. Add the spice mixture. Cook until the mustard seeds begin to pop, 10 to 20 seconds. Immediately add the tomato mixture. Cook, stirring occasionally, until the liquid is mostly gone and everything is browning, about 8 minutes.

5   Add the chickpea mixture and 1 cup or so of water, so it is somewhat soupy.

6   Cook, uncovered, over medium-low heat until the sauce begins to thicken, about 15 minutes. Taste and adjust seasoning. Does it need more salt? More lemon juice? A bit more cayenne? Continue cooking until the stew reaches the desired thickness—you can see how I like it by looking at the photograph.

7   Heat the remaining 1 tablespoon vegetable oil in a small skillet over high heat and cook the mustard seeds until they pop, just a few seconds. This is called tempering, and it is a great way to add a final layer of flavor. Drizzle the mustard seeds and oil over the chickpeas and serve, garnished with the cilantro.

chili borracho

VEGAN (IF YOU
CHOOSE VEGAN
GARNISHES)

GLUTEN-FREE
OPTION

SERVES 3 OR 4

1 HOUR

For me, chili is all about the beans, complemented by a savory sauce and plenty of tasty garnishes. I think adding grains and lots of vegetables just detracts from the main event. My version includes dark beer, dried chiles, and cocoa powder to create deep bass notes, reminiscent of Oaxacan mole. Brown Butter Cornbread (page 273) is a great accompaniment.

The pressure cooker is my favorite way to make chili. It allows me to cook the beans from scratch and include the bean cooking liquid as part of the broth. The pressure cooker requires about 8 cups of liquid for 1 pound of beans (consult your manual to be sure). This makes a soup rather than a thick chili, so I just drain off the sauce and quickly simmer it down to the right consistency, then add it back to the beans.

If you have the time, make this chili a couple of hours in advance, or even the day before you plan to serve it. The flavors only get better when they have time to rest.

If you don't have a pressure cooker, you can still make this dish. Just precook the beans on the stovetop and follow the rest of the instructions.

¼ cup olive oil
1 onion, finely diced
6 garlic cloves, minced
1 cup dried pinto beans, rinsed and picked over (or 2 to 3 cups cooked pinto beans)
1 cup dried black beans, rinsed and picked over (or 2 to 3 cups cooked black beans)
⅔ cup dried kidney beans, rinsed and picked over (or 2 cups cooked kidney beans)
2 whole chiles negro (dried pasilla)
2 teaspoons ancho chile powder
2 teaspoons dried oregano (preferably Mexican)
1 teaspoon ground cumin
¼ teaspoon ground cinnamon
1 tablespoon unsweetened cocoa powder
2 teaspoons kosher salt
1 (12-ounce) bottle very dark beer
1 (14.5-ounce) can diced tomatoes
Juice of 1 lime
1 handful minced fresh cilantro or flatleaf parsley leaves
Sour cream, minced onion, shredded cheddar, minced fresh cilantro or
   flatleaf parsley, and hot sauce, for garnish

▼ ▼ ▼

1 Heat the oil in a pressure cooker base or a 5-quart saucepan over medium-high heat. Add the onion and garlic and sauté until softened, about 3 minutes.

2 If using a pressure cooker, add the dried pinto beans, dried black beans, dried kidney beans, chiles negro, ancho chile powder, oregano, cumin, cinnamon, cocoa powder, salt, beer, and tomatoes. Add 6 cups water, cover the pressure cooker, and cook on high pressure according to manufacturer's suggested time and instructions; in my pressure cooker, it takes 33 minutes. Turn off and allow the pressure to release naturally. If not using a pressure cooker, use the cooked beans, skip the water, and simmer for 30 minutes.

3 Remove the lid and discard the whole chiles. Test the beans (all 3 types) to make sure they are done; if not, simmer until tender.

4 If using a pressure cooker, pour off most of the liquid into a saucepan and simmer the sauce briskly until it's reduced to about 1 cup. Pour the sauce back into the chili.

5 Add the lime juice and cilantro, mix thoroughly, then taste and adjust the seasoning. It will probably need more salt and possibly more chile powder.

6 Serve immediately, passing the garnishes so diners can customize the chili to their taste.

chickpea and green olive tagine

VEGAN

SERVES 2 TO 4

20 MINUTES

A tagine technically refers to a clay pot with a funnel-shaped lid traditionally used in Morocco, but it also describes any moist, spicy stew made with the spices typical of that region. This version uses *ras el hanout*, sumac, pomegranate molasses, preserved lemon, and marinated olives to build up big flavors quickly. All of these ingredients can be found at a Middle Eastern grocery or online from Amazon.

For the green olives, look for a type that is already pitted and marinated in a spice mixture. If you happen to find one with Moroccan or Middle Eastern spices, that is ideal, but Sicilian or even French styles will do fine. Your best bet will be at the olive bar of an upscale grocer rather than in a jar.

Serve this dish family-style over a big platter of steaming couscous for the most dramatic impact. You can add an oven-roasted vegetable such as cauliflower or winter squash to round out a Middle Eastern meal.

¼ **cup extra-virgin olive oil**
1 **medium onion, diced**
3 **cups home-cooked chickpeas (see page 99) or 2 (15-ounce) cans chickpeas,**
    rinsed and drained
1½ **teaspoons kosher salt**
1 **teaspoon hot red pepper flakes**
1 **teaspoon** *ras el hanout*
2 **tablespoons pomegranate molasses**
Half a preserved lemon, minced, plus additional if desired
1½ **cups pitted, marinated green olives (see headnote), cut in halves or thirds if large**
1 **tablespoon ground sumac, for garnish**
Minced fresh flatleaf parsley leaves, for garnish
3 **cups cooked couscous**

1   Heat the olive oil in a large skillet over medium-high heat. Add the onion and sauté until it is beginning to soften, about 2 minutes. Add the chickpeas, salt, hot red pepper flakes, *ras al hanout*, pomegranate molasses, and preserved lemon. Reduce the heat to medium-low and cook for 5 minutes more.

2   Stir in the green olives. Cook for 2 minutes more, then taste and adjust seasoning. You can add more minced preserved lemon if you like. Add a few tablespoons of water if needed to keep the dish moist, but it should not be at all soupy.

3   Transfer to a large serving bowl, garnishing with the sumac powder and parsley. Serve with the couscous. For a dramatic presentation, you can mound your couscous on a platter and spoon the tagine over it.

kimchi stew (kimchi jigae) with shiitake and daikon

Kimchi jigae is classic Korean home cooking that is simple enough to make for a weeknight dinner. The body of the stew comes from chopped kimchi, spiked with chile paste (*kochujang*, also spelled *gochujang*, available at Asian grocery stores) and miso. My version is made with daikon, shiitake mushroom caps, and tofu, but you can adapt the stew to just about any ingredients you have on hand.

Daikon is delicious in salads and pickles, but don't underestimate its value as a cooked vegetable as well. Heat brings out a sweet, tender side that is easy to like.

Serve this stew with rice and more kimchi for a simple meal, or add a collection of Korean side dishes (*banchan*) for a full feast (see page 218).

You'll find more information about vegetarian kimchi on page 48. Depending on your kimchi, this recipe as written may make quite a spicy stew, or you may wish to add additional chile heat.

1 medium-size daikon
2 tablespoons toasted sesame oil, plus additional for garnish
16 shiitake mushroom caps, cut into bite-size pieces
Half a white onion, diced
1 tablespoon grated fresh ginger
2 garlic cloves, minced
2 cups coarsely chopped vegetarian kimchi
2 tablespoons *kochujang*
2 tablespoons red miso
2 tablespoons soy sauce
3 cups water
Powdered chile pepper or hot red pepper flakes (optional)
1 pound firm tofu, cut into ½-inch cubes
2 scallions, white and light green parts only, thinly sliced, for garnish

1   Warm four serving bowls in a low (200°F) oven. Peel the daikon. Cut it in half lengthwise, then cut ¼-inch half-moons until you have 2 cups. Reserve the rest for another use.

2   Heat a large (at least 4-quart) saucepan over medium-high heat. Add 2 tablespoons of the toasted sesame oil. When it is hot, add the daikon and sauté for 1 minute. Add the shiitake and onion, and sauté until the onion begins to soften, about 2 minutes more.

3   Add the ginger, garlic, kimchi, *kochujang*, and miso, and stir. Cook for about 5 minutes, stirring occasionally. Don't worry if the *kochujang* and miso start as big blobs; after a few minutes they will soften and dissolve.

▼ ▼ ▼

4 Add the soy sauce and water. Bring to a boil, reduce to a simmer, and cook, stirring occasionally, until the sauce has thickened slightly and the flavors have begun to meld, about 15 minutes. Taste and adjust seasoning. If you'd like it to be spicier, you can add more kimchi or *kochujang*, or, if desired, a bit of powdered chile pepper or hot red pepper flakes. Gently stir in the tofu and simmer for 5 more minutes.

5 Divide among the serving bowls, garnish with an additional drizzle of sesame oil and the scallions, and serve immediately.

KOREAN SIDE DISHES (*BANCHAN*). No Korean meal is considered complete without a selection of *banchan*, which are small, room-temperature side dishes. They are generally served in small bowls placed in the middle of the table, and diners help themselves. There are hundreds of varieties of *banchan*; here are three very quick ones to try.

Bean sprouts with sesame oil: Bring a small pot of salted water to a boil and blanch 2 cups bean sprouts for 90 seconds. Drain, rinse in cool water, drain again, and pat dry. Toss with 1 tablespoon toasted sesame oil and a big pinch of sea salt. Let cool to room temperature.

Squash in sweet soy sauce: Halve and seed a small delicata squash. Cut into $\frac{1}{4}$-inch half-moons. Cover with water in a medium-size saucepan, bring to a boil, and simmer until nearly tender, about 5 minutes. Drain, then return to the saucepan. In a small bowl, combine $\frac{1}{3}$ cup soy sauce, $\frac{1}{4}$ cup sugar, 2 tablespoons rice vinegar, and 1 tablespoon peeled, grated fresh ginger. Pour over the squash and bring back to a simmer; cook until fully tender. Let cool to room temperature. If you like, stir in 1 thinly sliced jalapeño pepper. Serve with only a small amount of the liquid. You can also make this *banchan* with sweet potato.

Spicy stir-fried zucchini: Cut a small zucchini into $\frac{1}{2}$-inch dice. Heat 1 tablespoon toasted sesame oil in a small skillet over high heat. When it shimmers, add the zucchini, $\frac{1}{4}$ teaspoon kosher salt, 1 teaspoon *kochujang* (Korean chili paste), and $1\frac{1}{2}$ teaspoons peeled, grated fresh ginger. Stir-fry until crisp-tender, about 1 minute. Transfer to a bowl and stir in 1 teaspoon toasted black sesame seeds. Let cool to room temperature

main courses
from the oven

aromatic tofu packets

VEGAN

GLUTEN-FREE OPTION

SERVES 4

40 MINUTES

Imagine opening a present at the table and being greeted with a rush of aromatic steam redolent of lemongrass and ginger that makes you close your eyes with pleasure. Baking your food in parchment paper or banana leaves is just the ticket to that experience. (Banana leaves also impart a pleasant, grassy aroma.)

Rather than marinating the tofu in advance, I score it in two directions to open up lots of surface area for the seasoning to penetrate quickly. This also creates an interesting look, similar to some fish preparations.

One nice thing about making individual packets is that you can customize the spice level for each diner. For children, you may want to leave out the jalapeño and long pepper and add their favorite vegetables.

1¼ pounds firm or extra-firm tofu
¼ cup soy sauce (use a wheat-free version for gluten-free)
1 tablespoon mirin
1 teaspoon vegetable broth powder (gluten-free if needed; optional)
¼ cup water
1-inch piece fresh ginger, peeled and grated
1 stalk lemongrass, trimmed, pounded, and minced (see page 253)
2 jalapeño or other chile peppers (heat to your taste), seeded and thinly sliced
2 scallions, white and light green parts only, thinly sliced lengthwise
Half an orange or yellow bell pepper, finely diced
Freshly ground black pepper
2 pieces long pepper, crushed in a mortar and pestle
1 lime, cut into wedges

SPECIAL EQUIPMENT: 4 (10 x 12-inch) pieces parchment paper or banana leaf, to wrap the tofu and form an envelope; banana leaves can be found fresh or frozen at Mexican or Southeast Asian groceries and sometimes at Whole Foods

1   Preheat the oven to 400°F.

2   If using banana leaves, you must make them pliable first. Cut out any thick ribs and either boil them for 20 minutes or use tongs to run them over a hot flame.

3   Cut the tofu into 8 evenly sized slabs about ½ inch thick. Holding your knife at an angle to the surface of your cutting board, score each slice in two perpendicular directions, being careful not to cut all the way through, with cuts about ¼ inch apart. (Making angled cuts, rather than straight up-and-down ones, exposes even more surface area to the sauce.)

▼ ▼ ▼

4 Combine the soy sauce, mirin, broth powder (if using), and water. Place two pieces of tofu in the center of each piece of parchment paper or banana leaf, and spoon a tablespoon or two of the sauce over each one, gently working it into the score lines.

5 Evenly divide the ginger, lemongrass, jalapeño pepper, scallions, and bell pepper among the packets. Season each with several grinds of black pepper and a big pinch of long pepper.

6 Fold the top half of the parchment paper or banana leaf down over the tofu, then fold the bottom half up over the top; crimp the top and bottom halves together. Fold the open sides under twice to make a firm seal, moderately tight around the ingredients, but leave a bit of room for steam. Secure the sides with toothpicks. Place the packets on a baking sheet and bake for 20 minutes. If you are using parchment paper, it will turn quite brown; don't be concerned.

7 To serve, place each packet on an individual plate. Tell the diners to open them carefully and enjoy the aromatic steam. Pass the lime wedges.

LONG PEPPER. Long pepper is an unusual spice with a rich history. It grows primarily in Indonesia and was used in Europe as early as the 5th century BC. Long pepper has a floral aroma along with heat, and it numbs the tongue slightly, like Sichuan peppercorn. It fell out of favor as black pepper became common but has recently become available at better spice shops and grocery stores. You may find the Big Tree Farms brand from Bali, which is excellent.

Long pepper can be ground in a mortar and pestle or with an electric spice grinder.

If you can't find long pepper, substitute a mixture of black pepper, cayenne, and coriander seed. Sichuan peppercorn can also work, but use half the quantity called for in the recipe.

chermoula-stuffed eggplant

GLUTEN-FREE

SERVES 4

50 MINUTES
(20 MINUTES
ACTIVE)

The eggplants in this recipe are halved, and then each half is cut so that there is a "pocket" to rub with *chermoula* (a sort of North African pesto). The *chermoula* bakes into the creamy flesh, seasoning it. Then you add more *chermoula* just before serving so you can enjoy both the fresh and cooked flavors of the herbs and spices.

This isn't a large entrée; you'll want to serve it with generous quantities of couscous and chickpeas or a rice pilaf, yogurt, and salad.

2 medium globe eggplants (about 14 ounces each)
1 batch *Chermoula* (page 331)
Extra-virgin olive oil
Kosher salt
½ cup crumbled feta

1 Preheat the oven to 450°F. Grease a baking sheet generously with olive oil.

2 Trim and discard the stem ends of the eggplants. Cut the eggplants in half lengthwise. Using a knife, trim off about ⅛ inch off the bottom of each eggplant half, to remove some of the skin and create a stable base. Cut the eggplant halves almost in half again, parallel to the base, creating a pocket and leaving them attached by the last ½ inch at the base end.

3 Open up each eggplant half and rub the inside with a generous tablespoon of *chermoula*. Close the halves back up and put them on the baking sheet, cut side up. Brush the tops with olive oil and season with a generous sprinkle of salt.

4 Warm four serving plates or bowls. Bake the eggplant until completely tender and just starting to brown, about 30 minutes. Remove from the oven and place an eggplant half on each serving plate. Drizzle on the remaining *chermoula*, scatter the crumbled feta on top, and serve immediately.

main courses from the oven / 223

portobello and summer squash lasagna

The two most common varieties of vegetarian lasagna are those filled with spinach and ricotta and those layered with piles of watery vegetables. This version—with portobello mushrooms and summer squash—gives you a much more decisive flavor.

To slice the portobellos, pull off the stems and lay the caps flat on your cutting board. Hold your knife at an angle and carefully cut through them on the bias to make ⅛-inch-thick slabs with as much surface area as possible.

For this recipe I use no-boil lasagna noodles. They are the same as any other dried pasta, just rolled a little thinner so they can cook through right in the oven. You just need to be sure they are surrounded with enough sauce to absorb, so they'll soften as they cook.

Extra-virgin olive oil
4 medium crookneck or other summer squash or zucchini, cut lengthwise
  into ⅛-inch-thick slices
Kosher salt
4 large portobello mushroom caps, sliced ⅛ inch thick on the bias
1 (15-ounce container) fresh ricotta (Calabro is an excellent brand)
½ teaspoon nutmeg (preferably freshly grated)
Freshly ground black pepper
2 large eggs
1 onion, diced
2 garlic cloves, minced
2 (28-ounce) cans tomato sauce
Grated zest of 1 lemon
1 pound no-boil lasagna noodles (or regular lasagna noodles, cooked until
  barely al dente)
12 ounces mozzarella, grated
3 ounces freshly grated Parmigiano-Reggiano

1 Preheat the oven to 375°F. Heat 2 tablespoons olive oil in a large skillet over high heat. Add a single layer of squash and sauté until well browned on both sides, about 5 minutes. Transfer to paper towels and season with salt. Repeat with the remaining squash and with the mushrooms, adding more oil to the skillet as needed. Set aside.

2 In a medium-size bowl, stir together the ricotta, nutmeg, ½ teaspoon salt, and several grinds of black pepper. Beat in the eggs.

▼ ▼ ▼

3 Heat 3 tablespoons olive oil in a large saucepan. Add the onion and garlic and sauté until the onion is starting to soften, about 3 minutes. Add the tomato sauce, lemon zest, and 1 teaspoon salt. Simmer for 5 minutes. Taste and adjust seasoning.

4 Oil a 9 x 13-inch baking dish. Build the layers in the following way, from bottom to top. *Be sure to get the noodles quite wet if they are the no-boil type; they need plenty of moisture.* You'll probably have a bit of extra sauce.

- $1\frac{1}{2}$ cups sauce
- a single layer of noodles, one-third of the vegetables, one-half of the ricotta, 1 cup sauce
- a single layer of noodles, one-half of the remaining vegetables, one-half of the mozzarella, 1 cup sauce
- a single layer of noodles, the remaining vegetables, the remaining ricotta, 1 cup sauce
- a single layer of noodles, 1 cup sauce
- the remaining mozzarella mixed, with the Parmigiano

5 Cover the dish with aluminum foil and bake for 30 minutes. Remove the foil and bake until you can easily pierce the noodles with a fork and the sauce is bubbling around the sides—the internal temperature should be 170°F—about another 30 minutes. Don't overcook or the noodles will get soggy.

6 If the cheese isn't crispy and brown enough, finish judiciously under the broiler.

7 Allow the lasagna to rest for at least 15 minutes before serving, so it has time to set up a bit.

planning a meal: start with what's fresh

My favorite meals are those in which a particularly beautiful ingredient inspires the menu. This can happen any time of year, but the best seasonal meals seem to come from visits to the farmers' market, where you might see the most shockingly plump, dense eggplants or delicate strawberries still warm from the field. My policy is always to buy this spectacular produce and then find a way to highlight it in a simple meal.

Here are a few sample menus to get you started:

1 inspired by a beautiful radish

2 when the eggplant is perfect

3 asparagus three ways

4 asian mushrooms as the stars

5 the season's first broccoli rabe

See also Planning a Meal: Start with a Base Ingredient (page 153), and Planning a Meal: Start with the Culture (page 183).

over-the-top eggplant parmigiana

SERVES 6

1 HOUR
(40 MINUTES
ACTIVE)

For this no-holds-barred eggplant parmigiana, the eggplant is breaded with panko and pan-fried, layered with fresh mozzarella and homemade tomato sauce, finished in the oven, and then topped with a dice of fresh heirloom tomatoes. It makes a satisfying entrée, and you need only add a green salad to make a celebratory dinner.

I don't salt and drain eggplant for most uses, but it is worthwhile in this recipe. Extracting some of the liquid makes the eggplant fry up firm yet fork-tender. You don't want any mush factor in your parmigiana.

Here's a great tip for breading. Use one hand to put the eggplant in the flour, egg, and bread crumbs. Use the other hand to toss the eggplant in the bread crumbs and into the skillet. By keeping one hand for the wet stuff and the other for the dry, you avoid getting your hands breaded along with the eggplant!

The finest canned tomatoes for Italian dishes come from the area of San Marzano; look for that name on the can.

3 large or 5 smaller globe eggplants (about 4 pounds total)
Kosher salt
1 tablespoon extra-virgin olive oil
2 garlic cloves, minced
2 cups canned crushed tomatoes (preferably San Marzano)
1 cup all-purpose flour
3 cups panko bread crumbs
4 large eggs, beaten
Vegetable oil, for pan-frying
12 ounces mozzarella, thinly sliced
1 cup freshly grated Parmigiano-Reggiano
2 handfuls fresh basil leaves, coarsely chopped

TO SERVE
1½ cups diced vine-ripened tomatoes (only truly good, ripe tomatoes will do here; don't use those supermarket ones ripened with ethylene gas)
1 handful fresh basil leaves, coarsely chopped
Kosher salt
Freshly ground black pepper

▼ ▼ ▼

1 Peel the eggplants and slice lengthwise into planks a scant ½ inch thick. Layer in a colander with a heavy sprinkling of kosher salt between each layer, top with a plate, and weight with some cans. Set aside on a plate to drain for at least 30 minutes. Wipe off excess salt with a paper towel.

2 Heat the olive oil in a medium-size saucepan over medium-high heat. Add the garlic and sauté until fragrant, about 30 seconds. Add the crushed tomatoes and bring to a simmer. Reduce the heat and simmer for 15 minutes, while you make the rest of the recipe. Don't add salt, because the eggplant will still have residual salt from the draining process.

3 Set up a rack or baking sheet covered with paper towels for draining the fried eggplant. Butter a 9 x 13-inch baking dish and preheat the oven to 400°F.

4 Set up for dredging, with plates for the flour and bread crumbs and a shallow bowl for the eggs. Heat a good ¼ inch of vegetable oil in your biggest skillet over high heat. Working with two slices of eggplant at a time, pat them in the flour until they have a dry coating, then drag through the egg, and finally press both sides in the bread crumbs, covering thoroughly. Place them in the skillet, where they should start sizzling immediately. Don't pack them in too tightly in the skillet; leave yourself some room to work. Flip when brown, about 2 minutes, then brown on the other side. They should be fork-tender at this point (the oven time is just to melt the cheese, not cook the eggplant). Transfer the eggplant to the rack to drain. Repeat with the remaining eggplant, adding more vegetable oil as necessary.

5 To assemble, set down your first layer of eggplant in the prepared baking dish, and top each slice with a couple tablespoons of tomato sauce, a piece of mozzarella, a bit of Parmigiano, and a bit of basil. Build up three layers, finishing with cheese.

6 Bake until the cheese is thoroughly melted, about 20 minutes.

7 To serve: Toss the diced tomatoes with the basil and a pinch of salt. Put an eggplant stack on each plate, and top with ¼ cup of the tomato salad and a grind of fresh black pepper.

triple-smoky mac & cheese

SERVES 6 TO 8
AS A MAIN
COURSE

1 HOUR
(30 MINUTES
ACTIVE)

This grown-up macaroni and cheese was inspired by an incredible oak-smoked cheddar that I found at Seattle's historic Pike Place Market. I reinforce that flavor with smoked paprika and some chipotle in adobo. If you can't get a smoked cheddar, use regular cheddar and substitute smoked mozzarella.

You can prepare this macaroni and cheese ahead and refrigerate it, which makes it very convenient for dinner parties. Just wait until the last minute to add the bread crumbs, and allow additional baking time.

1 pound elbow macaroni
6 tablespoons (¾ stick) unsalted butter
¼ cup all-purpose flour
4 cups whole milk
Half an onion, finely diced
1 tablespoon smoked paprika
1 teaspoon fresh rosemary leaves, minced
1 canned chipotle chile in adobo sauce, minced, or ¼ cup Frontera brand
    chipotle salsa
1 teaspoon dried oregano
¼ teaspoon nutmeg (preferably freshly grated)
8 ounces smoked cheddar, grated, or substitute regular cheddar if you
    can't find smoked cheddar
8 ounces mozzarella (substitute smoked mozzarella if you're using regular
    cheddar), grated
Kosher salt
1½ cups Homemade Bread Crumbs made with 2 cloves minced garlic added
    (page 345)

1 Bring a large pot of salted water to a boil. Boil the macaroni according to package directions, draining when it is just becoming al dente. This will bake more in the oven, so don't overcook it. Drain, transfer it to a bowl, and toss with 2 tablespoons of the butter.

2 Preheat the oven to 350°F and grease a 9 x 13-inch baking dish.

3 Melt the remaining 4 tablespoons butter in a medium saucepan over medium-low heat. Sprinkle in the flour and whisk pretty constantly for 3 minutes. Whisk in the milk. Add the onion, smoked paprika, rosemary, chipotle, oregano, and nutmeg. Bring to a gentle simmer and keep cooking, whisking occasionally, until the sauce begins to thicken, about 5 minutes.

4 Reduce the heat to low. Whisk in the grated cheeses, a handful at a time, stirring each addition of cheese until melted. It is important to do this gradually, to avoid graininess.

▼ ▼ ▼

5 Taste the sauce and adjust the seasoning to your preference. It will probably need just a little salt, depending on the cheeses. Add more chipotle if you'd like it hotter. Remember that the sauce should be pretty intense, because it needs to flavor a full pound of pasta.

6 Stir the macaroni into the sauce. Pour the macaroni into the baking dish. Scatter the bread crumbs evenly over the top.

7 Bake until you can see bubbling around the sides and the bread crumbs are nicely browned, about 30 minutes. Let the dish rest for 5 to 10 minutes before serving.

CRUNCH.

"Crunch is so universally appreciated that whenever I finish a recipe, I ask myself, 'Is there any way to add a little more crunch?' Often it makes the difference between a dish that is merely good and one that is miraculous. In short, if in doubt, crunch it." —Chef Michel Richard

I couldn't agree more. Properly crispy latkes, the well-browned cheese atop lasagna, a simple but well-made corn quesadilla, or good Homemade Bread Crumbs (page 345) on a rich Brussels Sprout Gratin (page 248) are great favorites of mine that deliver a dry, toasted crunch.

Then there is the moist, refreshing crunch of fresh vegetable garnishes, like the carrot, daikon, and onion in my Rice Vermicelli (*Bun*) with Ginger-Grapefruit Sauce (page 156).

Pretty much everyone loves crispiness, whether it is the simple addition of crackers to soup, the all-encompassing chomp through a bowl of granola, the balanced crisp and soft of French fries, or the shockingly irreversible shatter of crème brûlée.

But why? Why do we love the crunch?

Chef Richard's answer is that our caveperson ancestors came to associate crunch with food that has been cooked; the browned flavors produced by the Maillard reactions that happen when protein and sugars are cooked together render it more nutritious and delicious.

I asked why people love crunch and crisp on the Herbivoracious fan page on Facebook and got some interesting answers. One reader perceptively suggested that we seek it because crispy is so often closely associated with the goodness of deep-fried fat and salt. Others pointed out the importance of contrast: Crispy is good, but crispy and soft in the same dish or the same bite can be transporting.

Then there is the sound. I think we enjoy eating most when it speaks to all of our senses. The sound of crunch travels right through our jawbones to our ears, adding an electrifying dimension to the experience.

Finally, there is the simple thrill of physically breaking through. The crispy crust first resists your teeth, then yields with a satisfying snap. Your jaw muscles actually work hard to render the food ready to swallow and digest. Crunchy food requires you to engage with the eating experience, and not just passively consume.

So let's not be careful out there, people. Let's throw caution to the wind, run that dish under the broiler, and finish it with bread crumbs or sesame seeds. Let's add a cracker or a chip, a tuile or croquant. Let's top it with cucumbers or radishes or thin rings of scallion. Let's make a little noise!

stuffed and baked polenta

SERVES 8

1 HOUR AND
15 MINUTES
(45 MINUTES
ACTIVE)

I love baked dishes when I'm entertaining or busy with kids, because they mind their own business in the oven while I take care of other things. This polenta is filled with a mixture of sautéed mushrooms and kale in a creamy tarragon-enhanced béchamel sauce and just enough cheese to make it seem rich without blowing your whole week's calorie budget.

Quick-cooking polenta will work just fine in this recipe. I particularly like the De la Estancia brand from Argentina, which has a pronounced corn flavor. But you can use any polenta that you like.

You can prepare this dish and bake it immediately or refrigerate it and bake it the next day. Just allow more time in the oven if it's been refrigerated.

Be sure to read the recipe through before starting, as it calls for the sauce and the polenta to be pre-cooked.

3 tablespoons olive oil
1 medium white onion, diced
4 garlic cloves, minced
1 teaspoon kosher salt
Hot red pepper flakes
2 pounds white mushrooms, sliced ¼ inch thick
1 bunch kale, stemmed and thinly sliced (about 4 cups packed)
Grated zest of 1 lemon
9 cups cooked polenta (3 cups uncooked, prepared according to package directions)
2 cups Tarragon Béchamel (page 324)
¾ cup freshly grated Asiago Fresco or provolone
½ cup freshly grated Parmigiano-Reggiano

1 Preheat the oven to 400°F using convection, or 425°F without convection. Grease a 9 x 13-inch baking pan with 1 tablespoon of the olive oil.

2 Heat the remaining 2 tablespoons olive oil in your largest skillet over medium-high heat; add the onion and garlic and sauté until the onion is translucent, about 2 minutes. Add the salt, hot red pepper flakes, and mushrooms, and cook, stirring occasionally, until the mushrooms are browned and most of their liquid has cooked out (the bottom of the pan will seem dry).

3 Add the kale and cook, stirring occasionally, until it is wilted and tender, about 10 minutes. Add the lemon zest. Taste and adjust the seasoning.

4 Spread half of the polenta in the bottom of the baking dish. If the polenta has cooled and solidified, you may have to squish it into place. Top with the mushroom mixture, then the béchamel sauce, and finally the remaining polenta. Scatter the grated cheeses on top.

5 Bake until hot all the way through and golden brown on top, about 30 minutes. Allow the dish to rest for 10 minutes before serving.

swiss chard and tomatillo enchiladas

GLUTEN-FREE
OPTION

SERVES 4

1 HOUR

These enchiladas are cheesy enough to be satisfying, but they're not the total gut bombs that plain cheese enchiladas can be. This recipe is my vegetarian version inspired by one from Rick Bayless.

If you haven't cooked with tomatillos before, this dish is a great introduction. They make incredible salsas, whether you use them raw, sear them before puree-ing, or as in this case, cook the puree. They have an intense, rounded flavor that is tart without being too acidic.

Most folks don't realize how good Swiss chard stems are. There seems to be an inclination to remove them, as you would from, say, collard greens, whose stems really are tough. But with chard, if you remove just the woodiest bit, chop the rest of the stem up fairly small, and give them enough time to cook, you'll discover just how delicious they are.

3 garlic cloves, peeled
1 to 3 jalapeño peppers (to taste), stemmed, halved, and seeded
1½ pounds tomatillos, husked and halved
Kosher salt
3 tablespoons vegetable oil
1 cup bean cooking liquid (see page 99) or vegetable broth (gluten-free if needed)
3 tablespoons sour cream
1 teaspoon sugar (optional)
2 large bunches Swiss chard
1 medium white onion, diced
¼ cup water
10 ounces Monterey Jack, grated
12 corn tortillas
¼ cup grated *queso anejo* or Parmigiano-Reggiano
Half a large red onion, cut into rings
1 handful fresh cilantro leaves

1 Combine the garlic, jalapeño peppers, tomatillos, and 1 teaspoon salt in a blender and puree until smooth.

2 Heat 1½ tablespoons of the oil in a medium saucepan over medium-high heat. Add the puree and cook it down, stirring frequently, until it's about as thick as an Italian tomato sauce, about 10 minutes. Don't let it scorch. Add the bean liquid and reduce the heat to a simmer. After 10 minutes, turn off the heat and stir in the sour cream. Taste; add more salt and the sugar if needed. If the mixture isn't thick enough, simmer a little longer. If it is too thick, add a bit more broth. Turn off the heat and allow to cool.

▼ ▼ ▼

3 To prepare the chard, strip the leaves from the stems and cut the leaves into ½-inch-wide ribbons. Rinse in a large bowl of water at least twice. Remove the toughest ends of the stems, rinse the remaining part, and chop into ½-inch lengths.

4 Heat the remaining 1½ tablespoons oil in a large skillet with a lid over high heat. Add the white onion and cook for 30 seconds. Add the chard stems and cook for 1 minute. Add the chard leaves and toss. If they don't fit all at once, add as much as you can, wait a minute until those leaves wilt, then add the rest. Add the water and 1 teaspoon salt; cover and reduce the heat to low. Cook, stirring occasionally, until the chard is thoroughly wilted and tender, about 15 minutes. Remove the lid and cook until most of the water has evaporated.

5 Preheat the oven to 375°F. In a bowl, combine the chard mixture with three-quarters of the Monterey Jack. Taste and adjust seasoning.

6 Wrap the tortillas in a clean, moist dishtowel and microwave for 2 minutes to soften.

7 To assemble, ladle 1 cup tomatillo sauce into a 9 x 13-inch baking dish. Dip a tortilla in the remaining sauce and then lay it in the dish. Fill it with about ¼ cup of chard filling, then roll it up and push it to one side, seam side down. Repeat with the remaining tortillas. Twelve will just fit snugly in the pan.

8 Pour another cup of sauce over the top, then top with the remaining Monterey Jack and the *queso anejo*.

9 Bake until the sauce is bubbling and the cheese is melted, about 25 minutes. Turn on the broiler and place the dish under the broiler, watching carefully, just until the cheese is browning a bit, 2 to 3 minutes. Remove from the oven, top with the red onion and cilantro sprigs, and serve.

baked penne with mushrooms and fontina

SERVES 4

**45 MINUTES
(30 MINUTES
ACTIVE)**

Jam-packed with mushrooms and spinach, this baked penne is a great alternative to macaroni and cheese. Because it is made with melted cheese instead of a bécha-mel sauce, the flavors of the mushroom and spinach shine.

I like to cut the mushrooms in quarters instead of thin slices for this dish. That allows them to brown nicely on the outside while retaining a satisfying chew.

You can use this recipe as a blueprint to make a wide variety of similar baked pastas. You can replace the penne rigate with any other medium-size extruded pasta; the cheese can be anything you fancy as long as it melts well, and the greens could be chard or kale.

**10 ounces spinach, tough stems removed
1 pound penne rigate
¼ cup extra-virgin olive oil
5 garlic cloves, minced
Half a white onion, thinly sliced
2 pounds white or cremini mushrooms, quartered lengthwise (cut smaller
   if necessary to make bite-size pieces)
Kosher salt
2 teaspoons dried oregano
½ teaspoon hot red pepper flakes
½ cup sweet vermouth
12 ounces fontina, cut into small cubes
Freshly ground black pepper
¾ cup freshly grated Parmigiano-Reggiano**

1   Bring a large pot of salted water to a boil and preheat the oven to 400°F. Lightly grease a 9 x 13-inch baking dish.

2   Put half of the spinach into a large metal strainer and carefully dunk it in the boiling water until it's thoroughly wilted, about 30 seconds. Drain very well and place in the baking dish. Repeat with the remaining spinach. (You can also microwave the spinach.)

3   Boil the pasta according to package directions; drain well and place in the baking dish. While it is cooking, continue with the next step.

▼ ▼ ▼

4 Heat 2 tablespoons of the olive oil in your largest skillet over high heat. When the oil is hot, add the garlic, onion, and half the mushrooms (or however much will fit in your skillet up to about a double layer). Season with ½ teaspoon salt, the oregano, and hot pepper flakes and cook, stirring occasionally, until the mushrooms are well browned on most sides but still meaty, not having given up all of their liquid. Transfer to the baking dish. Add the remaining 2 tablespoons olive oil and remaining mushrooms to the skillet and cook in the same fashion, adding another ½ teaspoon salt. When they are done, add the sweet vermouth and cook, stirring and scraping up any browned bits in the bottom of the skillet, for about 30 more seconds. Transfer the mushrooms, cooking liquid, and any juice and crispy bits in the skillet to the baking dish.

5 Add the fontina and several grinds of black pepper to the baking dish. Stir everything around thoroughly. If the dish is too full to stir, move some of the contents temporarily back to the skillet to make room for stirring, then return everything to the baking dish when well combined. Taste and add more salt if needed.

6 Sprinkle the top with the Parmigiano and bake until bubbly and browned, about 15 minutes. (You can prepare the casserole and refrigerate it, unbaked, for up to 24 hours, then bake when you are ready. The chilled dish will take 45 minutes to 1 hour to bake.)

side dishes

asparagus with nori butter

I devised this dish while interning at Canlis, a venerable Seattle fine-dining institution, where the kitchen uses much more classical French technique than I typically do in my home cooking.

I think you will like the nori butter. It adds an umami intensity and a slightly sweet funkiness that pairs beautifully with the asparagus.

The garnishes for this dish are nori strips, sesame seeds, Maldon salt, miso-lemon sauce, finely diced lemon zest, and chive tips. If you don't feel like making something this refined, you could just toss pan-roasted asparagus with the nori butter and salt and still have a delicious dish.

You can do all of the prep up to a day in advance and simply reheat the butter and blanched asparagus when you are ready to serve. If you have any of the nori butter or miso-lemon sauce left at the end, they are delicious on rice.

This dish works well with Japanese meals such as Chirashi Sushi (page 181) or with a main-course pasta like Pappardelle with Eggplant Ragu and Fresh Ricotta (page 172).

6 tablespoons (¾ stick) unsalted butter
1 sheet nori seaweed
24 spears beautiful medium-thick asparagus
Half a lemon
⅓ cup white miso
2 tablespoons mirin
Thin nori strips (buy them separately or cut them with scissors from a sheet)
Toasted sesame seeds
24 fresh chive tips
Flaky sea salt (such as Maldon)

1   Bring a pot of well-salted water to a boil and set up an ice bath (a large bowl filled with water and lots of ice).

2   Melt the butter in a small skillet. Crumple and tear the nori sheet into pieces and infuse over very low heat for 5 minutes. Remove from the heat and let stand for 15 minutes, then strain through a fine-mesh strainer. The nori butter can be stored overnight in the refrigerator.

3   Juice the lemon half and reserve the juice. Cut the juiced lemon shell in half again, squish the pieces flat on your cutting board, and carefully remove all of the membranes and white pith, leaving only yellow skin. Trim the sides to make two even rectangles.

▼ ▼ ▼

4 Blanch the lemon skins in the boiling water for 30 seconds, remove them with a slotted spoon, then shock them in the ice bath and drain on paper towels (leave the water boiling on the stove). Cut first into $\frac{1}{16}$-inch strips (fine julienne) and then into $\frac{1}{16}$-inch squares (brunoise). The lemon garnish can be stored overnight in the refrigerator.

5 Trim the asparagus to uniform length and use a paring knife to remove all the little random leaves that aren't part of the main tip. Blanch the asparagus until crisp-tender and bright green, about 3 minutes. The tip of a knife should go in easily but the stalks should offer a hint of resistance. Drain the asparagus, shock them in the ice water, drain again, and reserve. The asparagus can be stored overnight in the refrigerator, wrapped in plastic.

6 Whisk together the miso, mirin, and reserved lemon juice. Aim for a consistency that allows you to make a dot of sauce that will stand up on a plate, adjusting the liquid a bit to make it thicker or thinner. Put the sauce in a squeeze bottle. The miso-lemon sauce can be stored overnight in the refrigerator.

7 When you are ready to serve, have four warmed plates waiting, and preheat the oven or toaster oven to 500°F. Heat the nori butter in a saucepan. Bring the miso sauce back to room temperature, if necessary.

8 Brush the asparagus with the nori butter. Spread the asparagus on a baking sheet and reheat them in the oven (this should just take about 3 minutes).

9 To serve, arrange 6 asparagus spears in a neat row on a dinner plate. Drizzle on more of the nori butter. Add neat lines of nori strips and sesame seeds. Make 6 large dots of the miso sauce and top each one with a chive tip. Randomly place bits of blanched lemon zest on the plate. Repeat for the remaining 3 servings. Sprinkle liberally with salt and serve.

grilled chinese broccoli and lemon

VEGAN

GLUTEN-FREE
OPTION

SERVES 4

20 MINUTES

The Korean-French cuisine of chefs Seif Cherchi and Rachel Yang have had a huge impact on Seattle food culture. At Joule, they knocked my socks off with a dish of Chinese broccoli tossed with *Chermoula* (page 331) and grilled. My variation uses *kochujang* (a Korean chile paste, available at Asian grocers), which blends beautifully with the flavor of grilled fresh lemons. The lemons are sliced so thinly that you can eat them too.

If you aren't able to grill, you can also use a grill pan or your broiler to cook these greens. If possible, use the optional smoked salt to bring in some of those smoky flavors.

Chinese broccoli, or *gai lan*, is widely available at Asian markets. It has stems about the thickness of asparagus, tasty leaves that will crisp up on the grill, and small budding tops that resemble our familiar broccoli. The flavor is similar to that of broccoli as well. Be sure to get it scrupulously dry before tossing it with the sauce, to avoid dilution. If you can't find *gai lan*, broccolini makes a fine substitute.

Juice of 1 lemon
2 tablespoons *kochujang* (check the label to make sure it's gluten-free, if needed)
¼ cup extra-virgin olive oil
1 tablespoon toasted sesame oil
2 teaspoons smoked salt or kosher salt
2 teaspoons sugar
Freshly ground black pepper
3 garlic cloves, thinly sliced
1 shallot, thinly sliced
2 bunches *gai lan* (Chinese broccoli) or broccolini, washed and thoroughly dried
1 lemon, scrubbed and very thinly sliced (¹⁄₁₆ inch thick), seeded and ends discarded

1 Prepare an outdoor grill or preheat a grill pan or broiler. If using the broiler, set the rack about 4 inches below the heat source.

2 In a bowl large enough to hold all the ingredients, whisk together the lemon juice and *kochujang*, then gradually whisk in the olive oil and sesame oil to emulsify the dressing. Add the salt, sugar, black pepper, garlic, and shallot and whisk again. Taste and adjust the seasoning. It should be intensely flavored.

3 Add the *gai lan* and thinly sliced lemon and toss to coat generously.

4 Place the *gai lan* and lemons on the grill, perpendicular to the grid, or on a rimmed baking sheet if using the broiler. Cook, turning just once or twice, until the *gai lan* is starting to brown in spots, about 12 minutes. You should be able to pierce the stems with a knife without too much resistance, but they will be distinctly crisp-tender, not fully tender. Season with a bit more salt and a few grinds of black pepper, and serve hot.

brussels sprout and apple hash

This dish has those sweet and savory flavors that speak of fall, and especially of Thanksgiving. Although I think of it as a side dish that goes well with mac & cheese or a rustic soup and salad, I've also been known to fry up a plate just for myself, add a slice of toasted artisanal wheat bread, and call it dinner.

Many variations are possible. You could add toasted pecans, hazelnuts, or dried cherries; change the champagne vinegar to apple cider vinegar, sherry vinegar, or orange juice; or even replace the apple with a crisp pear.

3 tablespoons unsalted butter
Half a medium-size white onion, finely diced
Kosher salt
1 crisp apple (such as Pink Lady), peeled, cored, and finely diced
1 pound Brussels sprouts, bottoms trimmed and sliced about ¼ inch thick
    (about 4 cups sliced)
2 fresh sage leaves, thinly sliced
½ teaspoon minced fresh rosemary leaves
2 teaspoons champagne vinegar
2 teaspoons honey

1   Melt the butter in a large skillet over medium heat. Add the onion and a pinch of salt and cook until beginning to brown, about 4 minutes.

2   Add the apple and a pinch of salt. Raise the heat slightly and cook, stirring occasionally, until the apple starts to brown, about 2 minutes.

3   Add the Brussels sprouts, a big pinch of salt, the sage, and rosemary, and cook, stirring occasionally, until the sprouts are wilted and well browned, about 10 minutes.

4   Add the champagne vinegar and honey and toss to coast, scraping any delicious browned bits from the bottom of the pan. Taste and adjust the seasonings; it will likely need more salt, and you may also want to add more honey or vinegar to suit your taste. Serve hot.

brussels sprout gratin

SERVES 4

40 MINUTES
(25 MINUTES
ACTIVE)

You can make a gratin out of just about anything. Baked in a shallow dish, often with cream, until the top is crispy, a gratin is the essential forerunner of the great American casserole, but with fewer ingredients and a little more attention to detail. The gratin treatment brings out the gentle, sweet side of Brussels sprouts.

The downfall of many gratins is timing; you want the vegetable at the point of perfect tenderness at the same moment the sauce is appropriately thickened and the top crunchy. The best solution is to cook all three components separately and then combine them just long enough to get to know each other in the oven.

To get the Brussels sprouts ready for cooking, remove any tough or spotted loose outer leaves, so that you have a small, tight ball. Trim off a bit of the base but leave enough intact to hold the head together.

The Brussels sprouts can be blanched in a big pot of salted water, but they can easily get waterlogged, and you have to dry them very thoroughly to avoid diluting the cream. The microwave is probably the better way to cook the vegetables quickly and lightly without getting them soggy. Just be sure to keep an eye on them or you'll be in overcooked, cabbage-y, sulfur-smell territory.

In the same vein, I think it is better to make the reduced cream sauce on the stovetop, rather than counting on it to thicken in the oven. Unlike other dairy products, cream can be simmered to the desired thickness without scorching or breaking, producing a luxurious flavor and texture without adding any starch.

Although there are several steps in this recipe, you can actually prep the sauce, parcook the sprouts, and toast the bread crumbs at the same time, so the dish comes together quickly.

I like to serve this gratin with a comforting soup like White Bean and Kale Soup (page 94) or Celery Soup with *Fregola Sarda* or Israeli Couscous (page 86), or with an entrée portion of Classic Chopped Salad (page 111).

4 tablespoons (½ stick) unsalted butter
1 small white onion, thinly sliced
2 garlic cloves, thinly sliced
2 teaspoons minced fresh oregano or 1 teaspoon dried
2 cups heavy cream
1 teaspoon kosher salt, plus additional as needed
Freshly ground black pepper
Nutmeg (preferably freshly grated)
3 cups trimmed and cleaned Brussels sprouts (see headnote)
1 cup Homemade Bread Crumbs (page 345) or panko
½ cup grated Parmigiano-Reggiano or Grana Padano

1 Preheat the oven to 450°F.

2 Melt 2 tablespoons of the butter in a saucepan over medium heat. Add the onion and garlic and cook until the onion is beginning to soften, about 2 minutes. Add the oregano, heavy cream, and 1 teaspoon salt. Bring to a simmer, then reduce the heat to barely maintain a bubble. Cook, stirring occasionally, until the mixture has thickened enough to coat the back of a spoon, about 15 minutes.

3 When the sauce is sufficiently thick, add several grinds of black pepper and a few gratings of fresh nutmeg (or a nice pinch of pre-ground). Taste and adjust seasoning.

4 Meanwhile, put the Brussels sprouts in a microwave-safe bowl with a few tablespoons of water, cover with plastic wrap, pierce the wrap a few times with a knife, and microwave for about 5 minutes, stopping to stir occasionally, until you can just pierce the sprouts with a fork. If they start to smell cabbage-y, stop cooking. Drain and set aside.

5 Melt the remaining 2 tablespoons butter in a skillet and toast the bread crumbs with a pinch of salt until nicely browned.

6 Place the sprouts in a shallow gratin dish, preferably just big enough to hold them snugly in a single layer. Pour the cream sauce over them. Bake until you can see that the sauce is starting to bubble, 5 to 8 minutes.

7 Top with the bread crumbs and cheese, and return the dish to the oven until the bread crumbs are golden brown, about 3 more minutes. Serve hot.

five-minute indian-style cabbage

VEGAN OPTION

GLUTEN-FREE

SERVES 4

5 MINUTES

This cabbage side dish is great to have in your arsenal, because it comes together in 5 minutes flat and makes a big and flavorful addition to an Indian spread. I break out some variation of it when I'm making a curry, rice, and raita and feel the need for one more dish to round out the meal.

Everything in the cabbage family goes great with mustard, so mustard seeds are the primary flavoring. If you happen to have mustard oil, use that instead of the vegetable oil to intensify the mustard flavor. Be sure to have all of chopping done and your spices measured in advance, because once the mustard seeds hit the hot oil, you have to move quickly.

While the cabbage is delicious made with just mustard, cumin, turmeric, and cayenne, this dish lends itself to improvisation. You can change it up every time you make it by adding some—or all—of the optional flavorings.

1 tablespoon vegetable oil, clarified butter (ghee), or mustard oil, or more to taste
1 tablespoon black mustard seeds
½ teaspoon ground cumin
½ teaspoon ground turmeric
¼ teaspoon cayenne pepper
Optional flavorings: minced garlic, grated fresh ginger, unsweetened shredded
   coconut, sliced fresh chiles or dried hot red pepper flakes, garam masala
Half a head green cabbage, cored and cut into ¼-inch-wide strips
¾ teaspoon kosher salt
Fresh cilantro leaves or fresh lemon juice (or both), for garnish

1 Heat a large skillet or wok over medium-high heat. Add the oil, wait 10 seconds, and immediately add the mustard seeds.

2 As soon as the seeds start to pop, pull the skillet off of the heat and add the cumin, turmeric, cayenne, and any optional ingredients you may be using, and stir for 10 more seconds. Move quickly here so you infuse the oil with flavor but don't burn anything.

3 Add the cabbage and salt, return the skillet to the heat, and raise the heat to its highest setting. Stir-fry until crisp-tender, about 1 minute, or tender, 2 to 3 minutes, according to your preference. Taste and adjust the seasoning.

4 Garnish with cilantro or a squirt of lemon juice (or both) and serve hot.

FLAVOR PROFILES. When chefs talk about "flavor profiles," they mean the characteristic tastes and aromas that define a dish or a cuisine.

All food cultures have a set of ingredients that are used frequently in their dishes, with varying techniques and in different combinations. When you understand these profiles and work within them, you give yourself the freedom to improvise, knowing that you can't go too far wrong.

As you learn more about each cuisine, you'll become of aware of regional variations. For example, Sicily is known particularly for capers, pine nuts, pistachios, citrus, and North African spices, all of which are used much less in the cooking of mainland Italy.

Here are just a few national flavor profiles to get you thinking:

JAPAN
soy sauce, miso, rice vinegar, nori, kombu, sesame seeds and sesame oil, mirin, sake, wasabi

INDIA
clarified butter (ghee), every imaginable dried spice (but rarely dried herbs), cilantro, onion, mustard oil, ginger

SPAIN
garlic, olive oil, olives, smoked paprika (*pimentón*), lemon, tomato, saffron, sherry vinegar, flatleaf parsley

MEXICO
chile peppers, Mexican oregano, cumin, lime, garlic

THAILAND
fresh and dried chile peppers, coconut milk, ginger, cilantro, lemongrass, lime leaf, Thai basil, tamarind

red wine–braised cabbage

VEGAN

GLUTEN-FREE

SERVES 4

40 MINUTES
(10 MINUTES
ACTIVE)

I lived in Milwaukee for several years, and my downstairs neighbor was an elderly German woman who cooked cabbage for hours, until the sulfurous smells penetrated every corner of the apartment building. In spite of that trauma, I love well-prepared braised cabbage. The key is to cook it enough to be meltingly tender, but not so much that it starts to break down.

For a variation, use green cabbage instead of red, and replace the red wine with a dry white wine or a dark ale, adding a tablespoon of Dijon mustard in either case.

The exact sizes of onion, leek, and cabbage aren't critical in this dish. Just use what you have and I promise it will braise down into a luscious pile of tender vegetables. Serve with Crispy Polenta Cakes with White Beans and Morels (page 194) for a real treat.

2 tablespoons extra-virgin olive oil (butter is good, too, if you don't need the dish to be vegan)
1 white onion, thinly sliced
1 large leek, white and light green parts only, cut into thin half-moons and thoroughly rinsed
1 smallish red cabbage, cored and thinly sliced
1½ cups dry red wine
1 teaspoon caraway seeds
Freshly ground black pepper
1½ teaspoons kosher salt, plus additional as needed

1 Put the oil in a 4-quart or larger Dutch oven (or other pot with a lid) over medium-high heat. Add the onion and leek, and cook until the vegetables start to soften, about 3 minutes, stirring occasionally.

2 Add the cabbage, wine, caraway seeds, a few grinds of black pepper, and salt, and mix well. Bring to a simmer, reduce the heat to medium-low, cover, and cook until the cabbage is fairly tender, about 20 minutes.

3 Remove the lid and continue cooking until the cabbage is quite tender and the liquid is reduced to just about ⅛ inch on the bottom of the pot, about 10 minutes more. Taste and adjust seasoning, adding a little more salt if needed. Serve hot.

stir-fried corn with lemongrass

VEGAN
GLUTEN-FREE
SERVES 4 TO 6
20 MINUTES

Corn has a great affinity for the Southeast Asian flavors of lemongrass, lime, ginger, and chiles. Sautéeing it over high heat with these aromatics makes a bright, flavorful side dish. Try it with the Quinoa Cakes (page 193) for a perfect late-summer dinner.

This is one recipe where frozen corn won't do. If you try to use it still frozen, it will lower the heat too much, and if you defrost first, the kernels will be soggy.

3 tablespoons vegetable oil
Half a red onion, finely diced
2 stalks lemongrass, tender parts only, minced (see below)
1-inch piece fresh ginger, peeled and minced
3 garlic cloves, minced
2 kaffir lime leaves (optional)
2 or more small hot green chiles (optional), minced
2 medium yellow summer squash or zucchini, diced
1 yellow bell pepper, diced
Grated zest of 1 lime
Kernels from 5 ears sweet corn
1 teaspoon kosher salt
Juice of 2 limes
1½ cups halved cherry tomatoes
3 scallions, white parts only, thinly sliced
Freshly ground black pepper
Flaky sea salt (such as Maldon)

1 Place a wok or a large skillet over very high heat. When the wok is very hot, add the vegetable oil, onion, lemongrass, ginger, garlic, kaffir lime leaves (if using), and chiles (if using). Stir-fry until fragrant, about 1 minute.

2 Add the squash, bell pepper, and lime zest, and stir-fry for 1 minute. Add the corn and salt and stir-fry until tender, 2 to 3 minutes.

3 Stir in the lime juice and turn off the heat. Adjust the seasoning as needed. Remove the kaffir lime leaves.

4 Transfer to a serving bowl and top with the cherry tomatoes, scallions, a grind of fresh black pepper, and a few flakes of sea salt. Serve hot.

PREPARING LEMONGRASS. Remove and discard all but the bottom 3 inches, keeping only the nearly white portion. Trim ¼ inch off the root end. Remove the tough outer layers so you have only fairly tender stalk. Put that stalk on your cutting board and address it lovingly but firmly with the bottom of a saucepan or the side of a cleaver. Whack it several times, until it is rather flattened. Now mince the squashed bits, and it is ready to use in any recipe.

roasted purple cauliflower
with sherry vinaigrette

VEGAN

SERVES 6

**45 MINUTES
(15 MINUTES
ACTIVE)**

I invented this dish one day when I got off work at 2:45, and my wife informed me that we'd been invited to a potluck and needed to leave at 4:30. I knew we had nothing in the house, so I swung by the nearest store and grabbed the first interesting produce item that caught my eye: purple cauliflower.

The restaurant where I was working at the time, Café Flora, is well known for a vegetarian Caesar salad that uses fried capers to replace some of the saltiness that omnivores get from anchovies. I realized that the same capers would be great with roasted cauliflower, and I added a sherry vinaigrette to bring it all together.

You can certainly make this recipe with white, yellow, or green cauliflower. They all taste similar, so the difference is mainly visual.

FOR THE DRESSING
2 tablespoons sherry vinegar
1 tablespoon fresh lemon juice
1 garlic clove, minced
1/2 teaspoon kosher salt
5 tablespoons extra-virgin olive oil

FOR THE BREAD CRUMBS
1 cup Homemade Bread Crumbs (page 345)
2 garlic cloves, minced
2 tablespoons extra-virgin olive oil

FOR THE CAULIFLOWER
2 heads purple cauliflower (about 4 pounds total, before trimming)
3 tablespoons extra-virgin olive oil
1/2 teaspoon kosher salt
1/4 cup capers
1/2 cup vegetable oil
1/2 cup jarred roasted piquillo peppers or roasted red peppers, thinly sliced
Freshly ground black pepper
1 handful fresh flatleaf parsley leaves, minced, for garnish

1 Preheat the oven to 400°F using convection, or 425°F without convection.
2 *For the dressing:* Stir together the sherry vinegar, lemon juice, garlic, and salt in a small bowl. Drizzle in the olive oil, whisking continuously. Taste and adjust the seasoning, and set aside.
3 *For the bread crumbs:* Toss the bread crumbs with the minced garlic and olive oil, and set aside.

4 *For the cauliflower:* Break the cauliflower into large bite-sized florets. Peel the stem and chop into bite-size pieces.

5 Toss the cauliflower with the olive oil and salt, place on a rimmed baking sheet, and roast, tossing occasionally, until the cauliflower is quite tender with significant brown spots, about 20 minutes. You don't have real roasted flavor until you see those caramelized bits.

6 Meanwhile, rinse the capers and dry them well on paper towels. Heat the vegetable oil in a very small saucepan or skillet over medium-high heat. Carefully add the capers. Watch out for spattering! Fry until the capers are quite dark but not burned, about 1 minute, then remove with a slotted spoon and drain on paper towels.

7 When the cauliflower is done, let it cool on the baking sheet for a few minutes. Add the capers and red peppers. Toss with the vinaigrette, adding a little at a time until you reach your preferred level of saturation. I like it to be highly flavored but not drenched. Taste and adjust salt and pepper.

8 Set the oven on broil. Put the dressed cauliflower in an attractive, broiler-proof serving dish and top with the bread crumbs.

9 Place under the broiler long enough to make the bread crumbs nice and toasty, about 3 minutes. Garnish with the parsley and serve hot or warm.

lemony celery root (apio)

VEGAN

GLUTEN-FREE

SERVES 4

45 MINUTES
(10 MINUTES
ACTIVE)

Saying that the Sephardic relatives on my wife's side of the family like lemony foods is like saying that Superman has a firm handshake. Almost any vegetable can be served with enough lemon juice to make civilians pucker up in surprise. It took me a while to get used to this style of cooking, but now I adore it.

Celery root (also known as celeriac, or *apio* in Ladino, the Judeo-Spanish language my relatives speak) is perfect for this treatment. All you have to do is simmer the root in lemony water until it is tender and the liquid is reduced to a thin sauce. I like this dish best served cold, with good artisanal bread to mop up every drop.

This is a very simple side dish. It goes well with entrées that are based on cheese or pastry, as the bright lemony flavor will cut through any heaviness.

1 large celery root, peeled and sliced into generous ¼-inch-thick half-moons
1 carrot, peeled and cut into ¼-inch-thick rounds
1 tablespoon extra-virgin olive oil
Juice of 2 lemons
1 teaspoon sugar
1 teaspoon kosher salt

1   Combine the celery root, carrot, oil, lemon juice, sugar, and salt in a medium-size saucepan. Add just enough water to barely cover the vegetables. Bring to a boil, reduce the heat to a simmer, cover, and cook for 30 minutes.

2   Remove the lid and continue cooking until the celery root is completely tender, about 10 more minutes. Using a slotted spoon, transfer the vegetables to a serving bowl. Increase the heat under the saucepan and boil the liquid until it's reduced by approximately half. It won't be thick, as a sauce would be, but it will have a slight body to it. Taste and adjust the seasoning. Pour over the vegetables. Serve warm or chilled.

roasted cipollini onions and beets

VEGAN

GLUTEN-FREE

SERVES 4

65 MINUTES
(20 MINUTES
ACTIVE)

A slightly sweet-and-sour dressing (*agrodolce*, as the Italians call it) elevates this simple side dish of roasted onions and beets. It goes well with a savory tart, as a garnish on a plate of couscous, or over a sharp bitter green such as escarole.

Cipollini are small, rather flat onions that you can find at farmers' markets, Italian shops, or gourmet grocers. Don't confuse them with pearl onions, which are too small for this dish. You can also make this with golden beets instead of red ones, in which case use white wine vinegar instead of red so as not to ruin the beets' color.

1 pound beets
2 pounds cipollini onions
2 tablespoons extra-virgin olive oil
¼ cup red wine vinegar
1 teaspoon kosher salt, plus additional as needed
2 teaspoons sugar
Freshly ground black pepper

1 Preheat the oven to 400°F.

2 Peel the beets and cut into bite-size chunks (roughly ¾-inch cubes).

3 Remove a slice from the top and bottom of each onion, peel, and cut into chunks approximately the same size as the beet chunks.

4 Put the beets and onions in a roasting pan large enough to hold them in a single layer. Toss with the olive oil. Whisk together the vinegar, salt, sugar, and several grinds of black pepper. Pour this mixture over the vegetables and toss again.

5 Roast, tossing occasionally, until the vegetables are completely tender and caramelizing in spots, 45 minutes to 1 hour. Taste and add salt if needed. Serve hot or warm.

spicy tamarind-glazed potatoes

VEGAN

GLUTEN-FREE
OPTION

SERVES 4

30 MINUTES

There is a famous Thai dish known as son-in-law eggs. You'll get the joke if you realize that "eggs" in Thai refers to the same part of the male anatomy as *huevos* does in Spanish. To make son-in-law eggs, peeled hard-cooked eggs are pan-fried or deep-fried until the outside gets wrinkled and brown, and then they are halved and served with a spicy tamarind sauce.

My vegan variation uses small potatoes instead of eggs. The sauce is quite fiery, but the creamy flesh of the potatoes mitigates the pain. Be sure to warn your guests not to eat the whole dried chiles, or remove them before serving.

These potatoes are great as a side dish in an Indian meal. Or—and this might sound like crazy fusion-food talk—my wife and I have also been known to wrap them up in tortillas with refried beans and sour cream and make burritos.

2 pounds very small (2- to 3-bite) red-skinned potatoes
Kosher salt
4 tablespoons vegetable oil
10 thin, dried red chiles (such as chile de árbol)
2 garlic cloves, minced
⅓ cup minced shallot
¼ cup palm sugar (break it up before measuring) or dark brown sugar
3 tablespoons tamarind concentrate or 5 tablespoons sieved tamarind pulp
** (see page 261)**
½ cup water
1 tablespoon soy sauce (use a wheat-free version for gluten-free)
½ cup shelled unsalted peanuts, toasted
1 handful fresh cilantro leaves and tender stems
4 scallions, white and light green parts only, thinly sliced

1   Place the potatoes in a pot that holds at least 4 quarts. Fill nearly to the top with cold water and add 2 tablespoons salt. Place over high heat and bring to a boil, then lower the heat and continue to cook the potatoes until tender but not falling apart, usually about 10 minutes after they reach a boil. Drain.

2   In the same pot, heat 3 tablespoons of the oil over high heat. Add the potatoes and 1 teaspoon salt and cook, tossing occasionally and gently, until the potatoes are browned in spots, about 8 minutes. Remove the potatoes, leaving as much oil behind as possible.

3   Lower the heat under the pot to medium. Add the remaining 1 tablespoon oil, the chiles, garlic, shallot, and palm sugar. Cook for 1 minute. Add the tamarind concentrate, water, and soy sauce. Cook, stirring well, until the sauce is slightly sticky, about 5 minutes. Taste and adjust the seasoning; the sauce should be quite intense.

4 Add the potatoes and cook, tossing occasionally, until the sauce glazes the potatoes, about 5 minutes. Be careful not to let the sauce burn.
5 Just before serving, stir in the peanuts. Top with the cilantro and scallions. Serve immediately.

TAMARIND. Tamarind comes from the pod of a tropical tree of the same name. It has a tart, fruity taste that is beloved in Southeast Asian, Indian, and Mexican cuisines. It can be bought as whole pods, semi-dried pulp with seeds, or in concentrated thick-syrup form.

If you buy the pods or pulp, they must be soaked in boiling water. You then remove the skin, seeds, and strings and force the remaining pulp through a fine-mesh sieve. Honestly, this is a messy, sticky, tedious job. I generally buy the concentrate instead. The brand you will usually find is called Tamicon. Look for it at Asian or Indian groceries.

potatoes and chanterelles in red wine

GLUTEN-FREE

SERVES 2 TO 4

30 MINUTES

I came up with this dish when I had a pile of Rose Finn Apple fingerling potatoes from our garden, and I spotted magnificent chanterelle mushrooms at my favorite co-op. Sometimes the chanterelles I find are either half dried-up or soggy and on the verge of rotting. Not these—they were plump, firm, and fully arresting. My coworkers were a bit amused when I veered off from our afternoon coffee run directly into the store and returned to work with a big bag of those beauties.

This is simple to make; everything is sautéed until tender and caramelized, and then a quick pan sauce is made by deglazing with red wine and finishing with a little sweet butter. The result is rich and earthy, with a French feel. You can eat the mushrooms and shallots and then mash the spuds into the sauce to mop everything up.

This dish makes an elegant side to a main-course savory pie or pastry, or you could do a mushroom-themed meal of small plates, with Roasted Maitake Mushrooms in Smoky Tea Broth (page 80) and Chanterelle *Banh Mi* Bites (page 61).

This is one case where I wouldn't substitute regular button mushrooms, though morels would be delicious.

4 tablespoons (½ stick) unsalted butter
2 cups small fingerling potatoes or other small potatoes, cut up if larger than 2 bites
1 cup (or more) chanterelle mushrooms, thoroughly wiped clean
4 medium or 2 very large shallots, cut into large bite-size chunks
½ teaspoon minced fresh rosemary leaves
½ teaspoon kosher salt
½ cup water, plus additional as necessary
¾ cup dry red wine
1 handful fresh flatleaf parsley leaves, minced
Freshly ground black pepper

1 Melt 2 tablespoons of the butter in a medium skillet over medium heat.

2 Add the potatoes, mushrooms, shallots, rosemary, and salt, and toss to coat. Cook, stirring occasionally, for about 8 minutes, trying to get a little browning going but without burning anything.

3 Add the water, cover the pan, and reduce the heat to a simmer.

4 Cook, stirring occasionally, until the potatoes are tender, about 15 minutes, adding more water as needed to prevent burning.

5 When the potatoes are cooked, remove the lid and raise the heat to cook off any remaining liquid. Warm a serving platter in a low (200°F) oven.

6 Transfer all of the vegetables to the warmed platter. Pour the wine into the skillet and raise the heat to medium-high. Cook, stirring and scraping any browned bits off the bottom of the pan into the sauce. Cut the remaining 2 tablespoons butter into small pieces and whisk them vigorously into the sauce, which should have a nice sheen. This whole step should take just a couple of minutes, reducing and thickening the sauce slightly.

7 Strain the sauce if you prefer a more refined look. Spoon the sauce over the vegetables, top with the parsley and a grind of black pepper, and serve immediately.

non-traditional arroz verde

VEGAN

GLUTEN-FREE

SERVES 4

40 MINUTES
(10 MINUTES
ACTIVE)

The traditional recipe for *arroz verde* involves cooking rice with a puree of poblano peppers and herbs. It is truly delicious, and I'd choose it in a heartbeat over the typical red rice you find at Mexican restaurants in the United States. You can serve this with any of the Mexican entrées in this book, such as the Swiss Chard and Tomatillo Enchiladas (page 236) or the Grilled Tofu and Pepper Tacos (page 144).

One day when making *arroz verde* I asked myself, "Why am I cooking all of these delicious fresh herbs when their raw flavor is so perfect?" So I took a new approach. I omitted the poblanos and simply made a pesto-like puree of herbs, garlic, and a little oil. After I cooked the plain rice, I stirred in the herbs. The result was a rice that has a vibrant, fresh flavor and a color to match, and I've made it this way ever since.

The recipe calls for 2 cups of fresh herbs. I've given a suggestion in the recipe, but you can vary the herbs according to what you have available and what you are serving it with. Small amounts of chives and rosemary are also very welcome. Because the herbs are thoroughly pureed, you can use tender stems of parsley and cilantro as well as the leaves.

1½ cups medium-grain white rice or basmati rice
1 cup lightly packed fresh flatleaf parsley leaves and tender stems
½ cup lightly packed fresh cilantro leaves and tender stems
¼ cup lightly packed fresh oregano leaves
¼ cup lightly packed fresh mint or dill leaves
2 garlic cloves, coarsely chopped
¼ cup extra-virgin olive oil
1½ teaspoons kosher salt or flaky sea salt

1 Cook the rice in a rice cooker or on the stove according to package directions.

2 In a food processor, combine the herbs, garlic, and olive oil. Process until pureed.

3 Just before serving, stir the herb puree and salt into the rice. Taste and add more salt as needed. Serve hot.

jamaican rice and peas

VEGAN

GLUTEN-FREE

SERVES 4

40 MINUTES
(10 MINUTES
ACTIVE)

Rice and peas is a classic Jamaican dish, traditionally served on Sundays. But in this case, "peas" actually refers to kidney beans, pigeon peas, or cowpeas. The rice is richly flavored with coconut milk, garlic, crushed scallions, thyme, and, if you dare, a Scotch bonnet or habanero pepper. It goes well with *Dal Poori Roti* (page 139).

Even though the pepper is left whole, it will still infuse the dish with a subtle bit of heat if you choose to use it. For a bit more spice, cut a slit in the pepper, or, if you are really crazy, you can cut it up—wearing rubber gloves!

I prefer to make rice and peas in a rice cooker, but if you want to do it on the stovetop, the recipe offers that option.

If you make the beans from scratch, you can substitute 1 cup of the bean liquid for part of the water in the recipe for a "dirty rice" look with a slightly earthier flavor.

2 cups basmati rice (or 3 measures with the cup that comes with most rice cookers)
1 (14-ounce) can coconut milk
5 scallions, white and light green parts only
1½ cups cooked kidney beans (or other beans; see headnote), drained,
 or 1 (15-ounce) can kidney or other beans, rinsed and drained
2 garlic cloves, chopped
3 big sprigs fresh thyme
1 teaspoon kosher salt
Freshly ground black pepper
1 Scotch bonnet or habanero chile (optional; see headnote)

1 If using a rice cooker, put the 3 measures of rice in the pot, add the coconut milk, and top with enough water to reach the 3-cup line, plus ¼ cup more water. If using the stove, choose a pot with a tight-fitting lid and combine 2 cups rice, the coconut milk, and 2¾ cups water.

2 Crush 4 of the scallions with a rolling pin or the back of your knife. Add them to the pot, along with the beans, garlic, thyme, salt, a few grinds of black pepper, and the whole chile pepper, if using. Stir everything together.

3 If using a rice cooker, turn on and run a normal cycle. If using the stove, bring to a boil, cover, and reduce to a bare simmer; cook until all of the water is absorbed, about 15 minutes.

4 To serve, remove the whole scallions, thyme sprigs, and chile. Fluff the rice and turn out into a bowl. Garnish with the remaining scallion, thinly sliced, and serve hot.

red curry fried rice

VEGAN

GLUTEN-FREE

SERVES 4

20 MINUTES

Chunks of seared pineapple provide just a bit of sweet counterbalance to the complex heat of the red curry in this unusual fried rice.

You can make this dish with Thai jasmine rice, but I also really like it with basmati. The long grains fry up beautifully. Day-old rice is perfect, but if you don't have any, just make a fresh pot, spread it out on a baking sheet, and let it cool in the refrigerator for as long as possible. Steaming-hot rice is too moist on the outside to fry properly.

If you don't have homemade Red Curry Paste (page 348), store-bought paste can work in this too; if it is important that it be vegetarian, read the label carefully, as many of them contain shrimp paste. You can doctor it up with some grated fresh ginger to get a livelier taste.

This rice goes beautifully with Caramel-Cooked Tofu (page 189) or Crispy Vietnamese Crêpes (page 184).

1½ cups bite-size chunks fresh pineapple
¼ cup vegetable oil
Half a small white onion, finely diced
2 to 4 tablespoons Red Curry Paste (page 348, or use store-bought)
4 cups cooked and cooled jasmine or basmati rice (day-old if possible)
1 teaspoon kosher salt
1 handful fresh cilantro leaves or sliced scallions, white and light green
   parts only, for garnish
4 lime wedges

1 Heat a large skillet (preferably cast iron) or wok over very high heat. When the skillet is searing hot, add the pineapple and cook, stirring once in a while, until it gets some brown spots and the flavor intensifies, about 4 minutes. (The sugars in the pineapple will caramelize best in a dry skillet.) Transfer to a bowl and return the skillet to the heat.

2 Heat the oil in the skillet, and when it shimmers, add the onion. Cook for 30 seconds. Add the curry paste, and cook for 10 seconds. Add the rice, and break up any chunks, stirring to distribute the curry paste. Add the salt.

3 Continue to cook, stirring occasionally, for a few minutes. This dish tastes best if some of the rice is allowed to get brown and crispy.

4 Return the pineapple to the pan and stir it through the rice. Cook for a minute or so to reheat the pineapple. Taste and adjust the seasoning.

5 Garnish with cilantro or scallions. Serve with lime wedges.

PREPARING A PINEAPPLE. The best way to prepare a pineapple is to remove the crown, cut off the base, stand it up, and use a chef's knife to cut off the skin from top to bottom. Go ahead and cut deep enough to get all of the spiky bits—otherwise, you'll spend a ton of time picking out all of the "eyes." Cut the pineapple into vertical quarters and use your knife to remove the core from each quarter. The whole process only takes a couple of minutes, and at this point it's ready for final cutting as the recipe directs.

SALT. Salt is the most basic taste enhancer, and the one home cooks are most afraid of. I think there are two fears. First, in most cases oversalted food can't be easily fixed. So rather than take a chance, many cooks simply think, "Well, if they want more, they can just add it at the table." The problem is, food needs salt during the cooking process. The salt helps extract moisture and concentrate flavor, and it needs to be in the interior of the food when you bite into it.

Second, people are concerned about the link between sodium and hypertension. If you are worried about this, I can do you no greater service than to refer you to the chapter on salt in Jeffrey Steingarten's *The Man Who Ate Everything* (Vintage, 1998), which you should read anyhow because the whole book is informative and hilarious. Obviously, if your health-care professional has told you to minimize salt, you should listen, but if you are just doing it out of a general free-floating anxiety, read Steingarten's well-researched piece and see what you think.

To fully appreciate salt's role in making food appetizing, try a head-to-head comparison. Scramble two eggs with absolutely no salt, and two more with a couple of good pinches, and taste them side by side. Or spread a piece of good bread with unsalted butter, and then try it with and without a bit of salt sprinkled on top. In both cases, without the salt you have a sort of bland, neutral sweetness. The salt balances the sweetness and allows you to taste much more complexity and subtlety.

Good cooks salt food as they go and taste frequently. When sautéing, I do this as each group of ingredients is added to the pan. If you look through my recipes, you'll see that many steps include an instruction like "taste and adjust the seasoning" or "salt to taste." One of my great fears when writing recipes is that those instructions will be ignored, and salt will be only an afterthought.

Palates differ, ingredients differ, salts differ, and often what is needed is just a pinch or two—too little to be worth measuring. Keep an open container of kosher salt next to your stove, and add a bit at a time until you suddenly hear the flavors sing. With practice, you'll hear that chorus easily.

You'll notice I said kosher salt. I use it almost exclusively while cooking (as opposed to putting a final sprinkle on a finished dish—for that, see Finishing Salts, page 285), because the larger grain size makes it easier to pick up and distribute. For baking, you have to hope a recipe author tells you whether kosher or fine-grain table salt is intended, as they have different weights for the same volume. Even kosher salts can vary in weight by brand. Diamond Crystal Kosher Salt, which I prefer, weighs 3.2 grams per teaspoon; Morton Kosher Salt and table salt are much heavier, weighing around 5.4 grams per teaspoon.

persian rice pilaf with a crispy crust (chelow with tahdig)

GLUTEN-FREE

SERVES 6

2 HOURS AND
45 MINUTES
(15 MINUTES
ACTIVE)

Just about every culture that cooks rice has a crispy variation, whether it is the beloved crust on the bottom of the Spanish paella, fried rice in Chinese cuisine, or Indian *bhel poori* (a snack of crispy puffed rice, potatoes, and chutney). For Persians, the basic basmati rice pilaf with a crust is called *chelow*, and the crust itself is *tahdig*.

Although it is a bit more work than just tossing rice in the rice cooker and pushing the button, I think you will find the results more than worth the extra effort. You do need to have the forethought to soak the grain a couple hours in advance.

The crust on the bottom of the pot can be encouraged with a mixture of yogurt and egg, or a layer of sliced potatoes, or even flatbread. I've opted for the yogurt and egg approach in this recipe, which is based on the method explained in Jeffrey Alford and Naomi Duguid's wonderful book *Seductions of Rice* (Artisan, 1998).

I'm crazy about herbs in my rice, especially dill. Persians use copious quantities of herbs, sometimes even treating them like vegetables. Layering them into this pilaf makes it even tastier. You can serve this instead of couscous with Chickpea and Green Olive Tagine (page 215) or as part of any Middle Eastern meal.

2½ cups basmati rice
¼ cup plus 1 tablespoon kosher salt
4 tablespoons (½ stick) unsalted butter
1 large egg beaten with 2 tablespoons plain whole-milk yogurt
½ cup minced fresh dill, plus a sprig for garnish
½ cup fresh flatleaf parsley leaves
¼ cup thinly sliced scallions, white and light green parts only
1 teaspoon saffron crumbled into 2 tablespoons hot water (optional)
Flaky sea salt (such as Maldon)

1 Put the rice in a 5-quart Dutch oven or other good-size pot with a tight-fitting lid, cover with water by a couple of inches, stir in ¼ cup salt, and soak the rice for at least 2 hours. Drain thoroughly.

2 In the same pot, bring 4 quarts water to a boil; add 1 tablespoon salt. Add the rice and boil until is the grains are mostly tender with a slight bit of bite left in the center, 2 to 5 minutes. Drain and rinse with warm water. Set the rice aside.

3 Return the pot to the stove and melt the butter over medium-high heat. Stir ½ cup rice into the yogurt-egg mixture. When the butter stops foaming, spread the rice-yogurt mixture evenly over the bottom of the pot; it should immediately start sizzling.

▼ ▼ ▼

4 Mound the rest of the rice on top, layering in the herbs and scallions as you go. The rice should look like a small hill in the pot. Use a chopstick to poke a few holes in the mound to allow steam to move. Wrap the pot lid in a dish towel and cover the pot tightly (making sure the towel won't catch on fire!). Reduce the heat to medium-low and cook for 30 minutes. Taste a few grains to make sure they are fluffy. Use a fork to check that the crust has formed on the bottom of the pot. If not, raise the heat for a couple of minutes.

5 Scoop most of the rice out onto a serving platter. Mix 1 cup of the rice with the saffron mixture, if using, and spoon it over the plain rice (or mix it in if you prefer). Double-check the crust; if it has not fully formed, cook it a bit longer. It should be deep brown.

6 Lower the bottom of the pot into a sink full of cool water for a minute, which will help the crust release. Use a spatula to break the beautiful, crispy pieces into big shards and lay them over the saffron rice. Finish with a bit of flaky sea salt and a big sprig of dill.

brown butter cornbread

MAKES ONE
8-INCH
SQUARE PAN
OR 10 MUFFINS;
EASILY
DOUBLED IN A
9 x 13-INCH PAN

45 MINUTES
(15 MINUTES
ACTIVE)

Browning the butter before making this cornbread contributes a deep, warm taste. For bonus points, you can add a tablespoon of nonfat milk powder to the butter as it is browning. The extra protein increases the Maillard reactions that are responsible for so many of the flavors we love.

There are two main axes of cornbread variation: the ratio of cornmeal to wheat flour, and the decision to go plain or add things like corn kernels, onions, jalapeño peppers, cheddar, olives, and so forth.

I've seen cornbreads made with anywhere from 25 to 100 percent cornmeal; I like versions that are at least 50 percent cornmeal. I want to taste mostly corn, but when I go too far in that direction, the results are tasty but very crumbly. Fifty percent provides a good balance of tenderness and flavor. Use the freshest, best-quality organic stone-ground cornmeal you can find to maximize the flavor. A coarse grind is preferable.

As far as additions go, I don't have anything against them in principle. It's just that to me, the pure flavor and texture of cornbread with a big pat of sweet cream butter is so perfect, they seem an unnecessary distraction. However, if that's what you like, feel free to fold them into the batter just before baking.

This is the cornbread I serve when I make Chili *Borracho* (page 213).

8 tablespoons (1 stick) unsalted butter
1 tablespoon nonfat milk powder (optional)
2 large eggs
1 cup buttermilk
1 cup coarse stone-ground cornmeal
1 cup all-purpose flour
⅓ cup sugar
1 teaspoon kosher salt
½ teaspoon baking soda

1 Preheat the oven to 375°F and butter an 8-inch square pan (or 10 wells of a muffin tin).
2 Melt the butter in a small saucepan over medium heat. Reduce the heat to medium-low. Whisk in the milk powder, if using. Continue cooking until the butter turns a light brown and has a delicious, nutty aroma, 5 to 10 minutes. Do not skim; you want to keep all those browned milk solids.
3 In a medium-size bowl, whisk together the eggs and buttermilk. If you used the nonfat milk powder, press the brown butter through a strainer to break up any clumps. Drizzle the butter into the buttermilk mixture, whisking constantly to avoid cooking the eggs.

▼ ▼ ▼

4   In a separate bowl large enough to hold all the ingredients, whisk together the cornmeal, flour, sugar, salt, and baking soda.

5   Pour the wet ingredients into the dry mixture and stir just enough to form a batter. It's okay if there are a few lumps. Avoid overbeating, as this could make the cornbread tough.

6   Pour into the pan and bake until cornbread is golden brown and a toothpick inserted in the center comes out clean, about 25 minutes (17 minutes for muffins).

7   Serve forth while still hot, with lots of good sweet butter.

TALKING WITH MY BLOG READERS. This cornbread recipe gets lots of rave reviews, especially from hungry families with kids.

"I work at a summer cooking camp for 8- to 12-year old kids, and one day we made cornbread and gazpacho. I used your cornbread recipe, and really, it is the BEST EVER CORNBREAD! The kids went wild over this . . . they loved making it and even more they loved eating it! This browned butter thing really is magical."—Stephanie

"Having made this recipe Monday evening, I can attest to its greatness! My hungry teenagers and a couple of friends found the cornbread before dinner, and I was lamenting not making a second batch! Mom and Dad got one small piece each."—Barbara

"Recently made this for a wedding party dinner BBQ for 50 people and it was a hit! Comments were great and several folks sought me out to say it was the best item on the serving table."—GrayFeather

Don't forget, this same idea of using brown butter (especially with the extra flavor that comes from adding nonfat milk powder while browning) can be used in any recipe that calls for melted butter, including muffins, pancakes, and even some cookies.

desserts

maple pudding with spiced pecans

GLUTEN-FREE

SERVES 4

15 MINUTES,
PLUS CHILLING
TIME

Making pudding from a box is silly. It is the easiest thing in the world to do from scratch. All you have to do is bring milk to a simmer with cornstarch, sugar, and your choice of flavoring, and you are done. In this recipe, maple syrup serves as both the sweetener and the flavor, so it is even simpler.

You don't *have* to make the spiced pecans, but they do make this pudding a little special (you can also serve them as an accompaniment to the Cheese Course with Maple Pickled Pears on page 302). The smoked paprika adds a subtle background smokiness that makes them taste almost as if they were toasted over a wood fire.

I prefer Grade B maple syrup for most purposes. It is darker and more flavorful than Grade A.

FOR THE PUDDING
3 tablespoons cornstarch
2 cups whole milk
½ cup maple syrup (preferably Grade B)
Kosher salt

FOR THE SPICED PECANS
2 teaspoons sugar
½ cup pecans (halves or pieces)
¼ teaspoon ground cinnamon
Nutmeg (preferably freshly grated)
Smoked paprika
Kosher salt
2 teaspoons unsalted butter

1 *For the pudding:* Put the cornstarch in a bowl and whisk a small splash of milk into it until it makes a smooth slurry. Put the remaining milk into a saucepan and whisk the cornstarch slurry into it. Whisk in the maple syrup and a pinch of salt. Place over medium heat and bring to a simmer, stirring frequently. As soon as it reaches a simmer, you will see the pudding start to thicken. Remove it from the heat and pour into a medium bowl or four ramekins. Cover with plastic wrap and refrigerate until chilled and set.

2 *For the spiced pecans:* In a small skillet over medium heat, cook the sugar and pecans, stirring frequently, until the sugar is melted and the pecans are browned, about 5 minutes. Stir in the cinnamon, a few gratings of nutmeg, a big pinch of smoked paprika, a pinch of salt, and the butter. As soon as the butter is melted and has coated the nuts, remove from the heat and pour the nuts onto a plate to cool. They may stick together somewhat; simply break up the clusters with your hands at serving time.

3 Place about 2 tablespoons of the nuts on each portion of maple pudding and serve.

mango puffs with lemongrass-coconut pudding and black sesame

**MAKES 12
SMALL
PASTRIES**

1 HOUR AND
15 MINUTES
(20 MINUTES
ACTIVE)

These little two-bite desserts are a riff on classic fruit tarts, using an easy home-made coconut milk pudding instead of pastry cream. They are small enough to pass at a cocktail party, and the tropical flavors are pleasantly refreshing.

Black sesame paste is available at better Asian grocery stores, especially those that specialize in Japanese ingredients. It is similar to tahini, but thicker and sweetened and totally addictive. If you can't find it, you can omit it from this recipe and still have a delicious dessert.

FOR THE SHELLS
1 (17-to-20 ounce) package frozen puff pastry
1 large egg beaten with 1 tablespoon water
Sugar

FOR THE COCONUT PUDDING
1 stalk lemongrass
1 (14-ounce) can coconut milk
3 tablespoons sugar
Kosher salt
3 tablespoons cornstarch

TO ASSEMBLE
2 tablespoons black sesame paste
1 ripe mango, peeled and finely diced
Toasted black sesame seeds

1 *For the shells:* Preheat the oven to 400°F. Line a baking sheet with parchment paper or a silicone mat.

2 Unroll the puff pastry, allow to defrost for about 5 minutes, and cut out twelve 2½-inch circles. You may need one or two sheets of the puff pastry, depending on the brand. Wrap any remaining puff pastry tightly in plastic wrap and put it back in the freezer for another use. Place the pastry circles on the baking sheet and brush them with the egg wash. Sprinkle generously with sugar. Bake until puffed and golden brown, about 12 minutes. Set aside to cool.

▼ ▼ ▼

3   *For the coconut pudding:* Cut off and discard all but the bottom 3 inches of the lemongrass. Remove and discard the outer layer. Pound the lemongrass stalk to release the flavors, then chop it finely. Put the lemongrass, coconut milk, sugar, and a pinch of salt in a small saucepan over medium-low heat. Put the cornstarch in a small bowl. When the mixture is near a simmer, take a few tablespoons of it and whisk it into the cornstarch to form a slurry, then whisk that slurry into the saucepan. Whisking constantly, bring the mixture to a bare simmer and keep it there for 1 minute (you should see the pudding start to thicken). Remove from the heat and strain into a shallow bowl. Cover and refrigerate for at least 30 minutes, until cooled and thickened.

4   *To assemble:* Take one pastry shell and use a sharp paring knife to cut a circle out of the top, leaving a ⅜-inch rim all the way around. Carefully lift off the "lid" and reserve. Spoon in 1 tablespoon of the chilled pudding. Put ½ teaspoon black sesame paste in the center of the pudding. Spoon on 2 tablespoons of the mango and sprinkle with the black sesame seeds. Repeat for the remaining shells. Top with the reserved pastry lids and serve immediately.

PUFF PASTRY. You can find puff pastry in the freezer at many grocery stores. I prefer the flavor of brands that use all butter to those that use vegetable shortening. Another option is to make your own puff pastry. There are simplified methods for "rough puff" that you can easily find on the Web. It makes an enjoyable project and you'll learn a lot about pastry in the process.

raspberry-blueberry buckle

What is a buckle? It is a rustic American baked fruit dessert (usually made with berries) in the same general family as cobblers, crisps, crumbles, grunts, and slumps. (Rustic Americans were nothing if not picturesque in their nomenclature.) You make a quick cake batter, mix it with a raft of fresh fruit, top it with a little streusel, and bake. Apparently the name derives from how the streusel top buckles (bends and cracks) in the oven.

I love this buckle made with raspberries and blueberries when they are overflowing out of our farmers' market and refrigerator, but you can use any fruit that could live in a pie: pitted cherries, pears, peaches, apples—heck, even pineapple. Like its cousins, buckle seeks out vanilla ice cream, or just a pour of heavy cream.

I've adapted this recipe from the one in *Joy of Cooking*. For the cake batter, you can use cake flour or all-purpose flour, but my favorite option is whole-wheat pastry flour. It is low in gluten so the crumb will be tender, and you get a little bonus nutrition without any overt signs of eating a "health food."

FOR THE STREUSEL
½ cup sugar
6 tablespoons all-purpose flour
¼ teaspoon ground nutmeg (preferably freshly grated)
¼ teaspoon ground cinnamon
½ teaspoon kosher salt
4 tablespoons (½ stick) unsalted butter, cold and cut into small pieces

FOR THE CAKE
1¾ cups whole-wheat pastry flour
2 teaspoons baking powder
1 teaspoon kosher salt
4 tablespoons (½ stick) unsalted butter, softened
1 cup sugar
1 large egg
1 teaspoon vanilla extract
½ cup whole milk
1½ cups fresh raspberries
1½ cups fresh blueberries

1 *For the streusel:* Whisk the sugar, flour, nutmeg, cinnamon, and salt together in a small bowl. Add the butter and work it into the flour mixture with your fingertips until it resembles coarse cornmeal. It is fine if there are a few larger bits of butter. Refrigerate until ready to use.

2 *For the cake:* Preheat the oven to 350°F. Butter a 9-inch square baking pan.

3 Whisk together the flour, baking powder, and salt.

4 With a stand mixer or handheld mixer, beat the butter, sugar, egg, and vanilla until fluffy, about 4 minutes. Beat in the milk. Gradually add the flour mixture and beat on low speed until just mixed. Do not overbeat, as it will make the cake tough.

5 Gently fold in the fruit. It may seem like there is too much fruit, but don't worry. Spread the batter in the pan, and sprinkle the streusel evenly over the top.

6 Bake until the streusel is browned and a toothpick comes out clean, about 40 minutes. Let cool for 20 minutes and serve while still warm.

rustic peach and nectarine crostata

SERVES 6

1½ HOURS
(30 MINUTES
ACTIVE)

Crostata: pie without the fuss. It can be hard to make a pie (or tart) as pretty as the picture we all envision, cooling on Grandma's windowsill. Crostata takes my inability to make a precise pie and makes a virtue of it! All you have to do is roll the pastry out to a rough circle, layer the fruit in the center, then fold the edges over to make a beautiful, rustic tart.

Peaches and nectarines are a superb choice in midsummer, but you can use just about any fruit that suits your mood.

The recipe calls for you to sprinkle sugar over the pastry before baking. Sanding sugar, which has larger crystals, is ideal because it retains its texture in the oven, but regular granulated sugar will also work fine. You can find sanding sugar in the baking aisle of better grocery stores.

1 recipe Basic Pastry Dough (page 351), chilled for at least 1 hour
4 large ripe peaches and/or nectarines, cut into 10 to 12 slices each (no need to peel)
3 tablespoons unsalted butter, melted
2 tablespoons brown sugar
2 tablespoons granulated sugar (or sanding sugar if available)
Vanilla ice cream (optional)

1 Preheat the oven to 400°F. Line a rimmed baking sheet with a silicone mat or parchment paper.

2 Place the dough on a lightly floured board; flour your rolling pin and, working from the center out and rotating after each push, form a circle about 13 inches in diameter. Roll the pastry up onto your pin and unroll it onto the baking sheet. Refrigerate for 15 minutes.

3 Arrange the fruit in rings (or randomly) on the dough, leaving about a 1½-inch rim around the outside. Fold the rim up around the fruit. You can do it very rustically as it is in the photograph or, if you like, you can do a neater crimp.

4 Brush the edge of the pastry with melted butter and drizzle the rest over the fruit. Sprinkle the brown sugar on the fruit, and the granulated sugar on the pastry.

5 Bake until the juices are bubbling and the crust is nicely golden brown, 40 to 50 minutes.

6 Allow to cool for at least 10 minutes, then slice and serve, with a scoop of vanilla ice cream if you like.

WHY OVEN TEMPERATURE MATTERS. You might think it isn't that big a deal if your oven temperature is off by a little bit—say, 25 degrees. What's the worst that can happen? Maybe your muffins will bake a little faster or slower, but so what? Of course, at lower temperatures the inside has more time to cook before the outside is done, but again, for small variations in temperature, does it really matter?

Well, as Jeff Potter points out in *Cooking for Geeks* (O'Reilly Media, 2010), it turns out there is an important difference between 350°F and 375°F, and that difference has to do with sugar. At 350°F, sugar will turn only a very light caramel color, and the flavor is mostly just sweet. At 375°F, it becomes a dark brown caramel with strong caramel flavor.

So, for example, if you are baking shortbread, you probably want 350°F (or lower), and if you are baking something like Brown Butter Cornbread (page 273) and want it to brown, you need 375°F. So get yourself a good oven thermometer and learn the quirks of your own oven.

caramel apple french toast

SERVES 6

30 MINUTES

This dessert has some of the flavors of apple pie, including a slice of cheddar cheese (a.k.a. the best combination ever), but it looks a bit like a cheeseburger! For a fun and somewhat ambitious little party, you could serve it with the Cheddar-Battered Onion Rings (page 54) and Stout Chocolate Malt (page 298).

FOR THE FRENCH TOAST
1 cup whole milk
3 large eggs, lightly beaten
1 teaspoon vanilla extract
¼ teaspoon kosher salt
Ground cinnamon
12 pieces (2 x 2 x ½-inch) brioche or challah
½ cup vegetable oil

FOR THE MAPLE WHIPPED CREAM
1 cup heavy cream
3 tablespoons maple syrup (preferably Grade B)
Kosher salt

TO ASSEMBLE
2 tart apples such as Cortland or Granny Smith, peeled
4 tablespoons (½ stick) unsalted butter
1½ cups caramel sauce (store-bought or homemade), warmed
12 thin slices well-aged cheddar
Flaky sea salt (such as Maldon)

1 *For the French toast:* Whisk together the milk, eggs, vanilla, salt, and a pinch of cinnamon. Arrange the brioche slices in a shallow dish just large enough to hold them. Pour the custard over the bread and allow it to soak in for about 5 minutes, turning once.

2 Heat the oil in a skillet over medium-high heat. When the oil is shimmering, lift 4 slices of bread from the dish, let the excess custard drain off, and set them carefully in the oil. Cook, turning once, until well browned on both sides, adjusting the heat as necessary to make sure that they cook through before burning, 4 to 5 minutes total. Transfer to paper towels and cook the remaining pieces. Set aside.

3 *For the maple whipped cream:* Beat the cream, maple syrup, and a pinch of salt to stiff peaks in a mixer with a whisk attachment. Chill.

4   *To assemble:* Slice the apples ½ inch thick, avoiding the core. Melt the butter in a large skillet over medium heat. Cook the apples, turning, until tender and browned on both sides, about 5 minutes total.

5   To serve, pour about 2 tablespoons of the caramel sauce on each serving plate. On each plate, lay down one slice of brioche and top with 2 more tablespoons of sauce. Place an apple slice on top and cover it with 2 thin slices of cheddar. Sprinkle on a few flakes of sea salt. Add a second piece of brioche and a healthy dollop of the maple whipped cream, and serve immediately.

FINISHING SALTS. Finishing with salt can be the detail that turns a good dish into an amazing one. Something about having a few grains of salt meet the palate first is innately appetizing to most people. Think of a well-seasoned French fry: Salt hits your tongue, almost too much so for a second, and then the crisp shell gives way to the fluffy, mild potato. The effect is obvious with fried foods, but almost anything, from a salad to caramels to polenta, will appreciate a minuscule final sprinkle.

Italians have a concept of *capriccioso*, which they apply to chile flakes. Rather than mixing them in completely, they may add them at the last minute to get surprising little pinpricks of heat. Salt works in the same way: It can be more exciting to taste the individual crystals.

There are many wonderful finishing salts from all over the world. Some folks will disagree, but to me the taste differences among them (excluding smoked salts and herb-scented salts and so forth) are quite minor. What counts is appearance and texture. I have quite a few of these salts, but I wouldn't be sad if I could keep only Maldon. It is superbly flaky, adding an element of crunch as well as salinity.

If you have never bought a finishing salt before, you might choke on the idea of spending $7 for 8 ounces of salt. But remember, you are using it in tiny quantities. A single box of Maldon lasts me a couple months at home and adds pleasure to so many dishes. Give a box as a gift to a friend. He or she might look at you as if you are nuts but will thank you profusely later.

zabaglione with roasted plums

GLUTEN-FREE

SERVES 4

20 MINUTES,
PLUS COOLING
TIME

Zabaglione is similar to custard but is made with only egg yolks, sugar, and flavoring; no milk or cream is used. The yolks are whisked over a double boiler and incorporate a lot of air, becoming creamy, rich, and fluffy.

The traditional flavoring for *zabaglione* is Marsala wine. When possible, I like to use a spirit made from the same fruit I will serve it with instead, to intensify the experience.

This dish is spectacular when Italian plums are in season. Italian plums are a small and oval shaped, and are firm enough to stand up to a little cooking. If you can't find Italian plums, you can make this same dessert with peaches, pears, or even apples.

My favorite plum brandy (known as *slivovitz* in the Balkans, where it is quite popular) is made by Oregon's Clear Creek Distillery. If you can't find a plum spirit, you can use one made from another fruit or the traditional Marsala wine.

If you don't have time to chill the zabaglione, it is perfectly appropriate to serve it at room temperature.

12 Italian plums, halved and pitted
6 tablespoons sugar
4 large egg yolks
¼ cup plum brandy (*slivovitz*) or grappa mixed with ¼ cup water,
   or ½ cup Marsala wine
Kosher salt

1 Heat the oven the to 400°F. Place the plums on a rimmed cookie sheet (lined with parchment paper for easier cleanup) and sprinkle with 2 tablespoons of the sugar. Roast until the plums are browning and tender but not falling apart, about 15 minutes.

2 Bring about 2 inches of water to a bare simmer in a saucepan over medium-high heat. Reduce the heat to maintain a bare simmer. Combine the egg yolks, the remaining 4 tablespoons sugar, the plum brandy mixture, and a pinch of salt in a round-bottomed metal mixing bowl; whisk thoroughly.

3 Set the bowl over the simmering water—the base of the bowl should not touch the water—and whisk continuously. The egg yolks will begin to froth, lighten, and grow greatly in volume. If you sense that the yolks are at risk of scrambling, quickly remove the bowl from the heat and whisk to cool slightly, then continue. When soft peaks form, after 5 to 10 minutes, the *zabaglione* is done. Transfer to a clean bowl, cover, and refrigerate.

4 To serve, place 6 plum halves in the bottom of each glass. Give the *zabaglione* a quick whisk and spoon it on top of the plums. Serve immediately.

sesame-orange sablé cookies

MAKES ABOUT
48 SMALL
COOKIES

3 HOURS AND
35 MINUTES
(15 MINUTES
ACTIVE)

Doughs for sablé cookies are a bit like shortbread, but with granulated sugar providing a delightfully sandy texture. They can be flavored with anything from chocolate to matcha tea with good results. My version incorporates enough sesame seeds to create something that is almost a cross between a cookie and those sesame sticks you overindulged in at Aunt Peg's Super Bowl party. Serve these cookies with tea and a bar of good bittersweet chocolate for a real treat.

I'm generally cautious about using whole-wheat flour in desserts, reserving it for cases where the heartier flavor enhances the other ingredients. With sesame and orange zest, it is a natural fit.

If you have raw sesame seeds, toast them in a skillet over medium-low heat, stirring frequently, until lightly browned and fragrant. Don't walk away for long, as they can get burned and bitter in a heartbeat.

12 tablespoons (1½ sticks) unsalted butter, softened
1 cup sugar
½ teaspoon flaky sea salt (such as Maldon) or ¼ teaspoon kosher salt or fine sea salt
¾ cup toasted sesame seeds (white, black, or a mixture)
¾ cup whole-wheat pastry flour
¾ cup all-purpose flour
½ teaspoon baking soda
Grated zest of 1 orange or 2 mandarin oranges

1 With a stand mixer or handheld mixer, cream together the butter, sugar, and salt on medium speed until light and fluffy, about 3 minutes. Add the sesame seeds and beat for 30 seconds.

2 In a separate bowl, whisk together the whole-wheat pastry flour, all-purpose flour, baking soda, and orange zest. Add the dry ingredients to the butter mixture and beat on low speed just until the dough comes together, about 1 minute.

3 Turn the dough out onto a lightly floured board and knead for a moment to form a cohesive ball. Divide into two pieces. Roll each piece into a cylinder about 8 inches long. Be sure the dough is holding together well; if not, roll it a bit more firmly. Wrap the dough cylinders tightly in plastic wrap, firmly roll them on the counter a couple of times, and refrigerate at least 3 hours.

4 Preheat the oven to 375°F and line two baking sheets with parchment paper or silicone mats. Unwrap the dough. Using a sharp knife, cut each cylinder into generous ¼-inch slices. Place the cookies on the baking sheets, leaving 1 inch between each cookie.

5 Bake until golden brown, 14 to 16 minutes, rotating the pans top to bottom and front to back about halfway through the baking time. Let the cookies cool on the pans for about 2 minutes, then transfer to wire racks to cool completely before serving.

seckel pears with cinnamon pastry crumbs

SERVES 6

1½ HOURS
(20 MINUTES
ACTIVE)

This dish is essentially a deconstructed tart. The simple, cinnamon-spiked sandy crust is baked and then crumbled to serve as a base for a whole poached pear. The poaching liquid is simmered until it forms a caramel and then used to make delicious, crispy decorations.

Seckel pears look like toys, just about half the size of their larger brethren. They have a brief season toward the end of fall. Crisp like Boscs, they are fine for eating out of hand, but their delightful size makes them even better for surprising desserts. Of course, if you can't find Seckels, you can make this dessert with larger pears cut in half.

Be sure to provide diners with knives as well as spoons so they can cut the pear and gather the pastry crumbs along with the ice cream.

It isn't practical to make a much smaller batch of the dough, so you will end up with more pastry than you need for six pears. You can either make more pears or just bake the extra off as simple cookies. To make cookies, roll the dough into a 1½-inch-wide cylinder, wrap, refrigerate, then slice and bake at 375°F until golden brown, about 15 minutes.

12 tablespoons (1½ sticks) unsalted butter, barely softened
½ cup confectioners' sugar
1 tablespoon vanilla extract
1½ cups all-purpose flour
¾ teaspoon kosher salt
1½ teaspoons ground cinnamon
1¾ cups water
½ cup granulated sugar
½ cup pear brandy
6 Seckel pears, peeled except for the top ½ inch, stems intact
Vanilla ice cream

1   With a stand mixer or handheld mixer, beat the butter and confectioners' sugar until pale and fluffy, about 3 minutes. Add the vanilla, flour, salt, and cinnamon, and beat for about 20 seconds more, just until the flour is incorporated. Form the dough into two balls, flatten into disks, wrap tightly in plastic wrap, and refrigerate for at least 1 hour and up to overnight.

2   While the dough is chilling, line a baking sheet with a silicone mat or parchment paper. Bring the water, granulated sugar, and pear brandy to a simmer in a small, deep saucepan. Add the pears and simmer until tender, about 30 minutes. Remove the pears with a slotted spoon, and continue to simmer the poaching liquid until it is a dark brown caramel, about 15 more minutes. Using a spoon, drizzle the caramel in thin lines on the baking sheet and allow to cool. (You don't need all of it, just 20 lines or so.)

3 Preheat the oven to 375°F. Line a baking sheet with a silicone mat or parchment paper. Roll out one of the disks of dough on a lightly floured board to about ⅛ inch thick (the shape isn't important). Transfer to the baking sheet and bake until golden brown, about 11 minutes. Remove and allow to cool, then crumble the pastry to fairly fine crumbs. (Save the remaining dough for another purpose.)

4 To serve, place about 2 tablespoons of the crumbs in a mound on each dessert plate. Make a small hollow in the middle and rest a pear in each hollow. Put a small scoop of vanilla ice cream on each plate and garnish with a few lines of the hardened pear caramel. Serve immediately.

spectacular chocolate-espresso brownies

MAKES 10
LARGE OR
18 MEDIUM
BROWNIES

1 HOUR
(30 MINUTES
ACTIVE)

Brownies, of course, are one of those topics that cleave the population along multiple dimensions. Cakey or fudgy? Love the middle or the edges? Celtics or Lakers? For me, I like more of a cakey brownie, but it has to be very moist and dense cake. Middle. And the Celtics.

The outline of this recipe has a long lineage. I learned about it from Ina Garten, who had adapted it from the *Soho Charcuterie Cookbook* by Francine Scherer and Madeline Poley (William Morrow, 1983). I omit the walnuts, double the salt, upgrade the chocolate, and simplify the steps to use one fewer bowl. I also sprinkle half of the chocolate chips over the top of the batter instead of mixing them in, which gives you these incredible creamy chocolate rivers on the surface.

Instead of instant coffee, I use instant espresso. I've always been loyal to the Medaglia D'Oro brand, which I used to drink 20 years ago at 4 a.m., sneaking off between the first two sessions of meditation practice when there wasn't enough time to make a real cup. Now it wouldn't be my first choice to drink, but it tastes pretty great in baked goods. Another fine option is two packets of Starbucks VIA instant coffee (decaf or regular).

16 tablespoons (2 sticks) unsalted butter
1 (12-ounce) bag best-quality semisweet chocolate chips
4 ounces best-quality unsweetened chocolate, coarsely chopped
4 large eggs
5 teaspoons instant espresso powder (Medaglia D'Oro is good,
   or use 2 packets of Starbucks VIA instant coffee)
1 tablespoon vanilla extract
1 cup plus 2 tablespoons sugar
½ cup plus 2 tablespoons all-purpose flour
1½ teaspoons baking powder
1 teaspoon flaky sea salt (such as Maldon)

1 Preheat the oven to 350°F. Butter and flour a 9 x 13-inch baking dish.

2 Melt the butter, half of the chocolate chips, and the unsweetened chocolate in a bowl set over a saucepan of barely simmering water or in the microwave (being careful to stir occasionally). Stir until smooth, then set aside to cool for at least 5 minutes.

3 With a stand mixer or handheld mixer, beat together the eggs, instant espresso, vanilla, and sugar until thoroughly combined, about 2 minutes. Stir in the chocolate mixture, drizzling it in slowly so you don't cook the eggs.

4 Whisk the flour, baking powder, and salt together in a small bowl. Mix into the chocolate mixture, but don't overbeat.

5 Pour the batter into the pan and spread evenly. Distribute the remaining chocolate chips over the surface.

6 Bake for 15 minutes. Take the pan out of the oven and carefully give it a rap on the counter to force out bubbles. Return to the oven and bake until a toothpick comes out clean, 10 to 15 minutes more. Don't overbake! Let cool slightly before cutting and serving.

TALKING WITH MY BLOG READERS. I sent this recipe off for testing to a reader who also happens to be an old friend. Beforehand, she wrote, "I make a LOT of brownies—got a bit of a reputation of my own with those—so this'll be interesting." I was sweating a bit!

Turns out I didn't have to worry. The next day, I heard back: "Delicious—and my household has very high standards for brownies. We liked that while they were extremely dense and rich, they managed not to seem like fudge—kept a more cake-like identity. Rich chocolate taste, and a bit crumbly in a way that makes them a sensory pleasure to eat off the plate (or out of the pan) with one's fingers. Very satisfying indeed."

chocolate chunk bread pudding

I love to make sweet bread puddings with leftover challah or brioche, because those breads are already rich. This version is filled with molten chunks of bittersweet chocolate. How good is it? Let's just say I find myself eating less challah on Friday nights because I'm hoping there will be enough left over to make this for dessert the next day.

The critical thing to understand about bread pudding is that it is a custard, albeit one that's heavily garnished with bread. Once you realize that and treat it accordingly in terms of egg-to-milk ratios (2 eggs per 1 cup of milk) and baking temperature, you have a lot of freedom to tweak the components and be assured of making a great dessert.

I bake this bread pudding in one large dish, but you can also use individual ramekins. Another option is to use a water bath, the way you would for flan or crème brûlée.

4 large eggs
2 cups whole milk
2 teaspoons vanilla extract
⅓ cup sugar
Pinch of kosher salt
14 ounces challah or brioche, preferably slightly stale, most of the crust removed,
  cut into ¾-inch cubes
7 ounces high-quality bittersweet (about 70 percent cacao) chocolate, cut into
  good-size chunks (not a whole mouthful but a lot bigger than a chocolate chip)
Whipped cream, heavy cream, or vanilla ice cream

1 Preheat the oven to 350°F using convection, or 375°F without convection.
2 Generously butter a shallow 9 x 13-inch baking dish.
3 Whisk the eggs until the yolks and whites are well mixed. Whisk in the milk, starting with just a little at a time until the eggs are well incorporated. Whisk in the vanilla, sugar, and salt.
4 Place the cubed bread in the baking dish. Pour the custard evenly over the bread and toss lightly, trying to get it to absorb without squashing the bread too much.
5 Add the chocolate chunks and again toss gently to distribute.
6 Cover the pan with aluminum foil and bake until it reaches an internal temperature in the center of 185°F, about 45 minutes. You can also check for doneness with a fork or, as it gets close, by taking a bite. You want it to be well set, but not overcooked and rubbery.
7 Let it rest for 10 minutes and serve it forth. A bit of whipped cream, a drizzle of heavy cream, or a scoop of vanilla ice cream are all very welcome. If you want to whisk a bit of good bourbon into that cream, don't let me stop you.

caramelized raisin sundaes

GLUTEN-FREE

SERVES 4

25 MINUTES

There is nothing like a sundae to bring out the kid in all of us, but there's no reason it can't have adult flavors! Here, raisins are caramelized with butter, brown sugar, port wine, and orange zest to make a rich sauce that isn't too sweet. Fresh apple spiked with cinnamon adds a crunchy, slightly spicy counterpoint.

The raisins grow hilariously plump while cooking, blowing up like little zeppelins. Don't let that worry you; when they cool back down, they return to a normal size.

For a smooth variation, you can puree the sauce. It would also be delicious made with dried figs instead of raisins.

3 tablespoons unsalted butter
1 cup raisins (Thompsons work well)
¼ cup dark brown sugar
½ teaspoon kosher salt
1 cup port wine (tawny port is a good choice; don't use so-called cooking wine)
Grated zest of half an orange
Juice of 1 orange
1 tart apple, such as Cortland or Granny Smith
¼ teaspoon ground cinnamon
¼ teaspoon ground sumac (optional)
8 scoops high-quality vanilla ice cream

1 Melt the butter in a small saucepan over medium heat. Add the raisins, sugar, and salt, and cook for 5 minutes, stirring occasionally. Don't worry about the raisins growing amusingly plump; they will shrink later. The raisins should brown a bit, but don't let them burn.

2 Add the port, orange zest, and half of the orange juice. Bring to a simmer, then reduce the heat to maintain the simmer. Cook for about 10 minutes, stirring occasionally, until the sauce is thick enough to coat a spoon; when you drag a spatula across the bottom of the pan, it should leave a clear space for a couple of seconds. Remove from the heat and let cool until slightly warm (about 100°F). Taste and adjust the seasoning.

3 Just before serving, pour the remaining orange juice into a bowl. Peel, core, and finely dice the apple, adding it to the juice and tossing frequently to coat and minimize browning. Add the cinnamon and sumac, if using, and toss to coat.

4 To serve, put two scoops of vanilla ice cream in each bowl or sundae boat. Top each with one-quarter of the raisins and sauce, followed by a big spoonful of the apples. Serve immediately.

FORTIFIED WINES. Fortified wines are wines that have had distilled spirits, often brandy, added to raise the proof, preserve the product, and create new flavors. They are delicious as aperitifs or after-dinner drinks, in cocktails, and for making sauces.

You should always avoid fortified wines that are specifically designated as cooking wines. They are mass-produced, with awful flavors masked by vast amounts of salt. Your best bet is to buy mid-grade bottles for cooking, saving the expensive aged stuff for savoring straight. If you have the opportunity to taste a range of any of these wines, at either a shop or bar, you'll find that there is much to learn and appreciate!

Here are some of the most popular fortified wines:

PORT comes from the Douro valley of northern Portugal. There are many varieties; the most common are red and rather sweet, making mid-grade bottles especially suitable for dessert sauces.

MADEIRA is also from Portugal, specifically the Madeira islands. It is made in a unique way, by heating and oxidizing the wine for an extended period. (This method was developed after a ship carrying the wine sailed through the tropics and back!)

SHERRY is made in and around Jerez, Spain. It is aged in a series of barrels (the solera), in a process similar to the production of true balsamic vinegar. As with port, there are many styles, ranging from dry, pale fino to oxidized oloroso and sweet jerez dulce.

MARSALA comes from the Sicilian city of the same name and is produced in a way similar to sherry. It also comes in a range of sweetness levels and is frequently used in desserts as well as savory sauces.

VERMOUTH originated in Italy and France and is generally either white and dry or red and somewhat sweet. Both varieties are scented with a variety of herbs. The name is derived from the German word for wormwood, which is best known as an ingredient in absinthe, but vermouth doesn't actually contain wormwood. Dry vermouth is especially useful as a cooking wine, as it keeps for a long time in the refrigerator.

stout chocolate malt

SERVES 4

5 MINUTES

Porters, stouts, and other dark, intensely flavored beers can make incredible pairings with chocolate. They have similar roasted aromas that complement each other perfectly. In this twist on the classic malted milk shake, the malt acts as an additional bridge that has a natural affinity for both the beer and chocolate.

Try serving this shake with Cheddar-Battered Onion Rings (page 54).

2½ cups chocolate ice cream
½ cup stout or porter (I use Barney Flats Oatmeal Stout, but anything you like is fine)
5 tablespoons malted milk powder (preferably Carnation)

Combine the ice cream, stout, and malted milk powder in a blender and run at medium speed until creamy. Serve immediately.

sephardic doughnuts (buñuelos)

VEGAN OPTION

MAKES ABOUT
14 DOUGHNUTS

20 MINUTES
ACTIVE, PLUS
1 HOUR RISING
TIME

Buñuelos (also spelled *bimuelos*) are the rustic yeast-raised fried doughnuts that the Sephardic side of my family makes. For Chanukah, we have them with the traditional drizzle of honey; at any other time, I prefer them dusted with confectioners' sugar. There is also a Passover version made with matzoh, but that doesn't hold a candle to the flour-based doughnut.

The dough for *buñuelos* should be quite wet. This isn't a doughnut that you roll out. You wet your hands, grab a piece of dough, form a rough ball and poke a hole with your thumb, then drop it straight into the oil. The results are unfussy, light, airy, and altogether insanely delicious. They are so simple to make that you could stir up the dough in just a few minutes before dinner and fry them up afterward to entertain and thrill the kids.

> 1 package (2¼ teaspoons) active dry yeast
> 2 cups warm water
> 1½ teaspoons sugar
> 1 tablespoon vegetable oil, plus additional for deep-frying
> 3¼ cups all-purpose flour
> ½ teaspoon kosher salt
> Honey (or confectioners' sugar, for vegan or if you prefer)

1 In a large bowl, stir the yeast into 1 cup of the warm water and let it sit until creamy, about 5 minutes. If you don't see bubbles after a few minutes, the yeast is dead, and you'll need to start over. Mix in the remaining 1 cup water along with the sugar and 1 tablespoon oil. Slowly stir in the flour and salt, and keep stirring until you have a smooth, wet dough. Cover and let rise in a warm spot for at least 1 hour. (I've allowed it to go as long as 4 hours, stirring it down occasionally, and it only gets more delicious.)

2 Put 3 inches of oil in a pot suitable for deep-frying and bring the oil to 370°F over medium-high heat. Adjust the heat to maintain temperature. Line a tray with paper towels. Have a bowl of water ready.

3 Moisten your hands in the bowl of water and grab about 3 tablespoons of the dough. Quickly form it into a rough ball and poke a hole through the center. These are supposed to be rustic, so don't spend any time trying to make them perfect. Drop carefully into the oil. Repeat for as many as will fit comfortably in your pot without crowding. Fry until golden brown on one side, about 2 minutes, then carefully flip the doughnuts and brown the other side, about 1 minute more. Use a slotted spoon to transfer to paper towels.

4 Drizzle with honey (or offer honey for dipping) or dust with confectioners' sugar and serve piping hot.

apple-celery sorbet

VEGAN

GLUTEN-FREE

MAKES ABOUT
2½ CUPS,
ENOUGH FOR AT
LEAST 6 SMALL
SERVINGS
AS A PALATE
CLEANSER

6½ HOURS
(30 MINUTES
ACTIVE)

NOTE:
Glucose powder
is available from
cake-decorating
supply stores.
Citric acid and
xanthan gum
are available
at health food
stores. All of
these ingredi-
ents, as well as
sodium citrate,
are available
online from
amazon.com.

After I launched the Herbivoracious blog, I started hosting "underground" dinner parties to test out recipes and build my skills as a professional cook. I was trying to decide on a palate-cleansing sorbet flavor for one of these events, and I ran across an apple-celery combination from Michael Laiskonis, pastry chef of the New York restaurant Le Bernadin. The result was exactly what I wanted: bracing and not very sweet.

His recipe requires some ingredients that aren't readily accessible in a home kitchen, including a high-quality commercial apple puree. Via email, Chef Laiskonis helped me make the right substitutions, including using citric acid to keep my home-juiced apples from browning. Another amazing pastry chef, Dana Cree, who has worked at The Fat Duck, noma, and Alinea, suggested that I could use xanthan gum instead of sorbet stabilizer to keep large ice crystals from forming over a few days in the freezer.

Even though this recipe is more exacting than others in this book, I'm including it because it is a testament to the power of the blogosphere (where I came to know these chefs) to communicate and cross-pollinate ideas. And it makes a damn tasty sorbet, too.

I've given the ingredients in this recipe by weight because the extra precision is required to get the right results.

110 grams water
65 grams granulated sugar
35 grams glucose powder (see Note)
About 3 pounds flavorful heirloom apples, such as King, Goldrush, or Russet
2 grams (about ¼ teaspoon) citric acid or sodium citrate (see Note)
About 6 celery ribs
2 grams (about ¼ teaspoon) xanthan gum (see Note)
Celery leaves, for garnish

SPECIAL EQUIPMENT: Kitchen scale, juicer

1 Combine the water, granulated sugar, and glucose powder in a small saucepan and bring to a boil. Boil for 30 seconds. Cool, then refrigerate for at least 4 hours.

2 Peel and core the apples. Put the citric acid powder in a juicer container and juice the apples directly into it, stirring the juice once or twice. (This will help prevent any oxidation.) Strain, measure out 282 grams of juice, and drink the rest.

3 Juice the celery. Strain, measure out 117 grams, and drink the rest.

4 Combine the apple and celery juices in a blender with the chilled sugar syrup. With the blender running on low speed, remove the lid and sprinkle the xanthan gum into the vortex. Put the lid back on, raise the speed to medium, and blend for 5 minutes.

5 Process in an ice cream maker according to the manufacturer's instructions. It should turn nicely pale when it is sufficiently aerated. Transfer to a plastic container and freeze until firm enough to serve, about 2 hours. It will keep for about 48 hours in the freezer.

6 Serve small portions, each garnished with a celery leaf.

cheese course with maple pickled pears

This isn't so much a recipe as a reminder that a cheese course can be a fitting end to any meal. Lingering over small portions of beautiful cheeses with a thoughtfully made condiment and maybe a glass of port or sherry can feel much more intimate than eating a sweet dessert.

The most important thing you can do to make your cheese course delicious is to serve it at room temperature. This means that the cheese needs to sit out of the refrigerator, covered, for 1 to 2 hours depending on size. When good cheese is served cold, the complex flavors that you paid for are masked.

Whole books have been written about choosing cheeses. For small dinner parties, I suggest you keep it to two or three options, choosing quality over quantity. Three ounces total per person is sufficient, though you may need to buy more just to have a respectable-looking chunk. It is nice to have contrast, with soft, semisoft, and hard cheeses, made from a variety of cow's, sheep's, or goat's milk cheeses. My best advice is to find a cheesemonger whom you trust, ask for advice, and taste lots of samples.

These pears, quick-pickled with apple cider vinegar and maple syrup, are just one possible accompaniment to cheese. Spiced Pecans (page 288), good honey (preferably with pieces of honeycomb), perfectly ripe fresh figs, or a bit of marmalade are all terrific. Just keep it simple and don't overpower the cheese.

2 tablespoons apple cider vinegar
2 tablespoons maple syrup (preferably Grade B)
½ teaspoon kosher salt
Freshly ground black pepper
1 Bosc pear, peeled, cored, and finely diced or thinly sliced

1 Mix the vinegar, syrup, salt, and a few grinds of black pepper in a small bowl and microwave for 1 minute. Toss with the pears and set aside at room temperature for at least 15 minutes or refrigerate as long as overnight (bring to room temperature before serving).

2 Drain off the pickling liquid and serve the pears with your cheeses and bread or crackers. Leftovers can be used in grilled cheese sandwiches.

breakfast

buckwheat buttermilk pancakes

MAKES 10 TO 12
MEDIUM-SIZE
PANCAKES;
EASILY DOUBLED

20 MINUTES

Buckwheat pancakes have a place in the American imagination, but rarely at the breakfast table. You do occasionally find them at restaurants, but the percentage of buckwheat flour is so low that you can hardly taste it. That is a shame, because buckwheat adds a wonderfully warm, toasty, nutty flavor. (On the other hand, don't try to make 100 percent buckwheat pancakes; they will be flat and taste rather sour.)

My three-year-old and I make these a lot. Pancakes are a great way to introduce children to cooking because you can do the mixing in bowls on the floor, they are ready to eat in minutes, and most kids love them. Making them from scratch teaches your munchkins the value of home-cooked instead of prepackaged foods, and it gives you the opportunity to make them from healthier ingredients.

Because buckwheat flour doesn't contain gluten, it tends to make a flattish pancake. I counteract that tendency with buttermilk, which adds a lot of leavening power, so these pancakes rise high. This pancake batter should be fairly thick so that it has time to rise instead of spread when poured on the griddle.

The easiest place to find buckwheat flour is at your local natural foods store, often in the bulk section.

DRY INGREDIENTS
¾ **cup buckwheat flour**
¾ **cup all-purpose flour**
3 **tablespoons sugar**
1½ **teaspoons baking powder**
½ **teaspoon baking soda**
½ **teaspoon kosher salt**

WET INGREDIENTS
1½ **cups buttermilk**
3 **tablespoons unsalted butter, melted**
2 **large eggs**

Unsalted butter and maple syrup, for serving

1 *For the dry ingredients:* Put the flours, sugar, baking powder, baking soda, and salt in a mixing bowl. Whisk together to thoroughly combine.
2 *For the wet ingredients:* Whisk together the buttermilk, butter, and eggs in a second bowl. You can save a bit of cleanup by gently melting the butter in this bowl in the microwave, then whisking in the buttermilk and eggs.

3 Stir the wet ingredients into the dry mixture. Be careful not to overmix, or your pancakes will come out tough; it's okay if the batter has some lumps. If it is too thick, add a bit more buttermilk, but keep it on the thick side. If it is too thin, add a bit more of either flour.

4 Place a griddle (or two skillets) over medium heat. Rub it with a bit of oil on a paper towel. When the griddle is hot, ladle out about ⅓ cup batter to make circles about 5 inches in diameter. Cook until bubbles form on top and a peek underneath reveals a nice dark brown, about 1½ minutes. Flip and cook until the other side is done. (Adjust the heat as needed after your first batch. You want the pancakes to be dark golden brown and cook reasonably quickly but not burn before the inside is cooked.) You can keep them warm in a 200°F oven while cooking the rest of the pancakes.

5 Serve forth with plenty of soft butter and real maple syrup.

crunchy crusted yeast-raised belgian waffles

SERVES 4

10 MINUTES THE NIGHT BEFORE, THEN HOWEVER LONG IT TAKES YOU TO COOK WAFFLES IN THE MORNING

I believe that there are no bad homemade waffles, only good ones and great ones. A great waffle should have an ultra-crispy crust with a tender interior and some complexity of flavor, without being too sweet.

This recipe is closely based on Marion Cunningham's formula. The main change I've made is to use some rice flour in the batter. Because it is a pure starch, rice flour creates the most incredibly crunchy surfaces. I also add malt powder for a little mysterious background flavor. You can find Carnation malt powder at many groceries.

Yeast delivers a great taste and allows you to make the batter the night before and just let it hang out in the refrigerator. The next morning, you don't have to do anything more ambitious than turn on your waffle iron and ladle in the batter. You'll need a Belgian-style (thick) waffle iron.

You might want to make a double batch. Cool extra waffles in a single layer and then freeze them, well wrapped. If you reheat them in a toaster oven directly from the freezer, the original crust comes right back.

2½ cups barely warm milk (about 100°F)
1 package active dry yeast (2¼ teaspoons)
8 tablespoons (1 stick) unsalted butter, melted and cooled to just warm
2 large eggs, lightly beaten
1 tablespoon agave nectar or honey
1¾ cups all-purpose flour
¼ cup rice flour
¼ cup malt powder
1 teaspoon kosher salt
Unsalted butter and maple syrup, for serving

1 In a large bowl—one big enough for the batter to greatly increase in size overnight without making a mess—sprinkle the yeast over the milk, stir, and allow to proof until creamy, about 5 minutes.

2 Stir in the melted butter, eggs, and agave nectar. The butter will clump up; that's okay.

3 Stir in the all-purpose flour, rice flour, malt powder, and salt. Mix well. The batter will be thinner than typical waffle batter. Cover with plastic wrap and refrigerate overnight.

4 In the morning, give the batter a stir. Preheat your waffle iron and cook the waffles according to the manufacturer's instructions, being certain to bake them until quite brown for maximum flavor and the best crunchy exterior. As always, the first waffle is usually not the best, but pay close attention and adjust the time and temperature to achieve perfection. You can keep the waffles warm in a single layer in a 200°F oven while you finish cooking the batch. Serve with plenty of butter and maple syrup.

dutch baby with sautéed apples

I never knew what a Dutch baby was until my wife introduced me to this favorite from her childhood. It's an enormous, oven-baked pancake that puffs up theatrically, then just as suddenly collapses into a rich, custardy pie—similar to a clafoutis but less eggy. The preferred way to cook a Dutch baby is in a cast-iron skillet with a lot of butter in the bottom so that you get a little bit of a popover-type crust. Confectioners' sugar and a squeeze of lemon are the traditional accompaniments.

The sautéed apples are our house variation. For a savory twist, skip the apples and add modest amounts of grated aged Gouda cheese, sautéed onions, and *herbes de Provence* directly to the batter.

I especially like to serve this Dutch baby for brunch with company, because I can make the batter and sautéed apples in advance and then finish the pancake in the oven while I visit with my guests. If you want to do it that way, you can make the batter the night before and refrigerate it in the blender jar, giving it a last-second spin to reblend. The apples can be made an hour ahead of time and rewarmed just before serving.

5 large eggs
1¼ cups whole milk
1¼ cups all-purpose flour
Kosher salt
8 tablespoons (1 stick) unsalted butter
2 firm apples (such as Cortland or Gala), peeled, cored, and cut into 16 slices each
2 tablespoons brown sugar
¼ teaspoon ground cinnamon
Confectioners' sugar
1 lemon, cut into wedges

1 Preheat the oven to 425°F.

2 Combine the eggs, milk, flour, and a pinch of salt in a blender. Blend at high speed for 1 minute.

3 Put 6 tablespoons of the butter into a well-seasoned 12-inch cast-iron skillet or other large, oven-safe pan. Put the skillet in the oven.

4 When the butter is melted and sizzling, carefully pull the skillet out and swirl the butter around or use a brush to be sure the whole skillet is coated. Pour in the batter and return the pan to the oven. Cook until puffed and golden brown, about 18 minutes.

5 Meanwhile, melt the remaining 2 tablespoons butter in a sauté pan over medium-high heat. Add the apples and sauté until they start to soften, about 5 minutes. Add the brown sugar, cinnamon, and a pinch of salt, and sauté until fully tender and glazed, about 2 minutes more.

6 When the Dutch baby is done, carefully remove the skillet from the oven. Pat off any excess butter on top with a paper towel. Top with the apples and a generous sprinkle of confectioners' sugar. Since the skillet is really hot, you might want to plate this in the kitchen rather than bring it to the table. Offer lemon wedges on the side; they add a nice counterpoint to the sweetness.

caramelized pear and ginger scones

These scones are light and moist, with just enough pear and ginger flavor to be interesting but not overpowering. Make them for brunch and I guarantee your friends and family will be happy. My kids beg me to make them whenever we have company for brunch.

These would be just ridiculously good as the base for strawberry shortcake.

FOR THE PEARS
2 tablespoons unsalted butter
3 medium or 2 large crisp pears, such as Bosc, cored, peeled, and finely diced
1 tablespoon sugar
Kosher salt
2 teaspoons grated fresh ginger
¼ teaspoon ground cinnamon

FOR THE SCONES
5 cups all-purpose flour
1 tablespoon baking powder
1 teaspoon baking soda
½ cup plus 3 tablespoons sugar
1½ teaspoons kosher salt
16 tablespoons (2 sticks) very cold unsalted butter, plus 2 tablespoons
    unsalted butter, melted
1½ cups buttermilk, plus additional as needed

Unsalted butter and jam, for serving

1 *For the pears:* Melt the butter in a large skillet over medium-high heat. Add the pears, sugar, and a pinch of salt and cook, stirring occasionally, until most of the liquid has cooked off and the pears are starting to brown, about 6 minutes.

2 Add the ginger and cinnamon and cook for 2 minutes more. Transfer the pears to a plate and let them cool to room temperature before adding to the dough.

3 *For the scones:* Preheat the oven to 400°F. Butter two baking sheets or line them with silicone mats.

4 In a food processor, combine the flour, baking powder, baking soda, ½ cup sugar, and salt; pulse several times. Cut the cold butter into pieces and add to the processor. Pulse until the butter is broken down to oatmeal-size pieces (for flaky scones) or to a sandy texture (if you prefer tender, less flaky scones). Transfer to a mixing bowl.

5 Add the buttermilk and pears and mix with a wooden spoon, moistening all of the dry ingredients. You might need another 1 to 2 tablespoons buttermilk, but don't be in a hurry to add it;
you want the dough to just barely form a mass.

6 Turn the dough out on to a floured board and knead as briefly as possible to make a rough ball.

7 Flatten the dough into a rectangle about 4½ x 24 inches. Brush the top with the melted butter
and sprinkle with the remaining 3 tablespoons sugar. Cut into 6 even rectangles and then divide
each rectangle into 2 triangles. Transfer to the baking sheets, leaving 2 inches between scones.

8 Bake until quite golden brown, about 22 minutes. Cool for 5 minutes and serve with soft butter
and jam.

manouri cheese blintzes

Blintzes are one of those items that automatically make breakfast or brunch a little bit special. You can serve them with sour cream and brown sugar, or for over-the-top deliciousness, offer Rosemary-Blueberry Sauce (page 333) as an accompaniment.

While these blintzes are a fair bit of work, much of it can be done ahead. You can prepare, fill, and roll the pancakes, then refrigerate them until you are ready to fry them in butter and serve them up. Blintzes are very forgiving to make because they don't need to be as thin as crêpes, and rolling the pancakes hides any little imperfections.

Manouri cheese is a sheep's milk cheese from Greece, with a sweet, clean, dairy taste and texture very similar to drained ricotta. If you can't get your hands on it, use ricotta and reduce or eliminate the milk in the recipe.

FOR THE FILLING
1 pound manouri cheese, finely crumbled (or ricotta; see headnote)
1 large egg, lightly beaten
½ cup whole milk
5 tablespoons sugar
Grated zest of 1 lemon
Kosher salt

FOR THE BLINTZES
2 cups all-purpose flour
1 tablespoon cornstarch
⅛ teaspoon kosher salt
1½ cups water
1 cup whole milk
7 large eggs
4 tablespoons (½ stick) unsalted butter, plus additional if necessary

Sour cream and brown sugar and/or Rosemary-Blueberry Sauce (page 333), for serving

1   *For the filling:* Mix together the cheese, egg, milk, sugar, zest, and a big pinch of salt. Cover with plastic wrap and refrigerate until needed.

2   *For the blintzes:* Combine the flour, cornstarch, salt, water, milk, and eggs in a blender. Blend on high speed for 3 minutes. The batter should be quite liquid, much thinner than pancake batter. Refrigerate for at least 30 minutes and up to overnight. Just before making the blintzes, stir or blend briefly again.

▼ ▼ ▼

3 Line a baking sheet with parchment paper. Heat a 7-inch nonstick pan, crêpe pan, or omelet pan over medium-low heat. Grease the pan with a small amount of butter. Ladle in 2 to 3 tablespoons of batter and immediately tilt the pan in all directions to spread the batter out evenly, covering as much of the surface as possible.

4 Cook the blintz until it is well set and you can remove it with a spatula, about 1 minute. Do not flip it. Lay the blintz on a flat surface, allow it to cool for a few seconds, then spread a heaping tablespoon of the filling on the horizontal center of the blintz, about 1 inch from the front edge. Fold the front edge over the filling, then fold in the sides and roll it up like a burrito. Transfer to the baking sheet, seam side down.

5 Continue making all of the blintzes, adding a little more butter to the pan as needed. Once you get the hang of it, you can have the next one cooking one while you fill the previously made one. Transfer the filled blintzes to the baking sheet, making sure they're not touching each other. At this point, you can either finish cooking the blintzes and serve them or cover the baking sheet with plastic wrap and refrigerate the filled blintzes for up to 24 hours.

6 To finish the blintzes, melt the 4 tablespoons butter in a large skillet over medium heat. Working in batches, fry the rolled blintzes on each side until they're golden brown and crispy, about 4 minutes total. Keep the heat low enough to ensure that the filling will be cooked by the time the wrapper is done. Add more butter to the skillet if necessary.

7 Serve them forth with sour cream and brown sugar and/or rosemary-blueberry sauce.

DON'T FEAR FAT. I'm hardly the first person to observe that Americans have a crazy, conflicted relationship to fat. We love it, and we eat far more of it than probably just about any other country in the world. God knows we have plenty of obesity to show for it. At the same time, we fear it mightily, using terms like "sin" and "indulgence" as if there were a higher power monitoring our every fat gram.

More than anything, we don't like to see liquid fat on our food. A drizzle of extra-virgin olive oil over a plate of sautéed broccoli rabe or a small slick of ghee on the *chana masala* is thought of as greasy and repulsive, even though in Italy and India, respectively, those fats would be considered the mark of a wholesome, delicious meal.

The bizarre thing is, if you take 10 times that amount of fat and put it in a obscenely large slice from the Cheesecake Factory, most people will say, "Oh, just this once," and go right ahead. So that is what restaurant chefs do. They use (and frequently hide) quantities of fat that would make most home cooks blanch in horror, and then diners wonder why it is that the food tastes so good.

It is time for some sanity. You don't need to fear fat. You just need to learn how to use it and eat it in moderation. If you skip that cheesecake and the triple cheeseburger with fries, or at least eat them only occasionally, you can afford to have a decent amount of oil in your stir-fry and even a pat of delicious sweet-cream butter on your morning toast. That's one of life's best things, and there is no substitute.

Why does a little fat make food so good? There are three main reasons. Fat carries flavor, because it can dissolve aroma compounds that aren't soluble in water; it feels good in your mouth; and it transmits heat efficiently, allowing food to cook at temperatures higher than the boiling point of water. I'm not counting, of course, the more technical things fat does, especially in baking.

Try this experiment, either in your mind or in your kitchen. First, steam a big handful of green beans and toss them with salt and raw garlic, or garlic that has been roasted with no fat.

Now sauté some green beans in a very hot skillet with a couple tablespoons of olive oil and some salt. When the beans are blistered and have a few dark spots, add some thinly sliced garlic and cook for another minute.

Which dish tastes better? The steamed beans taste dull and vegetal. If you used raw garlic, it will be harsh and poorly distributed. The roasted garlic might be better but will likely be just sweet and anemic.

In the second dish, the oil will have picked up the flavor compounds from the garlic and distributed them throughout the food. The garlic will neither be as pungent as it would be raw nor as mild as it would be roasted. Its intoxicating aroma will have spread throughout your house, whetting everyone's appetite. The beans will have beautifully blistered skin, courtesy of the low-moisture heat transfer. And when you eat those beans, the small amount of oil on their surface will contribute a sense of richness that contrasts nicely with the vegetable itself. Done right, they should taste amazing. To my mind, that is easily worth the small increment in calories.

huevos ahogados

GLUTEN-FREE

SERVES 2

20 MINUTES

This simple Mexican egg dish has a picturesque name: *Huevos ahogados* means "drowned eggs." The reality isn't so violent; they have actually just been poached directly in a thin salsa. One nice bonus about this technique: If you have ever had trouble poaching eggs, it won't be a problem here. The salsa has enough body to keep the whites in a compact ball around the yolks. You'll feel like a poaching pro!

I'm pretty much a sucker for anything involving poached eggs, especially if there is something good to mop up the runny yolk. In this case it mixes in with the sauce and you mop it all up with a stack of soft corn tortillas. Let me go ahead and state the obvious: This is great hangover food.

You can use a jarred tomatillo salsa for this dish, or make the Swiss Chard and Tomatillo Enchiladas (page 236) and cook up some extra salsa so you can have these eggs the next morning.

2 to 3 cups tomatillo (green) salsa, slightly thinned if necessary (it should be about the consistency of tomato soup)
6 (6-inch) soft corn tortillas
4 large eggs
Flaky sea salt (such as Maldon)
Fresh cilantro sprigs

1   In a small saucier pan or deep skillet with a lid, bring the salsa to a simmer over medium heat. Reduce the heat to maintain a low simmer.

2   Wrap the corn tortillas in a clean, damp dishtowel and microwave for about 1 minute to soften them.

3   Carefully crack each egg and, working right above the simmering salsa, pull the halves of the shell apart and allow the egg to nestle into the salsa. You can also break each egg into a small bowl and gently tilt it into the sauce.

4   Once all of the eggs are in, cover the pan and cook for 3 minutes. Remove the lid and check to see if the whites are completely cooked. If not, re-cover the pan and check every minute until you don't see any more transparent white.

5   Using a big spoon, divide the salsa and eggs between two bowls. Hit them with a bit of sea salt and a few sprigs of cilantro. Serve with the warm tortillas to wipe your bowl clean.

mexican breakfast torta

VEGAN OPTION
SERVES 4
30 MINUTES

Tortas are Mexican sandwiches. They generally have a base of refried beans, which can be topped with just about anything. My version is made with soft scrambled eggs (or avocado, for vegans) and a moderately picante roasted poblano pepper, with a simple cabbage slaw for some added crunch.

The traditional roll for a torta is a *bolillo* or *telera*, either of which may be found at a Mexican market. If you are a vegetarian, you'll want to double-check the ingredients to make sure no lard is involved. Otherwise, you can use an American sandwich roll. It can have a thin, crispy crust or a soft crust, but the interior must be light and soft. Whatever you choose, it should not be hard to bite through.

You'll want to remove some of the interior of the roll to make a sort of trough that helps keep the fillings in place.

If you like, you can serve these tortas wrapped in waxed paper or aluminum foil; otherwise, offer a knife and fork, or your guests will be wearing a lot of their breakfasts! These sandwiches are a messy good time.

2 poblano chile peppers
1 cup thinly sliced red cabbage
1 tablespoon mayonnaise or vegan mayonnaise
1 tablespoon fresh lime juice
Kosher salt
4 *bolillo* or *telera* rolls (or substitute; see headnote)
6 large eggs or (for vegan) 1 avocado, peeled, pitted, and thinly sliced
2 tablespoons water
1 tablespoon unsalted butter
2 cups vegetarian refried beans, heated (refried black beans are great, too);
    add salt and/or ground cumin if needed
½ cup cotija cheese, crumbled (omit for vegan)
Fresh cilantro sprigs
Hot sauce

1 Preheat the broiler. Place the poblano peppers on a small baking sheet under the broiler. Broil, turning every minute or so, until blackened and blistered all over, about 10 minutes. Place in a small bowl, cover with plastic wrap, and let steam for 10 minutes. Remove from the bowl, allow to cool, peel, remove the stems, cut in half, and remove the seeds. (You may want to wear rubber gloves while working with the peppers to avoid getting spicy oil on your hands. It is okay if you don't get every bit of skin off.)

2 Toss the cabbage with the mayonnaise, lime juice, and a pinch of salt.

3 Cut each roll in half and pull out some of the soft bread inside to make more room for the filling. Lightly toast the rolls.

4 Whisk the eggs with ½ teaspoon kosher salt and the water. Melt the butter in a small nonstick skillet over medium-low heat. Add the eggs and reduce the heat to low. Cook, stirring frequently, until the eggs are no longer wet but still tender, about 10 minutes.

5 To assemble, line up the bottom halves of the rolls. Top each one with one-quarter of the refried beans and scrambled eggs (or avocado). If using avocado, season it with a generous sprinkle of salt. Add 1 roasted poblano half, some red cabbage slaw, a generous sprinkle of cotija cheese, and a few sprigs cilantro. Cut in half if desired and serve immediately, offering hot sauce at the table.

real home fries

VEGAN

GLUTEN-FREE

SERVES 2 TO 4

20 MINUTES

Homemade home fries (is that redundant?) are infinitely better than those you find in most restaurants, because at home you can get them really browned and serve them while they are still crispy. In restaurants, the potatoes are usually cut too large and cooked in a big pile on a flat-top griddle, where they mostly steam. Bah.

I like to make a whole meal out of these potatoes, serving them up with a couple of sunny-side-up eggs and, if it is late summer, thick slices of tomatoes from the garden. The yolk mixed with the potatoes and the tomato juices is sublime.

¼ cup vegetable oil
Half a white onion, finely diced
1 fresh chile de árbol or other chile pepper (optional), seeded and thinly sliced
1½ pounds potatoes (any kind), skin on, finely diced
1 teaspoon kosher salt, plus additional as needed
Flaky sea salt (such as Maldon)
Freshly ground black pepper

1 Heat your biggest skillet, preferably cast iron, over medium-high heat. You want a really big pan to maximize surface area. Add the oil, onion, and the chile, if using, and sauté for 30 seconds.

2 Add the potatoes and kosher salt, and stir to coat with the oil. Distribute into a single layer, or as close to that as possible. Every 3 minutes or so, flip the potatoes and onion with a spatula, trying as much as possible to get uncooked surfaces onto the skillet and of course maintaining the single layer. Cook until deep golden brown, 10 to 15 minutes total.

3 Taste and salt as needed. Serve immediately, while hot and crispy, topped with a few flakes of sea salt for texture and a few grinds of black pepper.

congee with crispy yuba

VEGAN

GLUTEN-FREE

SERVES 4

1½ HOURS
(15 MINUTES
ACTIVE)

Wherever rice is a staple, from China to India and all points in between, some form of congee is a beloved dish. Congee is simply rice that is cooked in copious amounts of water until it falls apart into porridge. It is often a breakfast dish and is also considered an excellent recuperative and restorative meal.

Congee is a blank canvas that can be topped by a vast range of accompaniments. It is usually best to include something crunchy, something green, something salty, and a small but substantial hit of protein. Besides my suggestions below, you might consider sliced hard-cooked egg, toasted and crushed peanuts, thinly sliced scallions, kimchi (see page 48), tofu, or pickled ginger.

You can also experiment with using less water and shorter cooking times for a congee that is thicker and less broken down. This approach is more common in Japan, where the porridge is known as *okayu*.

¾ **cup Chinese or jasmine rice**
9 cups water
Kosher salt
1 cup thinly sliced red cabbage
2 tablespoons rice vinegar
2 sheets (roughly 8 x 10 inches) *yuba* **(tofu skin)**
¼ **cup vegetable oil**
1 to 2 large shallots, cut into ⅛-**inch-wide slices and separated into rings**
8 sprigs fresh cilantro (leaves and tender stems only)
4 teaspoons toasted sesame oil
Flaky sea salt (such as Maldon)

1 Rinse the rice in two changes of water. Drain. In a pot that holds about 3 quarts, combine the rice, water, and 1½ teaspoons kosher salt. Bring to a boil, reduce to a simmer, and cover loosely, leaving a gap for some steam to escape. Simmer, stirring every 10 minutes or so, until it has become a creamy porridge with a consistency similar to a slightly thin oatmeal, 1¼ to 1½ hours. While the congee is cooking, you can prepare the toppings. When the rice is done, stir, taste, and add more salt as needed.

2 Toss the cabbage with the rice vinegar and a big pinch of salt and set aside to marinate.

3 Break the *yuba* into large bite-size pieces, place in a small bowl, cover with boiling water, and let sit for 5 minutes. Carefully drain, rinse with cool water, then spread the *yuba* out on paper towels and pat it dry.

▼ ▼ ▼

4 Put the vegetable oil in a medium skillet over medium-high heat. When the oil is hot, place the shallot rings in the oil in a single layer. Cook, tossing once or twice, until dark golden brown, about 3 minutes. Transfer with a slotted spoon to paper towels, leaving the oil in the skillet. Sprinkle a bit of kosher salt on the shallots.

5 Close to serving time, pat the *yuba* dry again and then cook over medium-high heat in the skillet you used for the shallots. You may need to work in two batches. The *yuba* will brown quickly and stick together somewhat like an egg. When it is golden brown, about 1 minute, transfer to paper towels and sprinkle with a bit of kosher salt.

6 To serve the congee, divide the porridge among four bowls. Top each with one-quarter of the *yuba*, one-quarter of the shallot, one-quarter of the cabbage (drained), 2 sprigs of cilantro, and 1 teaspoon toasted sesame oil. Add a generous sprinkle of flaky sea salt and serve immediately.

sauces, condiments, and basic recipes

tarragon béchamel

Béchamel is a fundamental sauce of milk thickened with flour cooked in fat. It can be elaborated with herbs, as I do here, as a sauce to be used in the Stuffed and Baked Polenta (page 235). It can also be enriched with cheese for mac & cheese or used as the base of a creamy soup. It provides richness without the excessive fat of a cream-based sauce.

This recipe will work just fine with 2 percent milk, but I can't recommend skim milk.

Tarragon is a powerful herb; a tablespoon of it is sufficient to flavor 2 cups of sauce. If you substitute other herbs, you will generally want to use a larger quantity.

4 tablespoons (½ stick) unsalted butter
3 tablespoons all-purpose flour
2 cups whole or 2 percent milk
Kosher salt
1 tablespoon minced fresh tarragon (in a pinch, you can use 1 generous
    teaspoon dried tarragon)

1   Melt the butter in a small saucepan over medium-low heat. Whisk in the flour and cook, stirring, for about 2 minutes, keeping the heat low enough to prevent the flour from browning.

2   Add the milk in a thin stream, whisking continuously. It will sputter at first. The most critical part of this process is at the very beginning; you must break up any lumps that form before adding a lot of liquid, or you'll be chasing them around the pan.

3   After all of the milk is incorporated, raise the heat to medium and bring to a very slight simmer. Add a generous ½ teaspoon salt and the tarragon.

4   Continue to cook until the sauce easily coats the back of a spoon, about 5 minutes more. Taste and adjust the seasoning, then remove from the heat and use immediately, or refrigerate for up to 1 day. If refrigerated, whisk and reheat gently. You may need to add a little more milk.

ACID MAKES YOUR FOOD POP. One person's "acidity" is another's "sourness." Scientifically, they are the same thing. The sour taste buds fire when an acid meets water and releases hydrogen ions in your mouth. End of chemistry class.

At least in the U.S., acidity is a quality frequently missing from home-cooked meals, especially in what we think of as comfort food.

I'm not speaking here of the cases where acid is needed for a technical purpose, like preventing the browning of peeled artichokes, or reacting with baking soda in a pancake batter. I'm talking about sour flavors, which have a place in almost any dish. Why is this?

First of all, acid stimulates the palate and the production of saliva. Just imagine sucking on a lemon for a second and I bet your mouth literally waters. That is the very definition of appetizing: You are physically preparing your body to eat.

Also, acid gives the sensation of cutting through fat. A sauce that might seem too rich without an acid is magically enlivened with it. The classic heavy French sauces, like hollandaise, mayonnaise, and béarnaise, all include an acidic component. You probably wouldn't enjoy eating a bowl of lettuce dressed with just oil, but oil with vinegar or lemon juice is a staple.

Finally, sourness balances out sweet or salty flavors. Think of a crêpe dusted with powdered sugar and a squeeze of lemon, or salty fries dipped in sweet-tart ketchup. Less obviously, even a basic vegetable or lentil soup delivers mostly sweet, earthy flavors. That same squeeze of lemon makes such a dish much more interesting.

For the best effect, consider the balance of flavors for the whole meal, not just a single dish. If dessert is going to be a tart cherry pie, maybe lemony white beans aren't the ideal appetizer. Your palate might become fatigued with the repetition of sour flavors.

There are many ingredients that can add acidity, including wine and any of the hundreds of wonderful vinegars on the market. Tomatoes, tamarind, *amchoor* powder (an Indian spice made from dried mango), most fruits (especially when underripe), and anything pickled will do the trick. So, too, does carbonation: CO_2 dissolved in water produces a little bit of carbonic acid, which is part of the reason seltzer is so refreshing.

As for citrus, don't forget to look beyond standard lemons and limes when flavoring or garnishing a dish. Grapefruits, mandarins, tangerines, pomelos, Meyer lemons, yuzu, and even Buddha's hand offer amazing variations.

There are also times when you don't want or need any more acidity in a dish but you still want some tang. In that case, consider citrus zest or kaffir lime leaves. Although they aren't significantly acidic, they have such a strong association with the fruits that they create a similar effect. The zest of a lemon added to a simple tomato sauce is a surprisingly delicious twist.

So remember to taste your food frequently throughout the cooking process. And once you are satisfied that the salt level is correct, ask yourself, "Would a little splash of acid wake this puppy up?"

lemon-mustard vinaigrette

VEGAN

GLUTEN-FREE

MAKES 6
TABLESPOONS
(ENOUGH TO
DRESS A LARGE
SIDE SALAD FOR
4 PEOPLE)

5 MINUTES

I've never understood why people buy salad dressing, when an infinitely more delicious, fresher, healthier homemade vinaigrette takes only a few moments to make. This is my go-to version, with fresh lemon juice instead of vinegar and a bracing dose of Dijon mustard.

The traditional ratio for vinaigrette is 3 parts oil to 1 part vinegar. Depending on the intensity of your vinegar, this tends to produce a rather subdued dressing. Especially with lemon juice, I prefer an approximately 2-to-1 ratio. That is what I've specified in this recipe, but you should always taste it and adjust to your preference, the particular salad, and the dishes that will accompany it.

If you can find Meyer lemons, they will give you an even better flavor than the standard grocery-store variety, and of course, you should use a tasty extra-virgin olive oil.

There are two advantages to adding a significant amount of mustard to vinaigrette. The first is obvious: It tastes good. The second is that it acts as an emulsifier, keeping the oil suspended in the vinegar. You can get away with combining all of the ingredients in a jar with a tight-fitting lid and simply shaking it well. It isn't necessary to drizzle in the oil while whisking, in the traditional fashion, nor do you need a blender.

Salad dressings need to be highly seasoned with salt. Your salad will be lightly dressed, so if there isn't enough salt to make a statement in the straight dressing, the salad will be underseasoned.

To taste a dressing, always lightly dip a leaf of lettuce in it, rather than sipping from a spoon. This will give you a clearer sense of how it will taste on your salad.

2 tablespoons fresh lemon juice
½ teaspoon Dijon mustard
¼ teaspoon fine sea salt
4 tablespoons extra-virgin olive oil
Finely minced fresh or dried herbs, minced garlic, minced shallot,
  or grated citrus zest

1 *Option 1:* Combine the lemon juice, mustard, salt, olive oil, and any optional seasonings in a small jar with a tight-fitting lid. Shake vigorously until emulsified, about 30 seconds.
   Option 2: Combine the lemon juice, mustard, salt, and any optional seasonings in a bowl. Drizzle in the olive oil while whisking continuously.

2 Taste and adjust the salt as needed, and add more lemon juice or olive oil to achieve a pleasing balance of acidity.

chimichurri (argentine parsley sauce)

VEGAN

GLUTEN-FREE

MAKES ⅔ CUP

40 MINUTES
(10 MINUTES
ACTIVE)

Chimichurri is the quintessential sauce of Argentina and deserves to be better known in northerly climes. It is somewhat like an Italian pesto, but made from parsley instead of basil and without the cheese or nuts to thicken it. Like pesto, it comes together in a food processor with just a few minutes of work.

The essential ingredients of chimichurri are parsley, olive oil, garlic, onion, salt, pepper, and something acidic. I embellish this version with cilantro, red onion, a bit of sherry vinegar, and a few capers. Other common additions are hot red pepper flakes, paprika, or dried oregano.

In South America, chimichurri is usually served with steak, but you can definitely make a home for it in a vegetarian kitchen as well. Its strong, herbaceous bite pairs well with the smokiness of grilled vegetables, cuts the richness of fried foods, or amps up the flavor of a mild dish such as polenta.

⅓ **cup extra-virgin olive oil**
1 garlic clove, finely chopped or put through a press
1 cup lightly packed fresh flatleaf parsley leaves
1 cup lightly packed fresh cilantro leaves
1 teaspoon kosher salt
¼ **teaspoon freshly ground black pepper**
1 tablespoon sherry vinegar
¼ **cup minced red onion**
1 tablespoon capers, preferably salt-packed, rinsed

1 Combine the olive oil and garlic in a mini food processor and run for about 1 minute. (If you don't have a mini food processor and want to prepare this in a full-size food processor, you'll need to make a double batch, as a large machine isn't effective with this small quantity.) If you don't feel like mincing the onion by hand, you can add it in chunks here, but it won't look as nice.

2 Add the parsley, cilantro, salt, pepper, and vinegar, and process until the ingredients are minced but the leaves still retain a bit of texture.

3 Remove the mixture from the food processor and mix in the onion and capers.

4 Let rest, covered, for at least 30 minutes, then taste and adjust salt, pepper and vinegar as needed. Chimichurri is best used shortly after it is made but will keep for up to 24 hours covered in the refrigerator.

sauces, condiments, and basic recipes / 329

chermoula

VEGAN

GLUTEN-FREE

MAKES ¾ CUP

10 MINUTES

Chermoula is typically used as a marinade for fish in its North African home territory, but it can also be a stuffing or sauce. I like to serve it with a harissa-spiked tagine of butternut squash and potatoes with chickpeas, or to make *Chermoula-Stuffed Eggplant* (page 223).

There are any number of versions of *chermoula*. Some use only cilantro, while others include parsley. Some folks use preserved lemon, while others prefer just the fresh juice. I get a little crazy and add smoked paprika instead of sweet paprika, as well as a bit of fresh ginger (some recipes call for dried, most none at all). You should feel free to adapt it to your mood and what you have on hand.

For a less assertive variation, omit the hot red pepper flakes and smoked paprika and use 2 teaspoons of mild chili powder instead.

Chermoula is traditionally made with a mortar and pestle, but a mini food processor works just great. Simply buzz all the ingredients until you reach the desired consistency, which should be a little coarse, not fully pureed.

1 bunch fresh cilantro, leaves and tender stems only
1 handful fresh flatleaf parsley leaves
4 garlic cloves, coarsely chopped
2 tablespoons smoked paprika
1 tablespoon ground cumin
2 teaspoons grated fresh ginger
½ teaspoon hot red pepper flakes
Big pinch of saffron
½ teaspoon coriander seeds
1 teaspoon kosher salt
3 tablespoons extra-virgin olive oil
Juice of 1 lemon or half a preserved lemon, coarsely chopped

1 Combine all of the ingredients in a mini food processor. (If you don't have a mini food processor and want to prepare this in a full-size food processor, you'll need to make a double batch, as a large machine isn't effective with this small quantity.) Process to a thick, moderately rough sauce. Alternatively, put the ingredients in a mortar and work them with a pestle into a moderately rough sauce.

2 Let rest for a few minutes or up to an hour. Taste, adjust the seasoning, and serve. *Chermoula* will keep covered in the refrigerator for at least 48 hours.

vegetarian nuoc cham

VEGAN

GLUTEN-FREE
OPTION

MAKES 1 CUP

10 MINUTES

Nuoc cham is the quintessential Vietnamese condiment, made of fish sauce seasoned with sugar, lime juice, garlic, and chiles. I use a little bit of kombu and soy sauce to infuse this vegetarian version with the oceanic, umami flavor that fish sauce would supply.

Serve this with Crispy Vietnamese Crêpes (page 184), or as an alternative to the ginger-grapefruit sauce in Rice Vermicelli (*Bun*) with Ginger-Grapefruit Sauce (page 156).

¾ **cup water**
2 **tablespoons sugar**
1 **small piece dried kombu seaweed**
1 **to 2 Thai bird chiles or serrano chiles, thinly sliced, or 2 teaspoons chile sauce such as sambal oelek or sriracha**
1 **tablespoon soy sauce (use a wheat-free version for gluten-free)**
6 **tablespoons fresh lime juice**
2 **garlic cloves, minced**
About 1 teaspoon kosher salt
¼ **cup julienned carrots (optional)**

1 Bring the water, sugar, and kombu to a simmer in a small saucepan. Turn off the heat and let stand for 10 minutes. Remove the kombu.
2 Mix in the chiles, soy sauce, lime juice, garlic, and salt. Taste and adjust the seasoning to achieve a balance of savory, salty, sweet, spicy, and sour. Stir in the carrots. You can serve this immediately or store it, covered, in the refrigerator for a few days.

rosemary-blueberry sauce

VEGAN

GLUTEN-FREE

MAKES ABOUT
1 CUP

30 MINUTES
(5 MINUTES
ACTIVE)

I first came up with this sauce to serve with Manouri Cheese Blintzes (page 313), but it is equally amazing on vanilla ice cream, cheesecake, or cornmeal pancakes. The key is using the right amount of rosemary to create an interesting balance without overpowering the fruit.

12 ounces fresh blueberries (about 1¾ cups)
¼ cup sugar
⅛ teaspoon minced fresh rosemary leaves, plus additional as needed
Kosher salt

1 Combine the blueberries, sugar, rosemary, and a pinch of salt in a small saucepan set over medium heat. When the mixture reaches a simmer, reduce the heat to low.

2 Simmer for about 15 minutes, stirring occasionally. Taste and add a little more minced rosemary if you so desire, and continue simmering the sauce.

3 When the blueberries have mostly broken down, dip a spoon in the sauce, allow it to cool, and see if it is thick enough, with a consistency somewhere between syrup and jam. If not, check again every 5 minutes until you are satisfied. Remove from the heat and transfer to a small bowl. Serve immediately, or let it cool and store in the refrigerator. It will keep for several days.

grilled pineapple salsa

VEGAN

GLUTEN-FREE

MAKES ABOUT
1½ CUPS

15 MINUTES

I like this salsa for its bright flavors and simplicity. It has just a few ingredients, and you can throw it together in a few minutes. It is fantastic with Grilled Tofu and Pepper Tacos (page 144) and, if you add lemongrass and/or ginger, it works well in a Southeast Asian context, too. It is also plenty tasty to polish off with a bag of chips at midnight; if there were a security camera in my kitchen, I could prove it.

You only need half a pineapple for this salsa; you can either double the recipe or save the rest of the pineapple for another use. This salsa will keep in the refrigerator for at least 2 days.

You can't use pre-cut pineapple chunks because they would fall through the grill grate, but you can use a whole pineapple that has been pre-peeled and cored if you like. Otherwise, to prepare a whole pineapple, cut off the top and bottom, stand the pineapple on one end and carefully remove the skin, cutting deep enough to remove all of the eyes, then make vertical cuts to create ⅜-inch-thick planks.

Be sure to grill the pineapple long enough to drive off some moisture and develop caramelized flavors.

Half a fresh pineapple, peeled and cut into ⅜-inch-thick planks (see headnote)
Vegetable oil
Kosher salt
Juice of 1 lime
2 tablespoons minced shallot
¼ to 1 jalapeño pepper (depending on your heat preference), seeded and minced
1 big handful fresh cilantro leaves

1 Preheat a grill or heat a grill pan over medium-high heat. Brush one side of each pineapple plank with vegetable oil and sprinkle on a little salt. Grill until dark grill marks develop, about 5 minutes. Oil and salt the other sides and grill until done.

2 Remove the pineapple planks from the grill. When they are cool enough to handle, cut out and discard the cores and cut the pineapple into ⅜-inch dice.

3 Combine the pineapple with the lime juice, shallot, jalapeño pepper, and cilantro. If not using right away, hold off on adding the cilantro so it stays bright. Taste and add salt, lime juice, or more jalapeño pepper as needed.

banana raita

GLUTEN-FREE
MAKES 1½ CUPS
5 MINUTES

Raitas are a family of yogurt-based condiments that can go with just about any Indian dish, from street food to a sumptuous banquet. They make a cooling complement to a spicy dish. Unfortunately, only the cucumber raita has become popular in America, but there are many other possibilities.

I like this banana raita because the flavors are at once familiar and surprising. First you get banana smoothie, only to have your taste buds surprised by mustard seed, jalapeño pepper, and scallion. Try this with the Indian Potato Fritters (*Aloo Tikki*) on page 70.

Make this raita close to serving time, so the banana stays nice and fresh.

1 ripe banana, peeled and finely diced
Juice of half a lemon
1 tablespoon vegetable oil
1 tablespoon black mustard seeds
1 cup plain yogurt
½ teaspoon kosher salt
½ teaspoon sugar
Half a jalapeño pepper, seeded and finely diced (optional)
1 scallion, white and light green parts only, thinly sliced, for garnish

1 Toss the diced banana with the lemon juice to prevent browning.
2 Heat the oil in a small skillet over medium heat. When the oil shimmers, add the mustard seeds and cook until they begin to pop and change color, about 1 minute.
3 In a medium-size bowl, combine the yogurt, salt, and sugar and blend thoroughly with a whisk or fork until smooth. Mix in the banana, mustard seeds, and jalapeño pepper, if using.
4 Taste and adjust the seasoning, garnish with the scallion, and serve.

indian sichuan pickle

VEGAN
GLUTEN-FREE
MAKES 1 CUP
5 MINUTES

Indian pickles are not very well known in America, but in their home country, they are served as part of just about any meal. A teaspoon or two of these intense pickles—made with anything from lime to garlic, preserved in mustard oil with lots of spices—adds a great degree of interest to even the simplest bowl of rice and dal or any Indian dish like *Chana Masala* with Mushrooms (page 209).

When I had half a can of Sichuan preserved vegetable left from making Sichuan Dry-Fried Green Beans and Tofu (page 186), it occurred to me that it wouldn't take much to convert those vegetables into a condiment that would be at home with Indian food. The result is piquant and delicious, and it takes only 5 minutes of work.

If you use pre-chopped Sichuan preserved vegetable from a can, be sure to rinse off the excess salt before using in this recipe.

1 tablespoon mustard oil or vegetable oil
1 tablespoon black mustard seeds
1 teaspoon cumin seeds
1 teaspoon fennel seeds
1 cup coarsely chopped Sichuan preserved vegetable (about 2 whole knobs)

1 Heat the oil in a small skillet over medium-high heat. When the oil shimmers, add the mustard seeds, cumin seeds, and fennel seeds, and cook until the mustard seeds start popping and the mixture is fragrant but not burning, about 1 minute.

2 Toss the seeds and oil with the preserved vegetable. You can serve the pickle right away or keep it in the refrigerator for several days.

cryo-pickled onions

VEGAN

GLUTEN-FREE

MAKES ABOUT
⅓ CUP

10 MINUTES,
PLUS A FREEZE
AND THAW
CYCLE (START
THE DAY AHEAD)

Aki Kamozawa and Alex Talbot, in their cookbook *Ideas In Food* (Clarkson Potter, 2010), have terrific chapters on pickling and on freezing food to modify its texture intentionally. I like to combine these two methods into something I call "cryo-pickling."

When you freeze a vegetable, ice crystals puncture the cell walls. A slow thaw allows water to drain out, resulting in a denser product with more concentrated flavors. If you freeze and thaw the vegetable in a pickling liquid, the pickling flavors have the opportunity to migrate in as the water goes out.

In this recipe, I cryo-pickle onions with *togarishi*, which is a Japanese spice mixture that includes chile peppers and orange zest; it is available at Asian markets in the table condiment section. You can serve the pickles with Pear and Gouda Salad (page 121) and use the pickling liquid as part of the dressing. They are also good on sandwiches or in a quesadilla.

Feel free to change either the vegetable or the marinade; this method is very flexible. How about cantaloupe with Sichuan peppercorns? Experiment and have fun!

⅓ **cup rice vinegar**
1½ **teaspoons kosher salt**
2 **teaspoons sugar**
¼ **teaspoon *togarishi* or hot red pepper flakes**
1-inch piece fresh ginger, peeled and thinly sliced
Half a medium white onion, thinly sliced

1 In a small bowl, whisk together the rice vinegar, salt, sugar, and *togarishi*.

2 Place the ginger and onion in a small freezer bag. Pour the pickling liquid over them, shake a bit, and seal, forcing out as much air as possible (see below).

3 Freeze for at least 12 hours, then thaw in the refrigerator. Once thawed, the pickled onions are ready for use and will keep in the refrigerator for at least a few days.

REMOVING AIR FROM A ZIPPER BAG. There is a clever trick for removing most of the air from a zipper-top plastic bag without a vacuum sealing machine, which I learned from Dave Arnold of the French Culinary Institute. It works best if there is some liquid in the bag.

Fill the bag and zip it shut except for the last ½ inch, and put your index finger in the gap. Fill a pot or sink with water to a level deeper than the bag is tall. Slowly lower the bag into the water, angled so that the sealed corner goes in first. You will see that air is being forced out of the bag. Just before water would start to flow in through the open corner, seal it up, and you are done.

onion chutney

VEGAN

GLUTEN-FREE

MAKES 1½ CUPS

30 MINUTES
(10 MINUTES
ACTIVE)

When I was a freshman in college, I ate lunch at one of the many fine Indian restaurants in Providence, Rhode Island, almost every day. This style of raw onion chutney was always on offer. Unfortunately, I've rarely seen it outside of the Northeast, and I didn't see it at all when I was in Delhi.

If you crave the sweet, pungent crunch of raw onion, you'll find this chutney addictive. It goes well with curries like the *Chana Masala* with Mushrooms (page 209) and, even better, with fried tidbits like Indian Potato Fritters (page 70) or pakora (which are like Indian tempura with a chickpea flour batter).

I like to add a couple drops of red food coloring to give this chutney a more attractive color and make it resemble the restaurant version. You can certainly skip this. If you would like to use natural food coloring, India Tree makes a nice set of them (available at Whole Foods or from amazon.com). You could also use a teaspoon of beet juice.

1½ cups very finely diced white onion or sweet onion
   (such as Vidalia or Walla Walla)
1 tablespoon vegetable oil
2 teaspoons black mustard seeds
½ teaspoon ground cumin
¼ teaspoon cayenne pepper
1 tablespoon tomato paste
1 tablespoon white vinegar
¼ teaspoon kosher salt
1 or 2 drops red food coloring (optional)

1   Soak the onion in a generous amount of cold water for 30 minutes. Don't skip this step; it removes a bit of the harsh bite.

2   Heat the vegetable oil in a small skillet over medium heat. When the oil shimmers, add the mustard seeds and cook until they begin to pop and turn gray, about 1 minute. Add the cumin and cayenne; 10 seconds later (before the cumin can burn) add the tomato paste, vinegar, and salt. Remove from the heat.

3   Drain the onion thoroughly, then stir the spice mixture into it. Stir in the food coloring, if using. Taste and adjust the seasoning. You may like a little more vinegar, salt, or cayenne. You can serve this right away or keep it in the refrigerator, covered, for up to 3 days.

tomato confit

VEGAN

GLUTEN-FREE

MAKES 40
TOMATO HALVES

3½ HOURS
(20 MINUTES
ACTIVE)

Turning mediocre tomatoes into tomato confit is like spinning straw into gold. Beautiful, summer-ripe, heirloom tomatoes don't need any gilding. But when life gives you a bunch of tomatoes that aren't perfectly ripe, a long, slow roast to concentrate the flavors makes magic. The end result isn't like a fully sun-dried tomato. The tomatoes are still moist and fleshy but with a super-intense flavor backed by a deep caramelized note.

You can fit about 20 plum tomatoes on a baking sheet. I like to do at least this many at once, and then use them over several days, for dishes like Cool Tomato and Buttermilk Soup (page 85), Tomato Confit and Roasted Garlic Bruschetta (page 52) or Corn and Tomato Confit Risotto (page 197). They are also tremendous simply tossed with pasta and sautéed garlic.

20 plum tomatoes or other tomatoes, peeled (see below)
3 tablespoons extra-virgin olive oil
½ teaspoon kosher salt
1 tablespoon minced fresh tarragon leaves (optional)
2 teaspoons fresh thyme leaves
4 thinly sliced garlic cloves (optional)

1   Preheat the oven to 300°F. Line a baking sheet with parchment paper or a silicone mat.
2   Cut each tomato in half lengthwise. Scoop out the seeds. A grapefruit spoon or a butter curler works well for this. (If you like, you can strain the seeds and drink the resulting thin juice as a cook's treat.)
3   Place the tomatoes, cut side up, on the baking sheet. Drizzle with the olive oil and sprinkle on the salt. Add the tarragon, thyme, and/or garlic, if using.
4   Roast, turning the pan occasionally, until the tomatoes are quite flat and much of the liquid is gone, about 3 hours. Take one out, let it cool, and taste it to be sure the flavor is quite concentrated. If not, let them cook longer.
5   Use immediately or pack the tomatoes with any juice on the tray into a storage container; they will keep for a few days in the refrigerator.

PEELING TOMATOES. Blanching makes it easy to remove the skins from tomatoes.

Bring a large pot of water to a boil. Remove the core of each tomato with a paring knife and cut a small X in the blossom end. Dump the tomatoes in the boiling water a few at a time, let them sit for about 10 seconds, then remove with a slotted spoon.

Once they're cool enough to handle, you can zip the skin right off. Peeling half a dozen tomatoes this way takes just a few minutes.

tomato jam with rosemary and saffron

VEGAN

GLUTEN-FREE

MAKES ABOUT
2 CUPS

1½ HOURS
(20 MINUTES
ACTIVE)

Tomato jam sounds kind of funny, right? But tomatoes are a fruit, after all. Cook them down with sugar and seasonings and you get a piquant jam, though it might seem more like a chutney.

Whatever you call it, this tomato jam is amazing on a grilled cheese with seriously sharp cheddar or with Chickpea Fritters (page 69).

You don't need picture-perfect tomatoes for this jam, so you might ask at your farmers' market to see if you can buy seconds that are a little bruised or otherwise unloved. At my market, they are about half the regular price. It is important to peel the tomatoes before making the jam, to avoid having unpleasant stringy bits in it.

1½ pounds ripe tomatoes, cored, peeled (see page 343), and diced
½ cup finely diced white onion
2 tablespoons fresh lemon juice
½ teaspoon very finely chopped fresh rosemary leaves
¾ cup sugar
¾ teaspoon kosher salt
Hot red pepper flakes
Saffron
Freshly ground black pepper

Combine the tomatoes, onion, lemon juice, rosemary, sugar, and salt in a saucepan. Season with a pinch of hot red pepper flakes, a pinch of crumbled saffron, and a few grinds of black pepper. Bring to a simmer. (Plenty of liquid will come out of the tomatoes, so you don't need to add any water.) Adjust the heat and simmer until thick and syrupy, about 1 hour. Taste and adjust the seasonings. You can serve this right away, or keep it covered in the refrigerator for up to 3 days. It tastes best at room temperature.

homemade bread crumbs

VEGAN

MAKES 2 CUPS

15 MINUTES

Homemade bread crumbs are a completely different ballgame from the canned grocery-store stuff. It is a very easy thing to grate dried-out bread in the food processor and then toast the crumbs with a little olive oil in a skillet. You'll be rewarded with tasty, crunchy goodness that can top a gratin, add body to a filling, or bread a fritter.

In a pinch, if you don't have any stale bread, you can make these with bread that is still soft. Just slice the bread, toast it, and let it sit for 15 minutes or so to dry out so that it can be grated.

Bread crumbs keep very well in the freezer. Just give them a quick re-toast in a skillet or toaster oven to revive their crunch.

This recipe is for a basic, all-purpose bread crumb. You can add crushed garlic or hearty herbs such as rosemary or sage to the olive oil for variety.

6 thick slices of stale bread
3 tablespoons extra-virgin olive oil
¼ teaspoon kosher salt

1 Grate the bread in a food processor, using the grating blade. Empty the crumbs from the bowl and replace the grating blade with the regular steel blade. Put the crumbs back in the processor bowl and process until the crumbs reach the desired texture. I like mine fairly coarse for general use but rather fine for breading.

2 Heat the oil in your largest skillet over medium-low heat. When the oil is hot, add the bread crumbs and salt. Toast, stirring frequently, until the crumbs are well browned and crispy, about 10 minutes.

3 Set aside to cool and use as needed. Store what you are not using immediately in a zipper-top plastic bag in the freezer.

japanese sesame salt (gomashio)

VEGAN

GLUTEN-FREE

MAKES ABOUT
½ CUP

10 MINUTES

I first learned about *gomashio* when my mom was on a macrobiotic diet. The diet didn't stick with me, but this Japanese sesame salt did. Some folks believe it can treat everything from an upset stomach to much more serious diseases. I find it simple and flavorful, whether or not it has any of the special healing powers attributed to it.

Gomashio is simply toasted unhulled sesame seeds ground with sea salt in about a 10-to-1 ratio. It is typically used as a table condiment, though there is no reason the cook can't apply it as a garnish as well.

I love *gomashio* on those simple, fortifying meals that consist of, say, brown rice and carefully steamed vegetables, maybe a little tofu, and a cup of miso soup. It is also good on edamame, and it is used on a classic dish of sticky rice with adzuki beans.

How you make *gomashio* depends on whether you believe that the traditional method produces superior results or somehow invests it with the aforementioned healing powers. Even if you don't hold those beliefs, though, perhaps you just enjoy doing things the slow way (which I completely support). So I'll give you both options: The traditional method requires a *suribachi*, a Japanese ridged ceramic mortar and pestle, available at Japanese grocery stores or on amazon.com. Alternatively, you can simply use a spice grinder and be done in seconds.

Sesame seeds contain a lot of oil, so it isn't hard for them to turn rancid. If you can't tell whether they've gone off from taking a whiff of the whole seeds, it should be quite apparent when you grind them. If they are even a tiny bit rancid, throw them out and go get a new bag.

Once made, *gomashio* will last a couple of weeks in a glass jar at room temperature.

1 tablespoon coarse sea salt
½ cup plus 2 tablespoons unhulled raw sesame seeds

1 Heat a medium-size skillet over medium-low heat.

2 Add the salt and toast for 3 minutes, stirring occasionally. (I don't know if this does anything, but it is traditional. You might see the salt turn gray.)

3 Remove the salt and add the sesame seeds to the pan. Toast, stirring frequently, until the seeds are fragrant and have turned a few shades darker, about 5 minutes. You will hear some popping. Be sure to keep the heat low enough to avoid any burning. If you burn the seeds, throw them out, wipe the pan clean, and start over. Remove the toasted seeds to a bowl and allow them to cool to near room temperature.

4 Grind the salt and sesame seeds together in a *suribachi* (Japanese mortar) or a spice grinder. I like it fairly fluffy but with some seeds that are not completely powdered.

5 Store in an airtight container at room temperature and offer as a table condiment.

red curry paste

VEGAN

GLUTEN-FREE

MAKES ABOUT
¾ CUP

30 MINUTES
(10 MINUTES
ACTIVE)

There is nothing wrong with using prepackaged pastes, but making curry paste from scratch is easy and addictive, and the aroma and flavor of your curries will be at a completely different level.

This version of a red curry paste originated with my friend Ivy Manning, who writes wonderful cookbooks. I've changed it only a bit, to use ingredients I most often have on hand.

This recipe makes more paste than you will probably use in a single meal. Freeze the excess and you will have the beginnings of two or three great dishes, such as Red Curry Delicata Squash (page 190) or Red Curry Fried Rice (page 268), waiting for you at a moment's notice.

6 dried New Mexico chiles, stems removed
½ cup boiling water
1 teaspoon coriander seeds
½ teaspoon ground cumin
1 teaspoon ground turmeric
2-inch piece fresh ginger, peeled and coarsely chopped
¼ cup coarsely chopped red onion
6 garlic cloves, coarsely chopped
Grated zest and juice of 1 lime
1 stalk lemongrass, tender white parts only, pounded and coarsely chopped
  (see page 253)
1 big handful fresh cilantro leaves and stems
½ teaspoon kosher salt
Freshly ground black pepper

1 Wearing rubber gloves, tear the chile pods into small pieces. If you like your curries hot, keep the seeds and ribs. If not, discard them.

2 Put the chile pieces in a blender. Pour the boiling water over them, cover, and let sit for 20 minutes or so. In the meantime, you can gather and prepare the rest of your ingredients.

3 Toast the coriander seeds in a dry skillet over medium heat until fragrant, about 2 minutes.

4 Add the coriander seeds to the blender, along with the cumin, turmeric, ginger, onion, garlic, lime zest and juice, lemongrass, cilantro, salt, and a few grinds of black pepper. Puree until you have a smooth paste, 3 to 4 minutes, stopping occasionally to scrape down the sides and top of the blender. If needed, add a little more water to get the paste to come together. This paste will keep for a day or two in the fridge, or you can freeze it for up to 3 months.

quick harissa oil

VEGAN

GLUTEN-FREE

MAKES ABOUT 5
TABLESPOONS

15 MINUTES

Harissa is the classic spice paste of North Africa, used in stews, as a rub, and as a condiment at the table. Oil infused with harissa is terrific for grilling vegetables, and I like it drizzled on soups. You can also use a small amount of this oil to spice up a vinaigrette for dressing salads or dipping bread.

If you happen to have harissa paste, you can make harissa oil by simply pureeing the paste with olive oil and straining. If not, you can make a quick approximation using this recipe. It will keep in the refrigerator for a few days.

Sumac is an intensely maroon powder with a mild tangy flavor. Look for it at a Middle Eastern market or online retailer.

½ cup extra-virgin olive oil
2 teaspoons sriracha, sambal oelek, or similar thick Asian chile sauce
1 teaspoon hot red pepper flakes
½ teaspoon ground cumin
½ teaspoon caraway seeds
½ teaspoon coriander seeds
2 teaspoons ground sumac
1 garlic clove, minced

1 Combine all of the ingredients in a small saucepan and warm over low heat for about 5 minutes. Do not allow the spices to sizzle; you don't want them to cook, just to get warm enough for their flavors to infuse the oil quickly. Remove from the heat and let sit for 5 minutes more.

2 Puree all of the ingredients with a stick blender or a mini food processor. Strain through a fine-mesh strainer. The oil is ready to use.

basic pastry dough

MAKES ENOUGH
FOR 1 (9-INCH)
TART

1½ HOURS
(30 MINUTES
ACTIVE)

I'd like to have a word with you people who are afraid of making pastry crusts. I've been there, and I can get you through this and have you making tender, flaky crusts. It really isn't difficult; you just have to focus on a few details.

- The butter and the water should be really, really cold.
- Spend only 1 to 2 minutes working the butter into the flour.
- Use just enough water to get the dough to form a shaggy mass.
- Work the dough just enough to form a ball.
- Refrigerate before rolling out, then let it warm back up just slightly.

Your goal here is to get well-distributed pockets of butter that will separate layers of the dough, while minimizing gluten development. To make sure the butter is really cold, I cut it into cubes and then put them in the freezer for a few minutes.

I really like to use a pastry blender, a simple hand tool (available in kitchenware stores and even in some groceries) with several blades that cut the butter into the flour. If you don't have a pastry blender, you can cut the butter into the flour using two dinner knives, or work it in with your fingers, or pulse the butter and flour together in the food processor, being sure to stop when you reach the "oatmeal" stage. The food processor can also mix in the water for you, as long as you are careful to process it very briefly.

1 cup all-purpose flour
¼ teaspoon kosher salt
6 tablespoons very cold butter, cut into small cubes
2 to 4 tablespoons ice-cold water

1 *Bowl method:* Combine the flour, salt, and butter in a mixing bowl. Using a pastry blender or your hands, work the butter into the flour until it mostly looks like coarse oatmeal. Limit this to at most 2 minutes. It is fine if there are still some larger chunks of butter.
Processor method: Combine the flour, salt, and butter in a food processor. Pulse for 2 seconds at a time, until it mostly looks like coarse oatmeal. It is fine if there are still some larger chunks of butter.

▼ ▼ ▼

2 *Bowl method:* Add 2 tablespoons of the ice-cold water. Work this in, tossing and stirring with a fork, for 1 minute, then try to press a piece together with your hands. If you can form a ball, you are done. If not, add more water, 2 teaspoons at a time, until you can make a big shaggy ball. You really want to err on the side of minimal water, and keep the total time for this step again to less than 2 minutes. It is fine if there is a little bit of unincorporated flour left at the bottom of the bowl. (The amount of water needed will vary depending on the moisture content of both your flour and your butter.)

Processor method: Sprinkle 2 tablespoons of the ice-cold water over the butter-flour mixture. Pulse just until a shaggy ball pulls away from the sides of the processor bowl.

3 Turn the dough onto a lightly floured work surface and gather it into a ball. Flatten the ball into a disk about 7 inches in diameter. Press any little cracks in the edge together—this will make it easier to roll out. Wrap it in plastic wrap, or better yet, put it in a 1-gallon freezer bag. Refrigerate for at least 1 hour and up to 2 days.

4 Remove the dough from the refrigerator and let it warm up a bit until slightly pliable. This could take anywhere from 5 to 20 minutes depending on how well chilled it is. While the dough is still wrapped, give it several cathartic thwacks with your rolling pin to get a head start on rolling it out. Now, unwrap it, put it on your floured board, flour your rolling pin, and roll out to the desired shape for your final recipe.

measurement equivalents

LIQUID CONVERSIONS

U.S.	Metric
1 tsp	5 ml
1 tbs	15 ml
2 tbs	30 ml
3 tbs	45 ml
¼ cup	60 ml
⅓ cup	75 ml
⅓ cup + 1 tbs	90 ml
⅓ cup + 2 tbs	100 ml
½ cup	120 ml
⅔ cup	150 ml
¾ cup	180 ml
¾ cup + 2 tbs	200 ml
1 cup	240 ml
1 cup + 2 tbs	275 ml
1¼ cups	300 ml
1⅓ cups	325 ml
1½ cups	350 ml
1⅔ cups	375 ml
1¾ cups	400 ml
1¾ cups + 2 tbs	450 ml
2 cups (1 pint)	475 ml
2½ cups	600 ml
3 cups	720 ml
4 cups (1 quart)	945 ml

(1,000 ml is 1 liter)

WEIGHT CONVERSIONS

U.S./U.K.	Metric
½ oz	14 g
1 oz	28 g
1½ oz	43 g
2 oz	57 g
2½ oz	71 g
3 oz	85 g
3½ oz	100 g
4 oz	113 g
5 oz	142 g
6 oz	170 g
7 oz	200 g
8 oz	227 g
9 oz	255 g
10 oz	284 g
11 oz	312 g
12 oz	340 g
13 oz	368 g
14 oz	400 g
15 oz	425 g
1 lb	454 g

OVEN TEMPERATURE CONVERSIONS

°F	Gas Mark	°C
250	½	120
275	1	140
300	2	150
325	3	165
350	4	180
375	5	190
400	6	200
425	7	220
450	8	230
475	9	240
500	10	260
550	Broil	290

NOTE: All conversions are approximate.

index

Note: Page references in *italics* indicate photographs.